P9-DGT-787

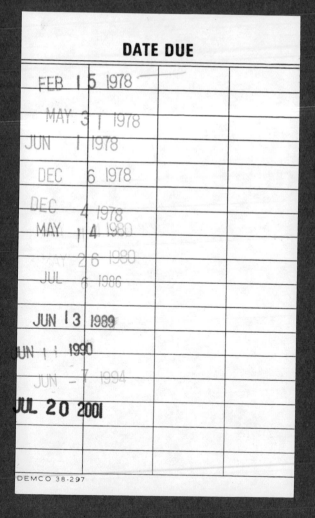

CONQUEST
AND
COMMERCE
Spain and England in the Americas

CONQUEST
AND
COMMERCE

Spain and England in the Americas

JAMES LANG

Department of Sociology
Vanderbilt University
Nashville, Tennessee

ACADEMIC PRESS   *New York   San Francisco   London*
A Subsidiary of Harcourt Brace Jovanovich, Publishers

Selections reprinted from Bernard Bailyn, "Politics and Social
Structure in Virginia," in *Seventeenth-Century America,* ed. James
Morton Smith, and from Edmund S. Morgan and Helen M. Morgan,
The Stamp Act Crisis, by permission of the Institute of Early
American History and Culture.

Selections reprinted, by permission, from John L. Phelan, *The
Kingdom of Quito* (Madison: Univ. of Wisconsin Press), © 1967
by the Regents of the Univ. of Wisconsin.

William H. Prescott, *The History of the Conquest of Mexico*
(1843), abr. and ed. C. Harvey Gardiner (Chicago: Univ. of Chicago
Press), © 1966 by the Univ. of Chicago Press. Selections reprinted
by permission.

Leslie Byrd Simpson, *The Encomienda in New Spain,* originally
published by the Univ. of California Press; selections reprinted by
permission of the Regents of the Univ. of California.

Selections reprinted from Earl J. Hamilton, *American Treasure
and the Price Revolution in Spain 1501-1650,* by permission of
Harvard University Press. Copyright 1934 by the Harvard
University Press.

ACADEMIC PRESS, INC.
111 Fifth Avenue, New York, New York 10003

United Kingdom Edition published by
ACADEMIC PRESS, INC. (LONDON) LTD.
24/28 Oval Road, London NW1

Library of Congress Cataloging in Publication Data

Lang, James.
    Conquest and commerce.

    (Studies in social discontinuity)
    Bibliography: p.
    Includes index.
    1.   Spain—Colonies—America.   2.   Spain—Colonies—
America—Commerce.   3.   Great Britain—Colonies—
America.   4.   Great Britain—Colonies—America—
Commerce.   I.   Title.   II.   Series.
F1411.L24   325'.37'094   74-17964
ISBN 0—12—436450—0

Contents

I
SPAIN
IN AMERICA

The history of Western Europe manifests a continuous tension between local patterns of culture and forces of concentration and centralization. The second feudal age (1050–1400) saw the growth of universities, the Papacy, craft guilds, and kingdoms, all comprehensive institutions of control that challenged the religious, economic, and political folkways of an earlier age. If the emergence of centralized Christianity under the aegis of Rome was one of the most striking developments of the second feudal age, the growth of the state dominates modern history. The Reformation weakened the autonomous power of the Papacy and placed new resources in the hands of ambitious princes who confiscated church lands.

In 1500, the advocates of royal power faced strong opposition. The feudal nobility and the clergy resisted attempts to reduce their authority. The common people, forced to surrender their resources (taxes, grain, labor, men, and loyalty) to the state, rebelled. Deliberative assemblies like the English Parliament, the French Estates General, and the Spanish Cortes often opposed the expansion of state power. Throughout the sixteenth and seventeenth centuries, the Crown provoked violent resistance as it increased its claims on the resources of society. Local groups were at times momentarily successful in thwarting central authority. But in the long run, the states of Western Europe repressed internal opposition and established bureaucracies to regulate their populations.

The power of the state was limited by its ability to extract resources from society. The growth of an international economy and overseas colonies presented the state that could regulate commercial activity with new opportunities. Between 1500 and 1713, there was a dramatic shift in the organization and control of the European economy. The commercial prominence of Venice, which centered on the Mediterranean and stretched overland into North and Central Europe, was eclipsed. The challenge of the Reformation to the dominion of Rome foreshadowed a sustained movement of political, economic and cultural power to the west and north. The new global economy that followed the voyages of discovery came to a momentary focus in Spain and Portugal. But commercial preeminence did not remain the monopoly of Iberia. By the mid-seventeenth century, com-

3

mercial dominance had moved to Northern Europe—to England, France, and Holland. State power was closely associated with commercial hegemony. Victory in the eighteenth-century imperial competition between France and England fell to England largely because England was the strongest state commercially.

The states of Western Europe brought elements of a common cultural heritage to the Americas. But from that common tradition, they constructed radically different societies. The kind of exploitable resources that existed in America, either available directly—silver and Indian labor—or developed over time—sugar and tobacco production—had a formative impact on the organization of colonial society. The creation of royal government was a response to the value and nature of the wealth that companies, colonists, and proprietors "discovered" or created in the New World. For the most part, royal governments did not direct the beginnings of colonization. This was the activity of Spanish conquistadores, English companies, Puritans and proprietors, Portuguese donatarios, French Jesuits and mercantile associations, and the Dutch West India Company. Only after these groups had enjoyed some success did the state act to claim its share of the wealth, often displacing the original agents of colonization.

Spain constructed the most extensive bureaucratic regime in America: not over the course of centuries but in a few decades. The immediate tangible assets of the Indies—precious metals and Indian labor—made a bureaucracy not only possible but necessary. If the Crown was to extract the resources of America, it had to control the societies that already existed there. This was a task that the Spanish Crown had undertaken previously in the reconquest of Granada, and it drew on this experience to establish royal government in the New World. Colonial Hispanic America cannot be studied without continuous reference to royal institutions.

In the sixteenth century, Spain's rivals devoted most of their energies to raiding her ships and her unfortified coastal settlements. The Portuguese in Brazil spent much of the century loading cargoes of dyewood at trading stations along the coast. No other European state conquered a settled agricultural population that could be so readily exploited as the Aztecs and Incas. In other parts of America, royal government developed more slowly in response to the spread of commercial agriculture. Colonial society in English America until the 1660s can be studied largely without reference to royal institutions. Indeed, only in the mid-seventeenth century did the value of commercial agriculture—tobacco in Virginia, sugar in Portuguese Pernambuco, tobacco and sugar in the West Indies—finally bring more decisive state control.

European states acted to regulate trade. This was especially true of Eng-

land. Navigation Acts, rather than executive government, initially defined the relationship of England to her colonies. As a result, particular groups of colonists—planters in Virginia and the West Indies, Puritans in Massachusetts—organized colonial society in terms of their own welfare. In respect to the role they played in organizing colonial institutions, Spain and England stand at opposite ends of a spectrum. The Spanish Crown tamed the encomanderos; the English Crown was unable to master the planters of Virginia and the merchants of Massachusetts.

In Quebec, a royal regime was not established until Louis XIV and Colbert acted to create a governor, intendant, and sovereign council in 1663. But while the French state actively involved itself in the direct administration of Quebec, it was unable to implement Colbert's policy of establishing a compact colony. Quebec did not become a supplier of needed raw materials like naval stores, nor was she able to provide the French West Indies with agricultural produce. The fur trade and the coureurs de bois, rather than the will of the Crown, determined the character of New France. In Brazil, the Portuguese Crown could not control the Paulistas. Only in the eighteenth century, when gold was discovered in Minas Gerais, did the Crown act to establish royal government in São Paulo. The Dutch West India Company, which maintained a series of trading stations from New Netherland to Brazil, was unable to secure its position in the face of English and Portuguese competition.

The nature of resources alone did not determine the role of royal government in America. The formation of national states in Western Europe was a dominant theme in the political history of the period. It is no accident, for example, that royal government was applied to Quebec during the reign of Louis XIV. The king and his minister Colbert were extending state control in France at the time. Exercising more direct authority in America was a corollary of statemaking in Europe. In England, the bureaucratic control of the Crown was weak, and the seventeenth-century program of royal centralization in America faltered badly.

As the organization of the state became more centralized in Europe, an attempt was made to duplicate this control in the colonies. The Bourbon reforms in America (1759–1800) were directly related to the reorganization of the state in Spain. Royal authority in Brazil was expanded as part of the enlightened state policy of the Marquis of Pombal (1750–1777). British policy after 1763 was an attempt to gain fiscal control in the colonies, thereby easing the financial burden of the state's enlarged empire.

As Britain and Spain attempted to redefine state authority in America, they provoked tenacious opposition and rebellion. Conflict between the state and its colonists over the control of Indian labor, silver, trade, taxes, *institutions, and offices was constant, whether it took the form of violent resistence or complex diplomatic maneuvering. But the form that opposition took depended on the way the colonial population was supervised by the royal government. In English America, the assembly provided a strong base for colonial resistence. This institution in turn provided a model for a unified, national political structure in the post-Independent period. In Spanish America, the royal bureaucracy managed political life. No comprehensive colonial institution was designed to act on behalf of landowners, miners, merchants, and manufacturers. Opposition to the policies of the Crown was filtered through a complex bureaucracy. When the royal bureaucracy was displaced by revolution, it proved extremely difficult to devise new institutions that could express the divergent interests of colonial society.*

I

The Beginnings

The English colonist in America, relentless and determined, conquered the land. His symbols were the axe and the plowshare, the tobacco leaf and Thanksgiving—an agrarian festival. The French colonist also conquered the land, but the rivers and lakes that ran over the land, he conquered as well. His symbols were the sturdy habitant, the *coureurs de bois*, the canoe. After a century, that struggle against the forest had hardly been engaged. The English and French colonists held the coastal flatlands and the fringes of lakes and rivers. It was a settlement frontier and a thin, fragile fur-trading frontier linked by forts and weightless canoes.

The Spanish came not as colonists but as conquerors. They came not to realize some distant future, not to stand on the margins of a continent for a century, but to master and subdue it in their own lifetime. They conquered not land but labor. Their symbols were the sword, silver, and Indian tribute. It was an Indian frontier, a labor frontier. The hegemony of the Spanish conqueror spread out and encompassed the available labor supply. Where there were no Indians, there were no Spaniards. The heart of the Spanish empire in America remained, for almost two centuries, the heart of the old Indian civilizations. The Spanish enterprise in the New World rested on an indigenous social order.

During the life of Hernan Cortés, Spanish control in America expanded from a few small Caribbean islands to extensive parts of two continents. But the *conquistadores* lost control of their own conquest. Cortés, who directed the conquest of the Aztecs, also witnessed the conquest of himself and his followers by the professional bureaucrats dispatched from Spain. That two such dramatic processes, a charismatic military conquest and an administrative, bureaucratic coup, should have occurred almost simultaneously suggests that the adversaries were in a sense twin-born. The scenario of conquest and control was a familiar pattern, and the Castilian monarchy developed a specific set of institutions to respond to such a challenge. Institutions that had proved to be powerful instruments of royal control in Castile—the viceroyalty, *audiencia, corregimiento*, and *real hacienda* (royal treasury)— found their way to the New World. Had this not been the case, it is difficult to believe that the process of royal consolidation could have occurred so rapidly. The conquest presented the Crown not with a new problem but with an old one, albeit with different dimensions. Similarly, the control of an extensive, agriculturally based labor force did not present a unique situation to the *conquistador*. The Indian population was divided into *encomiendas*, an institution of labor control previously established in Hispaniola and with antecedents in Spain itself. Consequently, as unprecedented as the conquest was in its very massiveness, it presented few problems outside the practical experience of either the Crown or the conqueror.

THE CROWN

The "Catholic Kings," Ferdinand and Isabella, consolidated the position of the Crown in Castile. Isabella reclaimed Crown lands seized by the nobility. The jurisdiction of royal justice was extended by the expansion of the *audiencia* throughout Castile. The *corregidor* became the instrument the Crown effectively employed to control the Castilian town. The powers of the Castilian Cortes were curtailed. The policy of the Catholic Kings was to become sovereign in Castile, the most wealthy and populous kingdom of the peninsula. To this end, the political power of the towns and the nobility was reduced or eliminated. The Cortes still retained some control over taxation but this power tended to become perfunctory. The nobility relinquished any claims to political sovereignty. But Isabella and her successors never attacked the economic base of the nobility. Tied securely to the land and the woolen industry and exercising in some cases seigneurial rights, the aristocracy still maintained a commanding position in the countryside. But political authority, the right to make laws and collect taxes, rested firmly in the hands of the monarchy.

The control of religious institutions was also secure. Isabella wrested control of the Inquisition from the Papacy. She began the task of reforming the Spanish Church assisted by her confessor Cardinal Cisneros. Ferdinand secured under the *patronato real* (1501, 1508) the right to appoint all ecclesiastics in the New World and to define the limits of their jurisdiction. The role of the church in Castile was clearly demarcated before the Reformation. The church was to be an institution of royal domination and a source of support both financially and politically, an ally and not a competitor. The Catholic monarchs

> had solved the problem of state building sooner than most of their contemporaries in Western Europe. In the revival of royal power, in the development of institutions of government, in the creation of a powerful military machine, in the reform of the church, all of which were accomplished or initiated within a single generation, Spain had a tremendous start on any of her rivals. [1]

It was Charles V, the young Burgundian Prince, who inherited the work of his Spanish grandparents. Charles was not simply King of Castile. In addition, he inherited the Crown of Aragon–Catalonia which included Sicily and Naples. He was also Prince of the Low Countries and heir to Hapsburg estates in Austria, the Tyrol, and Southern Germany. These acquisitions did not constitute an empire. They were a series of kingdoms united to his person. The preoccupation of his reign was the maintenance of this inheritance and the defense of royal power. The principal basis of Charles' support both financially and militarily was Castile where the foundations of royal power were secure. The New World belonged to Castile, and Castile possessed the most vigorous and aggressive machinery of state in Western Europe. The Crown's position was further strengthened when the resistance of Castilian towns and the Cortes to the rule of Charles V was broken in April of 1521. The Cortes did not regain control over the tax structure of the state.

Four months later, in August of 1521, Hernan Cortés completed the final siege and destruction of the Aztec capital, Tenochtitlan. Cortés and his contingent of followers had to contend with a monarchy acutely aware of its prerogatives in a conquest carried out on behalf of the King of Castile. The timing was consistent with the process of royal consolidation. Colonization and the subsequent extension of the bureaucratic machinery of state developed in Castile were tied together.

The followers of Cortés and Pizarro conquered, but like the conquerors of Granada and the descendants of Columbus, they were not to rule their conquest. Royal government rapidly advanced in the New World. Isabella

---

[1] John Lynch, *Spain under the Hapsburgs*, 2 vols. (Oxford, 1964–1969), vol. 1, *Empire and Absolutism*, p. 34.

displaced Columbus in 1502, appointing a royal governor in his place. The queen, concerned with every facet of society in America, issued extensive instructions to her governors. A comprehensive Indian code, the laws of Burgos, was drawn up by Ferdinand in 1512. Both monarchs took care to provide effective administration in their new kingdoms. Santo Domingo (Hispaniola) was made the seat of an *audiencia* in 1511. The extension of royal power to the vast area of two continents was a monumental task. But it was not a new task nor even a bold new policy. It was consistent not only with the policies and experience of the monarchy in Castile but was the fruition of three decades of careful control and observation in Hispaniola. Charles V and his advisors in the Council of the Indies were prepared to secure the rights of the Crown both in the New World and in Castile.

THE *CONQUISTADORES*

Although the Crown asserted its power and displaced many *conquistadores* from positions of political control, the *conquistadores* never attempted to establish independent kingdoms in the New World. While the coming of the first royal governor, viceroy, or *audiencia* was not greeted with rejoicing, it rarely provoked armed resistance. The great exception concerns the first Viceroy of Peru, who came as an agent of the Crown to enforce the New Laws. We shall consider the significance of this subsequently. Still, there was remarkably little formal opposition to the second conquest of America carried out by the royal bureaucrats dispatched by the Council of the Indies. To understand why this was the case, it is necessary to consider the social environment that produced the *conquistador*.

The settlement of the New World required royal approval. The Spaniards who undertook the conquest of Mexico were recruited from the islands (Santo Domingo, Cuba), where royal institutions were firmly established. Cortés, anxious to uphold his right to the spoils of conquest, carefully surrounded his actions with an aura of legitimacy. The expedition was carried out in the king's name. At Vera Cruz, Cortés formally established the first Spanish town on the mainland, appointing all the necessary town officials prescribed by Spanish custom and usage. Cortés was designated captain-general (governor and military commander) by his followers. He promptly sent a letter to Spain explaining his actions to the king. Cortés also made provisions to set aside the royal fifth (*quinto*), the king's share of all the gold and silver discovered in the New World. A decade later, Francisco Pizarro traveled all the way to Spain from Panama to acquaint the king with his discovery of Peru and to procure a capitulation from the Council of the Indies that would establish his legal right to carry out the conquest on behalf of the king. Only then did Pizarro return to Peru to begin the conquest.

Royal authority was an important reference point for the *conquistadores*. Experience demonstrated that royal officials, both civil and clerical, would follow in the wake of conquest. By the time of the conquest of Mexico, the role of the Crown in the New World was clear. The *audiencia*, established by the Crown in Mexico City (1528), provoked little opposition. The monarchy was simply asserting its legitimate rights.

Royal control spread throughout the areas of the conquest because Castile was well-equipped for the task. She was prepared not only by the role she had played in the conquest of the Iberian peninsula but also by virtue of the part she had played for over three decades in the settlement of Hispaniola and Cuba. In addition, the *conquistadores* were predisposed to accept royal control, as evidenced by the concern they showed to establish the legitimacy of their conquest in the eyes of the Crown and by their own self-definition as agents of the Crown. It is difficult to believe that the early *conquistadores* had much of an alternative. The deck was stacked in favor of the Crown. Its resources were not only political but religious and cultural as well. The Crown monopolized not only the right to fill political offices but through the church it controlled salvation. As the focal point of an aristocratic order—precisely that world of status and wealth the *conquistador* sought to enter—it controlled the mind as well.

The strong grip of the Castilian Crown in the New World was not due just to the array of officials and institutions that could be brought to bear upon the centrifugal forces of conquest. The Spanish empire in America was not simply an order of external constraints and social control. It was an internal, motivational order as well. The *conquistadores* were hardly the standard-bearers of a value system alienated from the social order of Spain. This was not the movement of a counterculture. Cortés and Pizarro came to the New World to acquire the resources to re-enter the old one with enhanced status and prestige. The Crown itself gave meaning to the conquest. The titles and *encomiendas* granted by the king determined social rank and gave public recognition to accomplishments. A social order in America that was not based on the authority of the Crown and the church would have violated basic assumptions about the nature of society.

Before embarking for Mexico, Cortés addressed his soldiers:

> I hold out to you a glorious prize but it is to be won by incessant toil. Great things are achieved only by great actions and glory was never the reward of sloth. If I have labored hard and staked my all on this undertaking, it is for the love

of that renown which is the noblest recompense of man. But, if any among you covet riches more, be but true to me . . . and I will make you masters of such as our countrymen have never dreamed of! You are few in number, but strong in resolution; and if this does not falter, doubt not but that the Almighty, who has never deserted the Spaniard in his contest with the infidel, will shield you, though encompassed by a cloud of enemies; for your cause is a just cause, and you are to fight under the banner of the Cross. Go forward then with alacrity and confidence and carry to a glorious issue the work so auspiciously begun. [2]

This is the speech of the *Reconquista,* and the man talking and the men listening are its heirs and descendants. These men are not institutional entrepreneurs or the harbingers of social change. They are attuned to the aristocratic seigneurial ideal. They respond to the images evoked by glory, renown, riches, masters, the infidel, the Almighty, the just cause, and the Cross. These men would conquer in the name of the king. They would expect to be rewarded, especially with *encomiendas;* they would not expect to face the task of building a social order by themselves. They looked to the Crown of Castile to be the lodestone of social organization providing justice, arbitrating conflicting claims, organizing commerce, collecting the royal tax on silver and gold, sending supplies, and taking responsibility for organizing the church and man's salvation. The Crown provided a secure point of reference for men surrounded by the vast population of an alien culture. It was the source of institutional life for men not primarily concerned with building new institutions. The Crown was the bastion of an ordered society.

During the aftermath of the conquest, the Crown intervened in the factional disputes between *encomenderos.* Where it did not perform this function immediately, as in Peru, complicated civil wars and vendettas resulted. Royal authority moored to a complex set of institutions became the essential ingredient, the primary focus in terms of which colonial society developed. In accomplishing this task, the Castilian monarchy performed the role it was equipped and determined to perform, but it was also

[2] William H. Prescott, *The History of the Conquest of Mexico,* abr., ed. C. Harvey Gardiner (1843: Chicago, 1965), p. 65. Prescott's account is based on the chronicle of Francisco López de Gómara. See López de Gómara, *Cortés, the Life of the Conqueror by His Secretary Francisco López de Gómara,* ed. Lesley Bird Simpson (Berkeley, 1964), pp. 24–25. It is possible that Cortés did not make such a speech to his troops. Gómara was not with Cortés at the time. But much of the chronicle is based on the testimony of Cortés, and the passage represents either what Cortés said or what Gómara thought Cortés should have said. In any event, the passage illustrates an interpretation of the meaning of the conquest by a contemporary of Cortés. The extent to which the Crown formed a reference point for the *conquistadores* can be seen in the letters of Cortés to the king. See A. R. Pagden, *Hernan Cortés: Letters from Mexico* (New York, 1971).

a role the monarchy was expected to play by those who were the object of royal control. Rarely was it necessary to use force against the *conquistador*. Instead, he complied to that external system of constraints and the internal motivational order that was the foundation of the monarchy.

THE NEW LAWS

The New Laws of the Indies were promulgated in a royal cedula by the Emperor Charles V in 1542. The Crown assigned the task of enforcing the New Laws and establishing viceregal government in Peru to Blasco Núñez Vela. Investigating the viceregal administration of Antonio de Mendoza in New Spain and proclaiming the New Laws in that kingdom was the mission of the royal visitor Tello de Sandoval. Several considerations prompted the Crown to issue the New Laws. The persuasive arguments of the Dominican polemicist, Bartolomé de Las Casas, were crucial. Las Casas appealed to the Crown's Christian duty to protect and safeguard the Indians entrusted by God to the monarchy. Undoubtedly the zealous arguments of Las Casas pricked the conscience of Charles V. A considerable amount of sincerity must be granted to the Castilian monarchy in this regard. The bulk of legislation issued throughout the colonial period designed to improve the treatment of the Indian population and to safeguard their welfare is impressive. The Crown was also moved by more pragmatic considerations. In 1542, the monarchy was concerned about the potential threat to royal authority, posed by the creation of an entrenched, hereditary aristocracy in the New World. The *encomienda*, an institution that granted the *conquistadores* unlimited access to Indian labor and tribute, provided the base for such a class. Yet, the expedient of legitimizing the right of the conquerors to Indian labor and tribute was precisely the measure used by the Crown to reward the men who had increased the domain of the King of Castile. The captains of conquest, such as Cortés and Pizarro, were conceded the right to grant Indian towns to their followers to be held in *encomienda* (encomendar: *v.*, *irr*, to charge, advise, to entrust, to recommend, to commend). The essential feature of *encomienda* was

> the official consignment of groups of Indians to privileged Spanish colonists. The grantees, called encomenderos, were entitled to receive tribute and labor from the Indians delegated to them. The Indians, though liable to the demands for tribute and labor during the effective period of the grant, were regarded as free for the reason that they were not owned as property by their encomenderos. . . . A grant of encomienda conferred no landed property. . . . [3]

[3] Charles Gibson, *The Aztec under Spanish Rule* (Stanford, 1964), p. 58.

Generally, the New Laws sought to regulate the treatment of Indians. The laws curtailed the enslavement of Indians, and terminated personal service. Indians were not to be used as carriers except where it could not possibly be avoided. The *audiencia* was enjoined to carefully investigate excesses committed against the Indians. But the most important provision of the New Laws was a direct attack on the institution of *encomienda* and hence the economic base of the *encomenderos*. It stated:

> Also we order and command that henceforth no viceroy, governor, audiencia, discoverer or other person, may give Indians in encomienda by our provision or by renunciation, donation, sale, or in any other form or means . . . but upon the death of the person holding the said Indians, let them be placed in our royal crown. . . . [4]

The institution of *encomienda* was to be abolished. The response came quickly.

The New Laws in Peru

In 1533, the Spaniards forcibly entered Cuzco, the seat of the Inca empire. But Inca resistance was intense, and the Spaniards faced serious uprisings throughout the 1530s. When the Spaniards were not fighting Indians, they fought each other. Peru was plagued with a series of civil wars pitting the followers of the two great captains, Francisco Pizarro and Almagro, against each other. Peace was not restored until the royal governor, Vaca de Castro, assisted by most of the great *encomenderos*, defeated the younger Almagro in 1542. At stake in these internecine battles was the distribution of *encomiendas*. With civil strife terminated, the governor undertook a final distribution of *encomiendas*. The truce in Peru was fragile. Opposition to the New Laws was complete. A prudent viceroy might have avoided overt conflict. But the new viceroy, Blasco Núñez Vela, was an uncompromising sort intent upon complete compliance to the royal will. His stance incurred armed resistance.

The *encomenderos*, led by Gonzalo Pizarro,[5] defeated and killed the viceroy in January of 1546. This was open rebellion, however reluctant the

---

[4] Lesley Byrd Simpson, *The Encomienda in New Spain* (Berkeley, 1950), p. 130.

[5] Francisco Pizarro brought several of his brothers to Peru. Hernando, the eldest, returned to Spain with his share of the treasure of Cajamarca. He died there in 1580 at the age of 80. Before he could be confirmed as governor of Peru, Francisco Pizarro was assassinated by the followers of Almagro in 1541. Gonzalo then inherited the leadership of the Pizarro faction. He opposed both the viceroy and the New Laws.

encomenderos may have been to take up arms against the vice-king.[6] Yet, this event does not necessarily run counter to the argument that the *conquistadores* accepted the framework of royal control. Royal judges, treasury officials, and a governor were already established in Peru by 1542. It was not the coming of a viceroy that led to the rebellion, but the intent of the viceroy to enforce the New Laws. Charles V abrogated a basic element in the understanding between Crown and conqueror when he issued the New Laws, namely, their right to exploit the Indian population. The *encomenderos*, to protect their own position within the new society, rebelled. The establishment of an independent state was totally out of character for a social group that "far from having any motive of dissent . . . opposed innovation in any form, either in Spanish culture or in the customs of the Indies."[7]

The New Laws violated the tenets of Spanish culture. Virtually all the men who participated in the conquest of the Indies were born in Spain. But they usually spent several years in the New World before embarking upon careers as conquerors. As a group, they were acutely aware of the prerogatives of nobility in Spain and were acquainted with practices in the Indies. The Crown of Castile never challenged the aristocratic control of land and labor in the peninsula. The peasantry remained, in many instances, under seigneurial jurisdiction. The New Laws, if enforced, would have directly linked the Crown and the Indian labor force, by-passing the *encomendero*. A society without the stabilizing force of a military–aristocratic order of *encomenderos* was untenable. This was precisely the argument of the *encomenderos* of New Spain. While the conquerors of Peru were not social theorists, the implication of the New Laws that defined the Indians as "free persons and vassals of the Crown" was, in effect, a social revolution.[8] As Prescott reported, "the conquistadores who had suffered the tortures of tantalus fighting, conquering, settling the new lands loudly demanded to see 'the clause of Adam's will which allowed the King of Spain to deprive them of their natural rights'."[9] Did not these natural rights entitle the *conquistadores* to dominate the Indian as the Spanish nobility dominated their peasants?

The New Laws diverged dramatically from established customs. *Encomienda* was outlined and sanctioned by royal decree in 1502. It was the

---

[6] William H. Prescott, *The Conquest of Peru*, ed. Victor W. von Hagen (New York, 1961), p. 367.

[7] James Lockhart, *The Men of Cajamarca* (Austin, 1972), p. 118.

[8] Simpson, *Encomienda*, p. 129.

[9] Prescott, *The Conquest of Peru*, p. 365.

traditional practice employed by the Crown to reward the conquerors. Cortés distributed *encomiendas* to his followers. The royal capitulation issued to Pizarro by the Council of the Indies in 1529 explicitly provided for the distribution of *encomiendas*. The New Laws sought to overturn an institution that became firmly rooted in the Indies during four decades of colonial experience. *Encomienda* was an integral part of the framework of royal control that connected the interests of the Crown to the welfare of its Spanish subjects in the New World. The Crown could dispatch its bureaucratic machinery: its *oidores* (judges), governors, treasury officials, viceroys, and ecclesiastics. But the disposition and use of Indian labor was to be a monopoly of the conquerors.

The revolt of the *encomenderos* in Peru was ɛ.ɪ attempt to maintain an essential cultural form. It was neither a harbinger of Spanish-American Independence nor a desperate effort to throw off the yoke of royal absolutism. The classical model of regicide provided by Cromwell and the Commonwealth was the product of another age, and the dynamic of a different cultural tradition. The *encomenderos* were willing to accept royal authority as long as their right to control Indian labor was not threatened. Pedro de la Gasca was commissioned by the king to restore order in Peru. He entered Peru in 1547, offering pardon for all and the repeal of the New Laws. Most of the *encomenderos* rallied to his side. In April of 1548, Gonzalo Pizarro was defeated. Royal government was restored and *encomiendas* were assigned to the victors. The *status quo ante* returned to Peru. The bureaucratic center lost the first major battle. The *encomendero* emerged victorious.

The New Laws in New Spain

The joint opposition of the royal bureaucracy, the church, and the *encomenderos* confronted the emissary of the king when he arrived in New Spain. The viceroy, Antonio de Mendoza, and the bishop, Juan de Zumárraga, prevailed upon Sandoval to suspend the New Laws until an appeal could be made to the Council of the Indies. Petitions and representatives of the *encomendero* class overwhelmed the Council. The Dominican chapter of Mexico City and Domingo de Betanzos, a friend of Las Casas, opposed their enforcement, arguing as follows:

> There could be no permanence in the land without rich men, and there could be no rich men without encomiendas, because all industry was carried on with Indian labor and only those with Indians could engage in commerce. Moreover, it was necessary to have rich men for defense against enemies and for protection of the poor, as was true in Spain and every other well-ordered Republic.[10]

---

[10] Simpson, *Encomienda*, p. 134.

In other words, if New Spain was to be like the mother country, a social hierarchy was required. Order rested upon hierarchy and social hierarchy rested upon the Indians. The aristocratic, seigneurial ideal pervaded colonial society. The Council of the Indies revoked the New Laws, thus preserving a basic aspect of Spanish society in America. Royal government would extend throughout the New World, but Indian labor, the original source of social stratification and economic power, was to serve the interests of colonists.

The history of the New Laws provides us with an example of what was to be a persistent aspect of Hapsburg domination. A royal cedula that challenged the local power structure would be passed by the Council of the Indies; facing serious opposition, the bureaucracy would delay implementation and appeal the cedula to the Council; the result would be a compromise adjusted to the realities of local conditions. We will examine this process in some detail subsequently. But let us first examine the structure of Indian labor.

THE SIGNIFICANCE OF INDIAN LABOR

Spaniards aspired to the social ideal of the landed nobility exempt from taxation. The men who participated in the conquest were no less attracted to this ideal than their compatriots who remained at home. James Lockhart has studied the 168 men who shared in the ransom of Atahuallpa at Cajamarca.[11] The majority of these men were either marginal *hidalgos* or upper plebians. Close to half were functionally literate. In view of their social rank, they could hope to secure titles of nobility if successful in the Indies. The treasure allotted at Cajamarca sufficed to support the *conquistadores* for life. Following the siege of Cuzco, some 60 of these men returned to Spain. They actively sought honors and titles, an activity in which most were successful. Similarly fortunate in the accumulation of honors and titles were the men who remained in Peru. For the most part, the men of Cajamarca vastly improved their social status. They achieved the goals of the Old World by reference to their achievements in the New World. Spain could be approached from America.

The success story of the *conquistadores* is based upon the social systems they subdued. Indian craftsmen produced the objects of precious metal that the Spaniards melted down. The *encomienda* was based upon the pre-Conquest organization of labor. The conquerors had seized a skilled, organized peasantry. They became its new masters. This fact helps to ac-

---

[11] Lockhart, *Men of Cajamarca.*

count for the rapid development of an aristocratic class in the Indies. The conquerors did not clear land. They did not build their own dwellings. They were not the calculating organizers of commercial agriculture. They were the masters of a productive economic system. In a single generation, an empire was created in the Indies that could accommodate most of the social groupings known in Spain. *Hidalgos,* professionals, merchants, artisans, women, priests, and slaves all came to the New World, in representative numbers, during the immediate post-Conquest period.[12] However, they entered a society that preserved the aristocratic, seigneurial ideal by perpetuating the *encomienda,* an institution made possible by the social organization of the Indian population. The *conquistadores* were the disseminators of cultural forms consistent with the social environment they engaged. Had this not been the case, the mode and result of Spanish colonization in the Americas would certainly have been different. In those marginal areas of the Spanish empire where a readily exploitable, agriculturally based labor force did not exist, as in Argentina, the pace and structure of development stands in vivid contrast to the achievements of Cortéz and Pizarro.

THE STRUCTURE OF INDIAN LABOR

The Council of the Indies revoked the New Laws, but the strength of the *encomendero* class in New Spain and Peru had reached its apex. The New Laws were momentarily neutralized. However, the long-term trend was toward a drastic reduction in the significance of the *encomienda* as an institution of labor control. The goal of the *ecomenderos* to establish themselves as a stable, economically secure, hereditary aristocracy—the nightmare of the Crown—was never realized. *Encomienda* could probably have withstood the attacks of the Crown. It could not survive the precipitous decline in the native population and the subsequent contraction of its tribute and labor base. The population of central Mexico continued to drop from the period of the conquest until the mid-seventeenth century.

Between 1519 and 1600, the Indian population fell by over 75%.[13] Especially dramatic were the great plagues of the 1540s and 1570s. They profoundly affected the economic and social organization of New Spain. Had

---

[12] James Lockhart, *Spanish Peru, 1532–1560; A Colonial Society* (Madison, 1968), p. 221.
[13] Woodrow Borah, *New Spain's Century of Depression* (Berkeley, 1951), p. 11 (Ibero–Americana 35).

the Indian population of 1519 remained relatively stable, the history of New Spain would certainly have been different. As it was, the society had to constantly adjust to a decreasing labor supply. By the 1570s, there was an acute labor shortage. The equilibrium between Spanish and Indian culture was continually shifting, creating grave instability in both. The effect on native culture and pre-Conquest institutions was disastrous. The more inclusive units of Aztec society were eradicated. Local, less comprehensive, fragmented units survived.[14] The ability of Aztec society to respond to the conquest was progressively undermined and demoralized. The Aztec empire disappeared in the mortality rates of the sixteenth century. A more striking case of cultural devolution and simplification can hardly be found.[15] The net result of depopulation in New Spain was the eclipse of both Indian culture and the *encomendero*. The desire of Cortés and his followers to be the lords of a great Indian civilization was forever undone. It scarcely outlived the first generation of conquerors. A new colonial aristocracy emerged unrelated, for the most part, to the early *encomenderos*. It was predominantly a land-based aristocracy recruiting labor through new institutions—the *repartimiento* and debt peonage.

While the abolition of the *encomienda* was stalled in 1542, the Crown succeeded in gradually restricting the institution. The level of tribute was progressively regularized. In 1549, labor services were curtailed, limiting the role of *encomienda* in agriculture. The royal offensive against *encomienda* occurred in the wake of the disastrous plague of 1545–1548. The Crown moved to restrict an institution that had already proved to be inadequate to feed the population of Spanish towns and cities. Recruitment of non-*encomienda* Indians to work on a rotational basis in the public interest had already started. The royal attack on *encomienda* was somewhat gratuitous, for the *encomienda* was a dying institution. For the next half century, *repartimiento* was the major means of supplying labor for work in Spanish agriculture and in the construction of public works. The *encomendero* was reduced from the master of the Indian population to the pensioner of the Crown.

The *repartimiento* system (repartir: *v*, to distribute, to allot) was organized as follows:

Population records were first collected for each contributing community, and from these a percentage quota, at first approximating two percent of the tributaries, was

---

[14] Gibson, *Aztecs under Spanish Rule*, pp. 403–409.
[15] For a theoretical discussion of "devolution" see Charles Tilly, "Clio and Minerva," in *Theoretical Sociology*, ed. John C. McKinney and Edward A. Tiryakian (New York, 1970).

computed. Each community was then expected to furnish its assigned number of workers each week. . . . Every Monday morning the Indians from the towns of each repartimiento area assembled at a given distribution point. [Indians were issued to the Spanish farmers] in accordance with the amount of wheat each had under cultivation. . . . On the afternoon of the second Monday, the Indians received their pay and were released to return to their communities. Their places were immediately taken by a new group, which had been collected, assigned and delivered in the same manner. [16]

This system worked without undue hardship on Indian communities. Initially, Indians held in *encomienda* were not liable for the *repartimiento*. As *encomiendas* escheated to the Crown, Indians were placed under civil magistrates, the *corregidores*. Thus, an increasing percentage of Indian labor was made available for the *repartimiento*. Based on the customary labor organization of the Indians, *repartimiento*, in its early stages, does not appear to have adversely affected the social organization of Indian communities. However, the plague of 1576 ushered in another period of adjustment as the ratio of the Spanish and Indian population was again drastically altered. The construction of cathedrals and palaces, projects characteristic of the first part of the century, came to a halt.[17] Food shortages were experienced in Mexico City. The Indian population continued to fall in almost every decade until 1620. As a result, the surviving population was overburdened with demands for its labor. The *repartimiento* quotas rose, sometimes to 10%. The disintegration of native communities was accelerated as demands for labor and tribute increased. The population that remained was congregated into larger units, and depopulated villages were abandoned. Thus, more land became available for Spanish commercial agriculture. It was during this period (1570–1650) that land ownership by Spaniards organized into large estates, or *haciendas*, attained its dominance.

As the deficiencies and the burdensome character of the *repartimiento* became manifest, it attracted the hostility of the Crown. *Repartimiento* was terminated in 1601, but without effect. In 1609, provisions were made to phase out the institution, but again, the royal legislation did not have the intended result. The Viceroy of New Spain appears to have been successful in terminating the institution by decree around 1633.[18] In the Audiencia of Quito, the royal legislation against *repartimiento* led the viceroy to invoke the standard formula—"I obey but I do not comply."[19]

[16] Gibson, *Aztecs under Spanish Rule*, pp. 226–227.
[17] Borah, *Century of Depression*, p. 31.
[18] Gibson, *Aztecs under Spanish Rule*, pp. 233–236.
[19] John L. Phelan, *The Kingdom of Quito* (Madison, 1967), p. 81.

Repartimiento, or the *mita*, as it was called in Peru, ended not because of royal cedulas but because it was gradually supplanted by a more stable and efficient labor institution, debt peonage and the *hacienda*.

Under the *hacienda* system, Indians were no longer forced to contribute labor services. Instead, laborers either established permanent residence on the *hacienda* or lived within an Indian community but hired themselves out to the *hacienda*. In theory, Indian labor could now choose its employer. The wheat farms of the central valley of Mexico had employed such labor since the 1580s. By viceregal order, private Indian workers, called *"gananes"* (ganar: *v*, to win, to profit, to gain, to earn, to get ahead of), were exempted from labor services owed to the Indian community. The *hacienda* attracted its workers away from the overburdened Indian community. Workers escaped community obligations by becoming *gananes*. In return, they were paid, but their primary labor obligation was now owed to the *hacienda*. While the *hacienda* seriously undermined the Indian community, it did offer advantages to Indian workers:

> To Indian workers the hacienda offered solutions to economic conditions not to be found elsewhere. As monetary values came to occupy a greater role in Indian society . . . the hacienda offered a regular or irregular income. To Indians who had lost their lands (largely, of course, to haciendas) the hacienda provided a dwelling and a means of livelihood. Under conditions permitting tiny margins between income and sustenance, the hacienda was an institution of credit, allowing Indians freely to fall behind in their financial obligations without losing their jobs or incurring punishment. [20]

The *hacienda* was the culminating institution in the history of Indian labor. It was less coercive than the labor systems it replaced. Although Indian workers were nominally free to choose their employer, the extension of credit and the contraction of debt probably inhibited mobility. Yet, debt peonage may not warrant the pernicious reputation it has acquired. In colonial times, the contraction of debt was a demand of labor rather than a sinister plot of the *hacendado*. This was certainly true in the mining industry where workers would refuse employment unless they were advanced substantial sums. In the valley of Mexico, during late colonial times, less than half of the *hacienda* workers were in debt and many of these owed only small sums.[21] The *hacienda* attracted Indian labor because it offered positive advantages. The role of indebtedness was less important. The emergence of the *hacienda* is symbolic of the economic

---

[20] Gibson, *Aztecs under Spanish Rule*, p. 225.
[21] Ibid., pp. 253–255.

shift that occurred in the New World. Native agriculture had given way to an agricultural system dominated by Spaniards.

THE EFFECTS OF POPULATION DECLINE: SUMMATION

Depopulation radically altered colonial society. The sequential development of labor institutions—*encomienda, repartimiento,* and *hacienda*—was a direct response to the rapid decline of the Indian population. The shift in labor institutions upset the social hierarchy. The *encomendero* class was undermined. The *encomienda* became progressively irrelevant to the social history of the New World. By the 1570s, most of the large *encomiendas* in the central valley of Mexico had reverted to the Crown. The discontented second generation of *encomenderos* could not find support for their disaffection in the ranks of the new Creole[22] elite who successfully adjusted to the changing economic environment.[23] Landholding and the organization of agriculture and cattle-raising provided a new base for the colonial aristocracy.

The crown may have won the struggle against the *encomendero*. But the *hacienda* won the battle to control the Indian labor force. Landowners circumvented Indian legislation that ran contrary to their interests. Labor systems responded to the demands of the dominant white population and not to the theories of the Council of the Indies. The Crown, for example, made little headway against *repartimiento* until *hacienda* and debt peonage had resolved the problem of a labor shortage. The official goal of a free, voluntary labor force was never realized. In spite of numerous cedulas to the contrary, a labor supply was always made available even to support the notorious and prison-like *obrajes,* the textile sweatshops of the New World. Employers could always find royal officials willing to disregard both the letter and the spirit of the law. If the colonial elite remained staunchly loyal to the Crown during the period of an acute crisis in labor supply, it was in no small measure due to the fact that the commercial landowners, mining interests, and *obraje* managers controlled the outcome and, for the most part, enjoyed the support of the bureaucracy.

---

[22] A Spaniard born in America was called a "Creole" or "*Criollo.*" The term did not imply a mixed racial ancestry. Spaniards born in the parent country were known as "*Peninsulares.*"

[23] Lesley Byrd Simpson, *Many Mexicos* (Rev. ed., Berkeley, 1971), pp. 129–149.

The relationship between the Spanish and Indian communities in the New World was fundamentally altered by depopulation. The Indians lost their land. Although land that was depopulated was to be redistributed to surviving Indian communities, depopulation occurred faster than land could be alotted. The regrouping of the remaining population into compact communities (*congregación*), a policy justified on the basis of administrative and ecclesiastical efficiency, made now tracts of land available for Spanish use, regardless of cedulas prohibiting their usurpation. Spanish commercial agriculture also received an impetus from the inability of Indian agriculture to support the needs of the white population. By the beginning of the seventeenth century, the Indian population found itself hemmed in by the encroaching *hacienda*. Whereas in the period following the conquest, an Indian society existed capable of maintaining elements of its pre-Conquest social organization, indigenous leadership succumbed to the same laws of mortality that affected the Indian masses. There was a flattening of the pre-Conquest system of stratification. While the basic resource of Indian culture, land, fell into the hands of the Spaniard, debt peonage further loosened the bonds that tied the Indian to the social structure of his community. Cortés had conquered a great Indian civilization. A century of depopulation and oppression yielded a demoralized and generally impoverished series of enclaves surrounded by the cultural institutions of an Hispanic world order—a legacy that remains to this day. Indian culture was unable to respond to Hispanization in any unified or creative manner. This was generally the case in New Spain.

The sequence of labor institutions in Peru followed the same overall pattern as that of New Spain, but the timing was different, and the drop in the Indian population not as severe. Not only did more comprehensive units of Inca civilization endure into the late colonial period, but Indian resistance was more intense and prolonged. It was not quelled until the capture and execution of the last Inca in 1572—a full half century after the fall of Tenochtitlan. Christianization was less thorough. The records of the *visitadores de idolatría* (clerical judges sent to investigate idolatry) attest to the tenacity of native religion and the existence of native priests as late as the eighteenth century.[24] The Inca nobility also survived. José Gabriel Tupac Amaru, who led the last Inca revolt (1780–1783), was a wealthy *cacique* (Indian chief or local ruler) who governed the Indians under his jurisdiction and collected the tribute owed to the Crown. He made use of many Inca institutions that survived the con-

---

[24] John Rowe, "The Incas under Spanish Colonial Institutions," *Hispanic American Historical Review* **37** (1957), pp. 156–191.

quest. José Gabriel, as a descendant of the Inca royal family, was exempt from tribute and personal service. He wore the dress of an Inca nobleman; operated a transport service; had a large cacao estate; and was heir to the marquisate of Oropesa granted by the king to the Inca royal family. He was also educated in a school established for the sons of Inca noblemen. After the revolt of Tupac Amaru, the Inca nobility was ruthlessly and totally annihilated.[25] Such were the tender mercies of Bourbon enlightenment.

Generalizations regarding the effects of depopulation based on data from New Spain can only approximate conditions in Peru. The survival of native priests, the Inca nobility, and a less servile class of Indian officials into the late colonial period points to the maintenance of a more complete Indian culture in Peru. The social organization of the Inca was less fragmented, and community life less dissipated. If we must qualify statements about the Indian population, then it is probably true that the effect of depopulation on the *encomendero* class in Peru was also less pronounced. The interaction between labor supply and labor organization, the social history of the *repartimiento* and the *hacienda*, must also differ considerably from the case of New Spain. A comparative study of this kind would certainly be worthwhile. At issue is the stability of the colonial elite and the integration of Indian and Hispanic culture.

---

[25] Lillian Estelle Fisher, *The Last Inca Revolt 1780–1783* (Norman, 1966), pp. 22–31, 348–383.

II

Royal Government in America under the Hapsburgs

Royal government had to counteract the challenge to its authority that came from centers of power in the colonies. In this respect, the Spanish monarchy faced a situation common to any colonial enterprise. Each colonial administration in America shaped the relationship between local authority and royal control in its own way. The problems were parallel, but the process of development and dissolution was specific to each.

The initial phase of Hapsburg control in the New World took the form of a prolonged offensive that attempted to bring under its administrative and judicial purview the huge expansion of empire secured for the monarchy by the *conquistadores*. This movement coincided with the apogee of Spanish power in Europe and the vigorous reigns of Charles V (1517–1556) and Philip II (1556–1598). The seventeenth century witnessed a progressive waning of royal initiative. Those aspects of royal administration that threatened the social and economic position of Creoles, or were directed against the illegal profits of royal officials, were neutralized or circumvented. The ability of the monarchy to extract resources from America declined. This situation was reversed by the Bourbons. Energetic

25

Map 1 The viceroyalties of New Spain and Peru, and the *Audiencias* of the sixteenth and seventeenth centuries. (Dates for the establishment of the *Audiencias*.)

reforms were initiated under Charles III (1759–1788), which increased royal revenue substantially and reduced the role of the Creoles in the governing of the Indies. The Bourbon reformers reconquered the New World. But the nineteenth-century revolts mounted a decisive counterattack that revealed the strength of local interests alienated from the Bourbon government. The empire collapsed.

THE TOWN

The municipal town council (*cabildo, ayuntamiento*) was a political institution of immense importance in the immediate post-Conquest period. One of the first acts of Cortés was the founding of a town. The early conquerors had the authority to do so. Designated as an *adelantado* (adelantar: *v.*, to advance, to move forward, to progress) by the Council of the Indies, Francisco Pizarro was expected to create municipal organization in the king's name. The *adelantado* had the right to appoint the first members of the *cabildo*, both those who were to carry out judicial functions—the *alcaldes*—and those who acted as councilors but did not have judicial jurisdiction—the *regidores*. Subsequently, the *alcaldes* were usually selected by the *regidores*. The procedure for selecting *regidores* varied considerably. One common practice was for the *adelantado*, and later the *corregidor*, to choose new members of the *cabildo* from lists drawn up by the retiring *regidores*. This procedure was followed by Pizarro in Lima. Other towns may have experienced comparatively greater freedom in the selection of *regidores*. The trend, however, was to involve agents of the royal bureaucracy in the selection process.

The establishment of a town was a solemn occasion. Frequently, it involved the designation of *vecinos* (town members eligible to attend open meetings of the *cabildo*) and the distribution of *encomiendas*. Towns in Spanish America did not "emerge." They were planned in accordance with a definite ritual. A site was chosen by the founder; the central plaza was marked off and from this point the town was laid out in grids, and individual lots were allocated to *vecinos*. The establishment of the town was legalized in a formal document drawn up by a notary and signed by the founder and *vecinos*.[1] The town was the center of Hispanic culture, the core of economic and political life. It retained its importance throughout the colonial period.

---

[1] See John P. Moore, *The Cabildo in Peru under the Hapsburgs* (Durham, 1954), pp. 48–64. See also Clarence Haring, *The Spanish Empire in America* (New York, 1947), pp. 158–178.

An instrument of domination, the Spanish town was planned to control
the countryside. The minority white population consciously located itself
in protected centers that could be supplied and served by the Indians.
Towns were also created to control trading routes and to dominate the
production of precious metals. The ability of the Spanish Crown to impose its bureaucratic machinery over the vast territory of the conquest
and to continue such domination for almost 300 years must, in no small
measure, be attributed to the settlement pattern symbolized by the town.

A population concentrated in towns was certainly more accessible to
royal control than one dispersed throughout the hinterland. The Spanish
empire was an empire of towns. The number of important towns in any
administrative area was limited. The greater the economic or political
significance of a town, the more likely it was to experience direct royal
intervention in its affairs. On the other hand, relative insignificance was
often the best guarantee that a town would retain all of its privileges unrestricted by subsequent clashes between the cabildo and various bureaucratic bodies. Santiago and Buenos Aires, for example, considered to be
marginal and undesirable places, convened the cabildo abierto (opened
cabildo) numerous times during the Hapsburg era. Santiago retained the
privilege of electing its regidores by purchasing all the offices from the
Crown.[2]

If the great symbol of the English colonist is the frontiersman clearing
the land, the symbol of the Spanish colonization should be the adelantado
pacing out the grids of a Spanish town. In striking contrast to the scattered settlements characteristic of Virginia and Massachusetts, Spanish
America was even more urban-centered than Spain.[3] It was the growth
of these centers that provided a market for Spanish goods and stimulated
the commercial agriculture of the hacienda. The society was organized to
serve the city because the masters of the New World were urban dwellers.
The economic subordination of the countryside to the city reflected the
social order. From their cities, the Spaniards strengthened and extended
their social organization.

Political administration in the immediate post-Conquest period rested
in the hands of the conquistadores. They held the seats on town councils
and the governorships of larger administrative units.[4] But as the Crown
consolidated its position in the New World, it displaced the conquistadores. Positions of political importance were filled by royal bureaucrats.

[2] Moore, Peru under the Hapsburgs, pp. 129–132, 95.
[3] James Lockhart, Spanish Peru, 1532–1560; A Colonial Society (Madison, 1968),
p. 227.
[4] James Lockhart, The Men of Cajamarca (Austion, 1972), p. 53.

Pizarro was assasinated by his rivals in 1541; a royal governor from Spain took his place. Cortés, although appointed governor and captain-general (military commander) of New Spain in 1522, found his authority reduced by royal officials. Financial responsibility was placed in the hands of treasury (*hacienda*) officials. In 1527, Cortés returned to Spain to answer charges leveled against his administration. Those *conquistadores* who managed to retain significant political positions in the aftermath of the conquest were unsuccessful in making such offices inheritable. Furthermore, several bureaucratic layers were successively superimposed on municipal organization. The great centers of Lima and Mexico City became the seats of both viceroyalties and *audiencias*; other important cities, such as Quito, Charcas, and Guadalajara became *audiencia* seats. Within the jurisdiction of the *audiencia*, important towns were organized into *corregimientos* presided over by a royal appointee, the *corregidor*. The important mining centers of Potosí in Peru, and Zacatecas in New Spain, were the centers of *corregimientos*. In addition, the ecclesiastical organization of bishoprics followed the same scheme. The *cabildo* saw many of its original *fueros* (privileges) pass into the hands of other bureaucratic units. Whereas the *cabildo* had selected its own *regidores*, members were now directly appointed by the king.

The "golden age" of the *cabildo* was in the first half century following the conquest. The scope of its jurisdiction and its potential for independent action was certainly limited thereafter. The issue was really the capacity of influential groups—merchants, landowners, miners, and *obraje* managers—to resist bureaucratic action directed against their welfare. While the Crown attacked the *cabildo* as the formal instrument of local power, other methods were found to protect important colonial interests. This is probably a better way to look at the "decline" of the *cabildo*, and we will return to it later. First it is necessary to map out the bureaucratic system through which the Hapsburgs ruled the New World.

THE COUNCIL OF THE INDIES

Final authority in matters relating to the New World rested with the Council of the Indies (*El Consejo Real y Supremo de las Indias*) and, of course, the king. The establishment of the Council in 1524 was consonant with Spanish practices of the period. Hapsburg administration was government by council linked to the person of the king via his secretaries. Conciliar government was specialized in terms of geographical jurisdiction; there was, for example, a Council of Castile and a Council of

Aragon. Councils could also be concerned with specific crosscutting functions such as the Council of the Inquisition or the Council of Finance. The bureaucratic machinery of the Hapsburgs was considerable. In the sixteenth century, Spanish administration compared favorably with that of other state systems.

Membership on the Council of the Indies typically included several appointees with extensive experience in the Indies. Every law or decree concerning administration or taxation was prepared by the Council in the name of the king, and dispatched with his signature. Papal Bulls were approved by the Council before promulgation in America. It exercised considerable influence over the selection of candidates to fill bureaucratic offices. No innovation in government or expenditure of revenue could be put into effect without its approval. The Council was a court of last resort for cases appealed from the *audiencia*; it supervised the *residencia* (review of an official's conduct at the end of his term), and periodically commissioned a visitor-general with full power to investigate all aspects of colonial life. The Council was the final adjudicator for all conflicts that occurred in the Indies.[5]

THE VICEROY

The viceroy occupied the highest bureaucratic office in the Indies. Chosen directly by the king, he usually had previous diplomatic experience in Europe. He was a noble of the highest rank and usually had political ties directly with the royal court. The viceroy was chief civil and military officer of the viceroyalty; he directed the treasury, appointed numerous lesser officials, and had supervision over justice. It was his responsibility to implement the substance of cedulas dispatched by the Council. As we have seen, the first viceroys had the difficult task of enforcing the New Laws. It was their task to oversee the organization of Indian labor. In brief, since the royal cedulas issued by the Council touched every phase of colonial life, viceregal administration concerned every aspect of imperial government. The viceroy, moreover, was not simply an executive. He exercised important discretionary powers. Not infrequently did a viceroy delay implementation of a royal cedula by invoking the formal clause, "*Obedezco pero no cumplo*" ("I obey but I do not comply"). Such was the response of Antonio de Mendoza, first viceroy of New Spain, to the New Laws.

---

[5] Haring, *Spanish Empire in America*, pp. 102–118.

There were many limitations on the authority of the viceroy. He was burdened with excessive correspondence. Not only was it necessary to keep the Council informed but he had to keep in constant communication with the *audiencias* under his jurisdiction. Many of his subordinates, such as the *corregidor, hacienda* officials (treasury), and the *oidores* of the *audiencia*, enjoyed the privilege of writing directly to the king. Indeed, *oidores* were often given secret instructions to inform the Council concerning suspect activities of the viceroy. It is extremely difficult to define precisely the powers of the viceroy, since his freedom of action often depended on the confidence placed in him by the king. Some viceroys were able to make appointments to offices usually filled only by the king. This privilege was denied to others. However, the most serious limitation on viceregal authority came from the *audiencia*.[6]

THE AUDIENCIA

The Hapsburg conception of the state was medieval. The most important aspect of sovereignty was justice. Consequently, the cornerstone of imperial administration was first and foremost a judicial tribunal, the *audiencia*. While the highest administrative unit may have been the viceroyalty, in terms of the practical administration of the empire, the *audiencia* had the greatest significance. It was the *audiencia*, and not the viceroyalty, that subsequently formed the nucleus for independent states.

By the end of the sixteenth century, there were eleven *audiencias*. The Audiencias of Santo Domingo, Mexico City, Panama, Guatemala, Guadalajara, and Manila were part of the Viceroyalty of New Spain. Those of Bogotá, Quito, Lima, Charcas, and Chile were attached to the Viceroyalty of Peru. Each *audiencia* was considered to be a separate kingdom united to the person of the King of Castile. It is a mistake to envision the *audiencia* as part of a centralized pyramid culminating in the viceroy. The pretorial *audiencias* of Mexico City and Lima, presided over by the viceroy, had no jurisdiction over other *audiencias*. Judicial appeals went from each individual *audiencia* directly to the Council of the Indies. In addition, each *audiencia* corresponded directly with the Council and often received specific orders from that body. The great distances that separated the *audiencia* seat from the viceregal capital reduced the personal authority of the viceroy. In practice, the viceroy tended to delegate a great deal of authority to distant *audiencias*. As it evolved, the *audiencia*

---

[6] Ibid., pp. 106–110. See also John Lynch, *Spain under the Hapsburgs*, 2 vols. *(Oxford*, 1964), vol. 1, *Empire and Absolutism*, pp. 180–192.

came to exercise critical administrative and legislative functions in addition to its judicial role.[7]

It is best to think of viceregal and *audiencia* authority as coextensive rather than as distinct units separated by clear divisions of responsibility. The *audiencia* was the council of the viceroy. The viceroy was president of the *audiencia* situated in the viceregal capital. It was the joint responsibility of the *audiencia* and its president, the viceroy, to ensure compliance with all royal cedulas. Difficulties arose when a viceroy attempted to act on his own without the support of the *audiencia*. In such a case, a war of correspondence was certain to be waged, with the Council serving as referee.[8]

As a court of law, the *audiencia* heard appeals from lower tribunals. It had final jurisdiction over criminal cases; civil cases could be appealed to the Council of the Indies. The viceroy was strictly prohibited from interfering with the judicial decisions of the *audiencia*, and unless he was a lawyer, he did not have the right to vote in judicial matters. The tribunal also had the right to issue ordinances of local application subject only to the approval of the Council. It is impossible to say whether the *audiencia* or the viceroy had greater authority. This depended upon the support the viceroy enjoyed from both the king and the Council, a fact that was sure to be known by the *audiencia*. Naturally, the authority of the viceroy was more pronounced in the viceregal *audiencia* kingdom.

The men who served on the *audiencia*, the *oidores* (oir: *v.*, to hear, to listen, to understand), were judges with law degrees from Spanish universities. They were career bureaucrats drawn from the urban professional class or from the gentry. Appointments were made by the Council of the Indies subject to the approval of the king. The Council consciously sought to support high standards and a genuine *esprit de corps* in the professional bureaucracy by means of an elaborate system of rewards, promotions, and penalties. An *oidor* appointed to a post in a minor *audiencia* could expect that, through faithful service, he would eventually be promoted to one of the more important *audiencias*. Initial appointments and promotions were based on some combination of academic distinction, previous experience, and family connections. A list of four nominations was submitted by the Council to the king when a position became vacant. Frequently, the king chose the first name. Rarely did he attempt to appoint someone not on the list. The Council was a very jealous guar-

---

[7] Haring, *Spanish Empire in America*, pp. 119–137. See also Lillian Estelle Fisher, *Viceregal Administration in the Spanish American Colonies* (Berkeley, 1926), pp. 1–44.
[8] Fisher, *Viceregal Administration*, pp. 131–173.

dian of professional standards. While connections at court were important, they certainly were not sufficient to guarantee an appointment. That
the Council insisted on academic qualifications and gave weight to previous experience can be seen in the case of the Audiencia of Quito. Of
the nineteen *oidores* and three *fiscales* (Crown attorneys) who served
in the Audiencia of Quito from 1598 to 1636, "every one had earned a
licentitate in law. Three had acquired doctorates. Eight oidores and two
fiscales had served in other audiencias in the Indies. The others had held
judicial offices in Spain."[9] There was also some guaranteed financial security. The widow of an *oidor* was entitled to half of her husband's original
salary for a year. If an *oidor* was permitted to retire because of old age,
he was eligible to receive a pension at full salary.[10]

The ideal *oidor* was the disinterested agent of the Crown. He was expected to be circumspect, remaining aloof from excessive sociability, especially with the Creole elite. He was to avoid entangling economic
activities or personal ties. To this end, an impressive amount of legislation
regarding the conduct of the *oidor* was sent to the Indies in the hope of
furthering the cause of disinterested government. The *oidor* and his children were strictly forbidden to marry residents of the *audiencia*. He was
not to involve himself in commercial activities, either personally or
through intermediaries. The *oidor* could not own real estate or engage in
mining, and he was not to serve as a godparent (*compadrazco*) or even
attend the weddings and funerals of residents in the *audiencia*.[11]

In spite of the expectations of the Council, most *oidores* did not conform to the ideals embodied in their job descriptions. They were involved
in commerce, owned property, invested in mining, and married Creoles.
To some extent, this can be attributed to the salary scale. While income
was substantial, it was just barely sufficient to support a life style com-
patible with the status of an *oidor*. Parsimony was not characteristic of
the *oidores*, and they usually were driven to find means to supplement
their salaries. The salary scale was rigid and did not adequately reflect
length of service. The principle of rotation in office was not strictly followed. The result was that many *oidores* served in the same *audiencia* for
ten years or more. Under such circumstances, it was almost impossible to
prevent *oidores* from sinking their roots deeply into Creole society.

The Council of the Indies, in addition to upholding professional stand-

---

[9] John L. Phelan, *The Kingdom of Quito* (Madison, 1967), p. 133. More generally,
see pp. 119–146; this chapter forms the foundation for many of my remarks.
[10] Ibid., pp. 149–150.
[11] Ibid., p. 153.

ards and specifying the requirements of professional conduct, monitored the behavior of its subordinates. On a routine basis, the president of each *audiencia* sent recommendations to the Council concerning *oidores* who merited promotion. The testimonials of both peers and superiors were important. Since correspondence was the lifeblood of the bureaucracy, any *oidor* was likely to have on file considerable documentation about his conduct in office. Still, the most significant machinery used to control subordinates consisted of the *residencia* and the *visita*.

By law, all *oidores* were subject to the *residencia* taken at the conclusion of their administration. They were required to reside in their districts for 60 days after leaving office. A special judge, the *juez de residencia* held a public inquiry into the conduct of the incumbent. Any charges of malfeasance were heard. One of the weaknesses of this system was that the *residencia* was often conducted by the *oidor's* replacement, who was inclined to be lenient.

The most dramatic means employed by the Council to check subordinates and enforce compliance was the commissioning of a visitor-general. Every official, but especially the *oidores* and the officers of the treasury, were subject to his scrutiny. The extensive powers of the visitor-general compensated for the weakness of the *residencia*. There was no time limit on the duration of the *visita*. The visitor-general listened to charges against officials in private, and collected evidence. From this testimony, he drew up a list of specific charges. The magistrate so charged defended himself before the visitor. If his defense was not satisfactory, the charges were forwarded to the Council where final sentence was passed.

The decision to commission a visitor-general was a serious one. It was an expensive and frequently excruciating experience for all concerned. Therefore, the Council of the Indies had recourse to the *visita* only in cases where it had reason to be discontented with the affairs of an overseas kingdom. The *visita* effectively shook up the bureaucratic structure. The visitor-general was empowered to investigate all aspects of colonial life; he could even suspend magistrates from office. But a particularly indiscreet visitor-general was likely to open a pandora's box of charges and countercharges that would remain unresolved for years.

THE TREASURY (*HACIENDA REAL*)

The exchequer in each *audiencia* was supervised by the *Junta Superior de Real Hacienda* (The Superior Junta of the Royal Treasury). The junta was a compendium of officials drawn from different bureaucratic agencies.

The viceroy, as chief financial officer of the viceroyalty, presided over the junta. But he shared control of the treasury with the senior *oidor* and the *fiscal* of the *audiencia* as well as with several treasury officials, usually the officer in charge of the collection of revenue, the paymaster, and the chief auditor. Subordinate treasury officials were located in the important towns of the *audiencia*, especially in ports and mining centers. There they collected the customs duties (*almorjarifazgo*) and the royal tax on silver production (*quinto, diezmo*). The sales tax (*alcabala*) was often farmed out for collection either to individuals or to corporate groups like the merchant guild (*consulado*) or the municipal council (*cabildo*). The revenue from Indian tribute was collected by the *corregidor*. After administrative costs had been met, the difference was remitted to the central treasury (*caja real*) in each *audiencia* capital. The salaries of the viceroy, *oidores*, and lesser officials were paid from the central treasury. Expenditures for defense and other approved activities were also made from the colonial treasury. The net balance was sent to Spain.

Treasury officials were, in theory, appointed by the Crown. Many treasury posts were held by Creoles. In Hapsburg times, the Crown clearly separated the supervision of finances from other aspects of administration; the treasury was to a large extent a separate bureaucracy. Its officials had the right to correspond directly with the Crown. Like the *oidores*, they could not engage in commercial activities. Still, treasury officials often played a significant role in the local economy. They extended desperately needed credit to the mining industry and financed the activities of merchants and *corregidores*.

THE CORREGIMIENTO

The principal units of local administration were the *corregimientos*, which varied considerably in both size and importance. They were governed from their chief town by a royal official called the *"corregidor."* The office of *corregidor* (sometimes referred to as the *"alcalde mayor"*) was associated with the municipality. In most instances, the *corregidor* was an integral part of town government, sitting regularly with the *cabildo*. He could intervene in town affairs to safeguard the public interest, and often had the right to confirm the election of *alcaldes* (town judges). Civil and criminal cases went by appeal from the town *alcalde* to the *corregidor*. Since the *corregimiento* could be quite large, containing several important towns, the *corregidor* was assisted by one or several *tenientes*. The primary responsibility of the *teniente* was often of a legal nature, especially if the *corregidor* was not a lawyer.

Although the office of *corregidor* was in principle a judicial one, he also had numerous legislative powers and could pass ordinances affecting local administration. The prerogative of framing local ordinances was shared with the *cabildo*. There was a definite symmetry between the *corregidor* and the *cabildo* that reflected the relationship between the viceroy and the *audiencia*. The *cabildo* and the *audiencia* were the councils of the *corregidor* and the viceroy, respectively. The *corregidor* had fiscal responsibilities, supervising the collection of certain revenues and fees that were deposited in the district *caja*, or treasury. There were the usual standards of conduct prescribed by the Council of the Indies, forbidding the *corregidor* to marry within his district, to appoint relatives to minor positions, to engage in commerce, or to hold real estate. While the *corregidor* was subject to royal appointment and approval, in practice, appointments were often made by the viceroy. A few *corregimientos* of exceptional importance were consistently filled directly by the king.[12] The term of office varied, but most of the time it did not exceed 5 years. The *corregidor* could correspond directly with the king. A few *corregidores* received salaries in the same range as that of the *oidores*. This, however, was exceptional; most *corregidores* did not receive a salary sufficient to cover their expenses. In the seventeenth century, many *corregidores* were Creoles. At the end of his term of office, the *corregidor* was subject to a *residencia*, but this mechanism of control was notoriously ineffective.

There were two types of *corregidores*. The *corregidores de españoles* had a significant Spanish and Mestizo population under their jurisdiction, while the *corregidores de indios* governed a population almost exclusively Indian. Initially, the office of *corregidor de indios* was envisioned as a counterweight to the *encomienda*. In New Spain, *encomiendas* that reverted to the Crown became *corregimientos* or parts of *corregimientos* administered by royal officials. In the long run, the creation of *corregimientos* did little to improve the treatment of the Indians. In fact, the *corregidor de indios* became an institution notorious for its exploitation. The *corregidores*

> were badly underpaid, and there was no regular promotion system by which an able administrator could expect advancement to a better post. Under these conditions, the only incentive to take on the job of corregidor was the opportunity for graft that the post offered because of the wide powers that went with it.[13]

---

[12] The practice respecting the appointment of *corregidores* varied considerably during the Hapsburg period. For a fuller discussion, see Guillermo Lohmann Villena, *El corregidor de Indios en el Peru bajo los Austrias* (Madrid, 1957), pp. 115–139.

[13] John Howland Rowe, "The Incas under Spanish Colonial Institutions," *Hispanic American Historical Review* 37 (1957): 162.

The *corregidores* became commercial monopolists, controlling the forced distribution of goods to Indian communities and sometimes dominating the sale of Indian agricultural products and handicrafts. They collected the Indian tribute that was owed to the Crown. If it was collected in kind, they "had it sold at auction, bought it in at half its market value up to the amount due for tribute, and then resold it at the going rate." [14]

MINOR OFFICES

Closely associated with the *audiencia* and the municipal *cabildo* were a series of minor posts remunerated mostly through the collection of fees for services rendered. They varied in prestige and importance. Attached to the *audiencia* was the office of *alguacil mayor*—the chief constable of the kingdom. Since all evidence and documentation presented to judicial bodies had to be notarized, there were numerous posts involving this function for both the *audiencia* and the general public. The *cabildo*, depending upon its importance, had a host of associated positions such as the inspector of the water supply, the inspector of weights and measures, police officers, surveyors, and overseers of the trade and craft guilds. On this level, Creoles predominated.

While this exposition of bureaucratic offices is tedious, it does indicate the pivotal position occupied by the Hapsburg bureaucracy in colonial life. Officialdom, whether self-interested or disinterested, was omnipresent.

BUREAUCRATIC ADMINISTRATION
IN THE INDIES

When the wife of Philip IV gave birth to a son in 1631, Quito received the news with great excitement. Antonio de Morga, president of the *audiencia*, played a key role in the celebrations that followed.

It took a month to prepare the fiestas which lasted for nine days, beginning on February 20, 1631. While the preparations were in progress, bullfights took place every afternoon. When Thursday, February 20, finally arrived, all the church bells of the city rang out to announce the beginning of the celebration. Every balcony in the main square was festively decorated with silks, taffetas and satins, all of them presumably once contraband merchandise. On each corner of the main plaza an elaborately decorated altar had been erected. ... The religious ceremony began

---

14 Ibid., p. 163.

with a splendid procession, in which the faithful carried the image of Our Lady of Copacabaña through the main square. The secular clergy, the seminarians, the regular clergy, the cathedral chapter and finally the bishop marched in front of the statue. Behind the image the civil authorities followed in order of increasing social importance, i.e., the city council, the inferior magistrates, the superior magistrates and the president of the audiencia. . . .

For the next seven days there were bullfights every afternoon. In the early evening each of the functional corporations, such as the shopkeepers, the silversmiths, the wholesale merchants, etc., at their own expense, provided the multitude with a pageant. On Friday afternoon, February 21, there was a splendid masquerade with grotesque costumes. On the following night the silversmiths entertained the capital with a pageant consisting of a cast of two hundred. On the eighth day it was the turn of the Indians to provide the entertainment.

The gaudy luxury with which the Quiteños celebrated the birth of the ill-starred heir to the Spanish throne cost the lavish sum of 50,000 pesos. [15]

This is a Baroque world of splendor and ceremony, a world in which the professional bureaucrat of our own time would feel decidedly uncomfortable. This is not a world of computers, typewriters, or clearly defined channels of communication that can be fruitfully approached from an initial perspective of goal specificity, or the functions of the executive. This is not a case study of a formal organization functioning within a larger context of norms and values. It would be more accurate to say that the bureaucracy itself provided the framework for colonial life. For the bureaucracy embodied a normative order in which compliance was reinforced through allegiance to the dominant universal symbols of Christ and King. To this end, the organization of a fiesta that reinforced the essential unity of society was as fundamental an obligation of the bureaucracy as promulgating a royal cedula. Every aspect of bureaucratic organization was surrounded by the aura of formal ceremony and ritual, be it the awesome retinue of the viceroy and his court or the ceremony of induction performed by the *cabildo* for the *corregidor*. The bureaucracy was organized not in terms of administrative functions but in terms of the highest attribute of kingship, the dispensing of justice. In addition, the bureaucracy embodied not only the presence of the King but the presence of Christ. There was little that could be rendered unto Caesar that was not rendered unto God.

Church and state were intermingled in the same structure of authority and control at all levels of the bureaucracy. The king appointed all archbishops, bishops, and abbots in the Indies. The king and the Council jointly administered and supervised ecclesiastical affairs just as they monitored the activities in, and appointments to, an *audiencia*. The viceroy,

---

[15] Phelan, *Kingdom of Quito*, pp. 179–180.

in his capacity as vice-patron of the church, made ecclesiastical nominations for parishes in Spanish and Indian towns. Bishops held membership on the Council of the Indies and were frequently chosen to serve as visitor-generals. At times, a Bishop might even act as viceroy. The mitre and the scepter were coextensive and mutually reinforcing. In its finest hour, the bureaucracy contained the centrifugal forces of localism and factional rivalry by integrating the diverse layers of society into a universal framework of salvation, kingship, and justice.

Certainly, loyalty to the king was not based just on religious socialization. But it should be remembered that colonial society supported not only an aristocratic ideal but an intense spiritual order as well. The New World had its saints; and Our Lady of Guadalupe, whose shrine was one of the most important in Spain, also appeared in the New World. The church records in the mountain villages of the north of Spain are filled with references to men who returned from the New World and rebuilt the local shrines of their villages.[16] In its dual role as the personification of both altar and throne, the Hapsburg bureaucracy exercised a magnetic attraction that maintained the political and religious loyalty of the New World for two centuries.

While the bureaucracy embodied a normative order and played an important role in helping to integrate a diverse society, the bureaucracy itself was not a unitary structure. The boundaries of authority were unclear, since the same responsibilities were allocated to different bureaucratic bodies. Accountability was difficult to define. Conflicts within the bureaucracy tended to end up in the lap of the Council of the Indies. For the bureaucracy presents us not with a hierarchical structure reflecting increasing and decreasing levels of authority, but with a series of roughly equal units counterbalanced in turn by other bureaucratic bodies. An overzealous viceroy would soon find himself facing the hostility of the *audiencia*, the archbishop, or the treasury service. The nominal subordinates of the viceroy could write on their own behalf to the Council. Many royal officials were the victims of successful defamation campaigns waged by their adversaries. The tendency of any single administrative unit to dominate the others was successfully prevented. This was government by consensus. King and Council, viceroy and *audiencia*, *corregidor* and *cabildo*, were to act in harmony. Frequently they did not. The result was intense bureaucratic conflict.

The Hapsburg tradition viewed overt conflict between competing eco-

---

[16] William A. Christian, Jr., *Person and God in a Spanish Valley* (New York, 1972), pp. 161–165.

nomic and political interests as fundamentally destructive—antithetical to the requirements of a well-ordered community. Ideally, the primary task of the bureaucratic order was the maintenance of social harmony based on the pursuit of common goals that were to the benefit of the entire society. The Crown did not face the agents of a colonial political order in a common institutionalized setting, since no formal institution expressed the opposition of local groups to royal policies. Rather than concentrating antagonistic groups in the same institution, Hapsburg political organization tended to scatter conflict across the entire range of bureaucratic institutions. In English America, a specific institution, the colonial assembly, provided a forum for intense internal conflict between competing colonial factions, and directly expressed colonial hostility toward the Crown. As the center of political life and the focus of incessant controversy, the assembly represents a different understanding of political organization.[17]

Conflict, naturally, was not absent in Spanish America. The opposition of particular groups to royal policy was directed into an informal system of evasion, cooptation, and collusion. Consequently, conflict in Spanish America during the Hapsburg era has an elusive quality. There was, for example, an undertone of hostility between Creoles and Peninsular Spaniards in the seventeenth century. But this latent conflict was often activated in extremely complex situations that involved the mutual hostility of bureaucratic bodies and royal officials. The great riot of 1624 in Mexico City is a case in point. The viceroy had attacked an illegal but profitable practice of *corregidores*. Since most *corregidores* were Creoles, this affected them as a class. At the same time, the viceroy precipitated a crisis with the archbishop. This allied the secular clergy, many of whom were Peninsular Spaniards, with the Creoles against the viceroy. The *audiencia* banished the archbishop from the city. The archbishop excommunicated the *audiencia* and the viceroy. The *audiencia* then lifted the decree of banishment against the archbishop. The viceroy imprisoned the *audiencia*. In the ensuing riot, the viceregal palace was burnt to the ground.[18]

The organization of the bureaucracy made concerted and unified action extremely difficult. Rarely did the bureaucracy present a solid front opposed to Creole interests. The overlapping of jurisdictions created a constant tension between bureaucrats. In volatile situations, the bureaucracy split in terms of local issues. This was a consequence not only of the

---

[17] A theoretical treatment of the relationship between social and political systems can be found in Guy E. Swanson, "To live in Concord with Society," in *Cooley and Sociological Analysis* (Ann Arbor, 1968), ed. Albert J. Reiss, Jr., 97–107.

[18] Lesley Byrd Simpson, *Many Mexicos* (Rev. ed., Berkeley, 1971), pp. 150–159.

fragmented organizational nature of the bureaucracy, but also involved the divided loyalties of the bureaucrats who were so enmeshed in the social networks of Creole society. The very diffuseness of the Hapsburg bureaucracy created a sponge-like structure that absorbed the energy of conflict. It is frequently very difficult to ascertain who the contenders in a conflict really were, what their motivation was, and what they hoped to accomplish.

While hostility between Creoles and Peninsular Spaniards was a common element in colonial life and usually an ingredient in any conflict, a clear-cut division between the bureaucracy and the Creole population did not develop during the Hapsburg era. This situation was also a consequence of the kind of role the bureaucracy played in colonial life. The bureaucracy exercised a moderating influence on the sporadic reforming sprees of the Council. Cedulas that threatened the position of the Creoles were almost certainly to be met with delaying tactics, evasion, or the standard formula, "I obey but I do not comply." Examples are numerous. In 1690, Charles II issued a decree pertaining to the organization of the *obrajes* in the Audiencia of Quito, where the woolen industry was the economic base of the Creole elite. The terms of the cedula would have led to the demolition of most of the *obrajes*, and would have injured other areas dependent on Quito for woolens. The viceroy did not enforce the cedula. He sent a defense of his actions to the Council. In 1684, the cedula was revoked. While the king did succeed in making sure that the accounts of the *obrajes* were audited by royal officials, the use of Indian labor remained subject to the demands of the local economy.[19] Bureaucrats had heavy investments in the *obrajes* that were jeopardized by the decree. The path of moderation served the interests of royal officials who were tied to colonial society both socially and economically.

The bureaucracy usually worked out some accommodation between royal demands and the complex of local pressures. Francisco de Toledo, the vigorous viceroy of Peru (1569–1581), was instrumental in establishing firm royal control in his turbulent viceroyalty. He strengthened the *corregidores* against the *encomenderos* and reorganized the royal treasury. But his actions were selective. He never implemented the prohibitions against the planting of vineyards and olive groves, and although he was specifically instructed to do so, he did not introduce the *alcabala* (sales tax) into the viceroyalty.[20] Outright defiance of the Creole elite could invite serious opposition. The Council of the Indies expected the bureaucracy to act

---

[19] Phelan, *Kingdom of Quito,* pp. 76–82.

[20] Arthur Franklin Zimmerman, *Francisco de Toledo: Fifth Viceroy of Peru, 1569–1581* (Caldwell, 1938), p. 77.

as chief arbitrator. It rewarded such behavior. Discretion in the Hapsburg empire was the better part of valor. Rarely did the Council look favorably upon impulsive or overzealous execution of instructions; a quiet administration was usually a good administration.

Juan de Manozca, the visitor-general sent to Quito in 1634, was selected from the ranks of the Holy Office of the Inquisition. He suspended virtually all the members of the Audiencia of Quito for illegal and corrupt activities. When word reached the Council of the Indies, Manozca was promptly recalled to Spain. He was recalled not because the Council felt that the charges against the *oidores* were unjustified (they were not), but because the visitor-general had acted without prudence and had, consequently, seriously disrupted the life of the *audiencia*. In suspending the *oidores* Manozca had, moreover, discredited the institution of the *audiencia* in the eyes of the people. A more cautious visitor-general was dispatched. Even a visitor-general was expected to be a mediator; while his responsibility was to safeguard the interests of the Crown, those interests were not served by provoking conflict detrimental to social harmony.[21]

The goals of the bureaucracy were not primarily utilitarian. The concern was not simply the increase of revenue or the more efficient exploitation of colonial society. This was also a normative order that sought to safeguard the mind and soul. Profit had to share the hierarchy of goals along with salvation, justice, and moderation. Colonial society was not run exclusively by the bureaucracy for the benefit of the royal exchequer. To a large extent, it was a shared society, if not *de jure* then certainly *de facto*. If the conquerors had been displaced as royal entrepreneurs by professional bureaucrats, the wealthy Creoles certainly continued to exercise considerable influence. The trend from the end of the sixteenth century to the period of Bourbon reforms was favorable to Creole influence.

Local power remained very strong in the New World even though the prerogatives of the municipalities had been curtailed in the sixteenth century. Although the Crown, in theory, controlled local patronage by direct appointment, the sale of public offices—prompted by the financial needs of the monarchy—returned many offices to Creoles in the seventeenth century that had been denied to them during the bureaucratic offensive of the sixteenth century. Notarial positions, *cabildo* seats, treasury offices, and *corregimientos* were all sold in the seventeenth century. Some of these offices, especially *cabildo* seats, became renunciable, meaning that the purchaser had the right to nominate his successor in return for another payment. As a result, many offices were passed from father to son. Elab-

---

21 Phelan, *Kingdom of Quito*, pp. 279–287.

orate procedures were established for the purchase and resale of offices which would ensure that the purchaser was qualified.[22] The sale or venality of offices was not the peculiar invention of Spanish administration. During the sixteenth and seventeenth centuries, most European states at one time or another had recourse to the sale of offices. Essentially, venality acted as a constraint on the powers of the state.[23] It transformed the nature of the bureaucracy. When an office was sold by the Crown, it became the instrument of the incumbent rather than a tool to implement royal policy. In particular, offices—especially those of the *corregimiento* and the *hacienda* (treasury)—became the financial instruments of individuals. This tendency was reinforced by the fact that officials often went into debt to purchase their offices. To recoup their investment, they engaged in economic activities forbidden by the Laws of the Indies. Venality weakened the control exercised by the Crown over its own bureaucracy:

> The bureaucracy in all but its highest reaches became the possession of propertied men, mostly Spaniards born in America (Creoles) and, to a lesser extent, immigrants from Spain. A vast network of interests came into being, flexible enough to admit newcomers with enough power or qualifications to claim a place at the trough, tenacious enough to resist efforts at displacement for two centuries, and effective enough to drain the resources of the empire, leaving rather little for the imperial government in Madrid. [24]

The sale of public offices became a vehicle for sustained Creole ascendancy. Creoles were able to purchase control of the *cabildo*. Although the municipality became in some instances a closed corporation, it was a corporation that mirrored the interests of wealthy Creoles. Apparently, the sale of offices neither destroyed the representativeness of the *cabildo* nor led to its lethargy. The study of the *cabildo* of Zacatecas (Mexico) shows that the important mining interests of the town were always represented on the council. The fluctuations of the industry that made and unmade family fortunes also guaranteed a change in the composition of the *cabildo*. When merchants began to play an important role in the extension of credit to miners, their names soon appeared on the council.[25]

---

[22] John H. Parry, *The Sale of Public Offices in the Spanish Indies under the Hapsburgs* (Berkeley, 1953), especially pp. 33–67 (Ibero–Americana 37).

[23] Gabriel Ardant, "Financial Policy and Economic Infrastructure of Modern States and Nations," *The Formation of National States in Western Europe*, ed. Charles Tilly (Princeton, in press).

[24] Woodrow W. Borah, "Representative Institutions in the Spanish Empire in the Sixteenth Century: The New World," *The Americas* 12 (January, 1956): 256.

[25] Peter J. Bakewell, *Silver Mining and Society in Colonial Mexico: Zacatecas, 1546–1700* (Cambridge, England, 1971), pp. 98–100.

The selection of *regidores* for the *cabildo* passed out of the hands of the king and returned to the power structure of the community. The office of *corregidor* underwent a similar transformation. Originally envisioned as the royal protector of the Indian against the avaricious *encomendero*, the *corregidor* became the exploiter of the native population. Progressively, the *corregidor* had become a creature of local patronage who purchased his office, rather than a direct appointee of the king and Council. The office provided a financial base for many Creole and Peninsular interests.

The sale of treasury offices was probably most detrimental to the Crown, since it adversely affected the collection of revenue and the remittances to Madrid. It is difficult to assess exactly how great the effect was. But if we can judge from the Bourbon reorganization of the exchequer, the effect of venality in the treasury service was substantial. The revenue from the *alcabala* increased dramatically under the Bourbons. The Bourbon reforms were directed against a corrupt treasury and sought to abolish the *corregimientos*. In no small measure, this reflected the degree to which these offices no longer served the interests of the Crown. Either they had fallen into Creole hands or informal agreements had hardened into custom by the eighteenth century. For example, in 1662, the *cabildo* of Zacatecas successfully resisted the attempts of the viceroy to inspect the accounts of the treasury officials. The town was anxious to protect the officers of the royal treasury because the treasury officials distributed salt and mercury (essential ingredients in the reduction of silver) on credit to the miners.[26] If the deputies of the viceroy had examined the ledgers, they would have discovered that the miners were substantially in debt to the Crown. Had the viceroy insisted on payment, many miners would have been ruined. Undoubtedly, by extending credit, the treasury officials would be generously repaid by the miners. The *corregidor* and *cabildo* of Zacatecas were also closely allied. The *corregidor*, Fernando de Valdés (1598–1601), protected miners from avaricious merchants who had extended credit but now attempted to foreclose. In return, he became the chief supplier of materials (*aviador*) for miners on better terms of credit. The arrangement benefited both:

> The curbing of merchant aviadores suited Valdés' own credit supplying activities very well. And after him most corregidores were also aviadores as far as can be told. Thus an accommodation was reached between the corregidor and the cabildo, which was directly representative of the powerful economic interests of the town. The corregidor "sold" the cabildo his political cooperation for a share in the mining wealth of the town, and the town "bought" his cooperation by allowing

---

[26] Ibid., p. 87.

him to operate as an aviador without protest. In this way, the interests of the town and the cabildo came to coincide very closely. . . . . If, then, the crown's intention in first replacing alcaldes majores in Zacatecas by a corregidor was in some way to improve probity in the government of the town, the object was soon lost, as was predictable, by the corregidor's selling out to local interests. [27]

Both these examples are representative of the kind of *ad hoc* informal systems that emerged throughout the empire, linking together structures of local power and bureaucratic officials in an intricately layered network of cooptation and collusion which attained over time the force of custom. Mediation between the content of directives and the reality of local conditions occurred at practically every level of bureaucratic administration. Cedulas directed toward the organization of Indian labor, the control of contraband trade, and the collection of taxes, especially the *alcabala* (sales tax), the *quinto* (silver tax), and the *almorjarifazgo* (tariff), had to run the gauntlet of Creole influence. Bureaucratic structures were still crucial reference points for social organization. But this framework was susceptible to considerable manipulation by local interests.

In utilitarian terms, the Hapsburg bureaucracy was not excessively burdensome on the Creole elite. Recent evidence suggests that Creoles held more important bureaucratic positions before the Bourbon reforms than previously believed. Creole *oidores* predominated in the Audiencia of Lima by the end of the seventeenth century.[28] But while Creole influence mounted throughout the seventeenth century, the power they exercised was always *de facto* and never *de jure*. Whether they served as *oidores*, coopted royal officials, or opposed royal cedulas, they never acquired the right to exercise power. They never possessed an institution that could legitimately give expression to that power. Perhaps this contradiction was less keenly felt in the Baroque world of the seventeenth century under the tutelage of an aging parent. The eighteenth century brought a new dynasty to power in Spain and a new conception of state and empire that invigorated the colonial bureaucracy. But if the eighteenth century changed Spain's understanding of empire, the revolt of English America and the French Revolution changed the Creoles' understanding of colony. The normative order disintegrated.

---

[27] Ibid., p. 94.
[28] D. A. Brading, *Miners and Merchants in Bourbon Mexico 1763–1810* (Cambridge, England, 1971), p. 36.

III

The Organization of Trade

THE MONOPOLY SYSTEM

Trade between Spain and the Indies was a royal monopoly. The *Casa de Contratación* (House of Trade) was established in 1503, antedating the Council of the Indies. Isabella and Ferdinand kept a watchful eye on the development of commerce, limiting participation to the merchants of Seville. This policy of restriction was eased by Charles V, who opened nine Castilian ports to the Indies trade. But the increasing importance of precious metals in the trading cycle gave a new impetus to restriction. The *Casa*—placed under the jurisdiction of the Council of the Indies— and the merchant guild of Seville (*consulado*), regained their former importance. The *Casa* emerged as a government bureau responsible for all phases of the Indies trade. It licensed all ships and merchants participating in the trade, controlled the movement of passengers and goods, enforced the edicts pertaining to trade, received the precious metals remitted to the Crown from colonial treasuries, and collected the *avería* (convoy tax).[1] While outgoing vessels could register with the *Casa* in

---

[1] Clarence H. Haring, *Trade and Navigation between Spain and the Indies in the Time of the Hapsburgs* (Cambridge, Mass., 1918), pp. 117–120.

47

either Cadiz or Seville, all returning vessels were required to disembark at Seville. This measure reflected the Crown's desire to control the inflow of silver by confining its importation to a single port. Between 1550 and 1570, silver imports registered in Seville grew from 7 to 23 million pesos.[2] As the value of silver imports rose, so did the solicitude of the monarchy to defend its precious cargo.

Hostility between Spain and France during the second quarter of the sixteenth century spilled over beyond the Atlantic into the Caribbean. French corsairs seriously endangered Spanish shipping. As early as 1537, a royal fleet was dispatched to ensure the safe passage of silver shipments to Spain. A system of annual fleets gradually developed in response to the pressure of French corsairs—and later in the century, English and Dutch privateers—attracted to the Caribbean by the magnet of precious metals. The merchant guild of Seville, anxious to maintain its monopoly, steadfastly supported such a development. By the 1560s, the fleet system had attained its definitive form. Two fleets sailed annually. The Peruvian fleet stopped at Cartagena and Portobello. Goods landed at Portobello were usually transported across the Isthmus of Panama where they were reloaded for shipment along the Pacific coast. From Cartagena, merchandise was often carried overland to such centers as Bogotá and Quito. The New Spain fleet, in addition to touching at the port of Veracruz, also serviced the Greater Antilles, stopping at Puerto Rico, Santo Domingo, and Cuba. Commercial transactions occurred at the ports of disembarkation where the famous fairs were held. Silver remittances were loaded onto the fleets. Both *flotas* assembled in Havana, then returned in combined strength to Spain. While annual fleets were the ideal, a year was often skipped. Toward the middle of the seventeenth century, a period of economic depression in Spain, the fleets sailed irregularly.

The rationale that sustained the *flota* system was the importance of both protecting the silver shipments and preserving the royal monopoly on trade with the Indies. Spanish merchants were to supply the Indies with foodstuffs and manufactures. These would be paid for in silver and with colonial products such as hides, cochineal (red dye), and sugar. Silver always remained the chief colonial export. The trade was to be carried on Spanish ships manned by Spanish sailors. The profits from the trade were to accrue to the royal treasury and the merchants of Castile. This system was progressively undermined: by the financial burden of the

[2] Jaime Vicens Vives, *An Economic History of Spain* (Princeton, 1969), p. 324. Trans. Frances M. Lopez–Morillas from the Spanish edition, *Manual de historia económica de España* (Barcelona, 1964).

fleet system that fell on the shoulders of Spanish merchants, by the inability of Spanish industry to supply colonial markets, by the circumvention of the fleet system through contraband channels, and by the internal diversification of the colonial economy that reduced the demand for Spanish products. As Spain's share in colonial trade declined, so did silver imports.

Trade between the Low Countries and Spain increased when both were joined under the rule of Charles V. At that time, the Low Countries had the largest merchant marine in Europe, and Spain had the second largest. The trade centered on Antwerp, where Spanish products such as raw wool, salt, iron, and olive oil, as well as certain colonial products like cochineal, sugar, and hides, were exchanged for a wide variety of northern products, notably: linen cloth, tin, quality fabrics, naval stores, fish, and cereals. Many of these products from Northern Europe were reexported to the Indies. Through much of the sixteenth century, Spain was an entrepôt where the products of the Indies, Northern Europe, and Spain were collected, often via Antwerp, and reexported. However, since most of her exports were primary products, Spain had a balance-of-payments deficit that was met by the exportation of silver. The combined influence of the *mesta* (wool producers' organization) and merchants who found it more profitable to export raw wool than finished Castilian cloth seriously damaged the export of Spanish textiles.[3] In addition, the fiscal policies of the Crown were often damaging to Spanish trade since customs duties, viewed primarily as revenue measures, often fell heaviest on exports.

The tremendous expansion of Spanish commerce in the sixteenth century was not based on the steady growth of the Spanish economy. Rather, her prosperous commercial enterprise was based on her role as "middle man" between Europe and America. In the context of the larger European economy, Spain remained an exporter of primary products and an importer of manufactured goods. The Spanish commercial empire was not established on a very firm foundation. Serious difficulties began with the revolt of the Netherlands (1567), a crisis precipitated by the imperial policies of Philip II (1556–1598). The Low Countries were principal markets for Spanish wool, and Dutch shipping supplied Spain with cereals and naval stores. Antwerp was part of an international commercial network that linked Spain to the Indies. In the two decades following the revolt, Spanish trade links with Northern Europe were under constant pressure not only from the Dutch but from the English and French as

---

[3] John Lynch, *Spain under the Hapsburgs*, 2 vols. (Oxford, 1964–1969), vol. 1, *Empire and Absolutism*, pp. 115–116, 143.

well. The Spanish carrying trade with Northern Europe was seriously damaged and the ports of the northern Spanish coast were in decline. The growth of English sea power and the harassment of the Indies trade by the Elizabethan "sea dogs" added to the cost of fleet defense.

The products of Northern Europe continued to come to Spain, but now more than ever, they were carried in foreign vessels. Notwithstanding, the Indies trade continued to expand. Total tonnage increased from about 17,000 toneladas in 1540 to about 32,000 in 1585.[4] Silver imports jumped during the same period from 8 to 32 million pesos.[5] The size of ships also changed. The mean size until 1560 was about 100 tons. After this period, ships of 300 tons became common.[6] The north of Spain was the center of shipbuilding, constructing over 80% of the ships involved in the trade from 1520 to 1580.[7] Until 1570–1580, Spanish exports of food-stuffs, particularly oil, wine, and grain, dominated the Indies trade.[8] Trade with the New World, in terms of shipping, sailors, profits, and products, remained a Spanish monopoly until the period following the defeat of the Armada in 1588.

Besides the religious and political significance of the Armada, it also embodied a commercial struggle. Economically, the Armada was launched to defend the Spanish trade monopoly with America. If Spain could neutralize England, she could significantly reduce the threat to Spanish shipping in the Caribbean. The Armada also represented the last serious Spanish bid to clear the sea lanes for Spanish commerce in Northern Europe. This was especially important given the shifting nature of demand in the Indies. Increasingly, the Indies demanded the products of Northern Europe. The merchants of Seville had as much at stake in the Armada as those of the Spanish north coast. The Armada was composed of vessels and men usually employed in the *flotas*. The defeat of the Armada was a serious blow to Spanish commerce. Not only did Spain fail to regain her position in the Northern trade, but Spanish shipping began to lose its dominance in the Indies fleet itself. The proportion of foreign vessels in the *flotas* rose from 5.9% during the period 1579–1587 to 21.3% in the years 1588–1592.[9] The reliance of the north coast shipbuilding industry on imported naval stores not only subjected the enterprise to shortages during wartime, but also increased the cost of the finished product. But the de-

---

[4] Ibid., p. 355, Table E.

[5] Vicens Vives, *Economic History of Spain*, p. 324.

[6] Ibid., p. 327.

[7] Lynch, *Spain under the Hapsburgs*, vol. 1, p. 155.

[8] John Lynch, *Spain under the Hapsburgs*, 2 vols. (Oxford, 1964–1969), vol. 2, *Spain and America*, p. 185.

[9] Ibid., p. 168.

cline of the Spanish monopoly in America was not due only to the defeat of the Armada. A combination of factors converged after 1590 to steadily undermine the position of Spanish merchants in the Indies trade.

THE DECLINE OF THE INDIES TRADE

By the 1590s, the shift in the trading cycle began to reverberate through the Indies trade. The colonial economy, especially in New Spain, had become more diversified. It now produced a significant proportion of the wine, olive oil, and wheat consumed by the domestic market. Gradually, the demand for Spanish agricultural products had given way to a demand for the manufactured products of Northern Europe. For a while, this situation was under control. Foreigners brought their manufactured goods to Andalucia and bought Spanish products: wine, olive oil, and fruits. This left a large trade gap bridged by Spanish merchants from the profits made on both the Spanish and foreign products they shipped to the Indies. From the Indies trade, then, they balanced the deficit and made a profit.[10] As the seventeenth century progressed, foreign merchants penetrated the Spanish end of the trade. More foreign vessels were employed in the fleets. After 1623, they accounted for about one-third of all the ships involved in the Indies trade.[11] A bankrupt monarchy allowed foreigners to acquire naturalization rights that permitted them to participate directly in the Indies trade, a privilege that, of course, had to be bought. By the end of the seventeenth century, a majority of the merchant aristocracy of Cadiz was composed of foreigners. As the locus of the trade moved from Seville to Cadiz, contraband activities increased. Cadiz had direct access to the sea. Foreign merchants met the fleet after it left the harbor. Merchandise was transferred at sea, avoiding customs duties in the process. Foreign merchants had at their disposal a superior clandestine network that allowed them to participate in the trade while avoiding the liabilities that afflicted the established Spanish merchant.[12]

The Tax Structure and Decline

The policies of the Crown and the financial system that supported the *flotas* endangered Spanish commerce. Large amounts of private silver

---

[10] Ibid., p. 171.

[11] Huguette and Pierre Chaunu, *Seville at l'Atlantique 1504–1650,* 8 vols. (Paris, 1955–1959), vol. 8, p. 1563. Cited in Lynch, *Spain under the Hapsburgs,* vol. 2, p. 189.

[12] Lynch, *Spain under the Hapsburgs,* vol. 2, pp. 170–173.

were appropriated by the Crown in 1620, 1629, 1635–1638 and 1649. The growing tendency of the Crown to sequester private silver, issuing *juros* (interest-bearing notes) to Spanish merchants in return, injured the capitalization of the trade.

The *avería* was an ad valorem tax based on the cost of defending the fleet. The rate rose steadily during the first half of the sixteenth century. The *avería* was farmed out to the *consulado* of Seville. In 1585, the *avería* was averaging about 1.7% on the value of goods carried by the Indies fleet. This increased to an average rate of about 6% during the years 1602–1630.[18] The augmentation of the *avería* led to wholesale fraud as merchants sought to avoid the registration of their goods. Merchandise was carried illegally on the escorting armadas, and officials were bribed on both sides of the Atlantic. In particular, the amount of unregistered silver multiplied to avoid both the *avería* and confiscation in Seville. As fraud increased, so did the *avería*. During the 1630s, the *avería* reached 35%. The tax system had disintegrated. The *consulado* of Seville went bankrupt on the *avería* contract of 1640. Thereafter, it refused to handle the tax, and the state was required to resume its administration. The Crown encountered the same problems faced by the *consulado*. If it raised the *avería*, the increment was countered by more fraud. The *avería* was subsequently dropped. After 1660, fixed quotas were paid by the merchants of Seville and the Indies, with additional subsidies coming from the royal treasury.

The rise in the *avería* reflected Spain's continued involvement in international conflicts. The Twelve Years Truce with the Dutch ended in 1621. Spain, already embroiled in the Thirty Years War (1618–1648), renewed hostilities with the Dutch. She now faced the militant hostility of the Dutch West India Company, founded as an instrument of war. Dutch privateers harassed Spanish shipping. In 1628, the Dutch captured an entire fleet. The Dutch offensive in the Caribbean led to the disastrous *avería* rates of the 1630s. The *flota* system was trapped in a vicious cycle. By safeguarding the silver shipments, the fleets provided financial resources that were indispensable for the support of Spain's international wars. But war required greater security for the silver shipments. Defense costs steadily mounted, cutting into the profits of Spanish merchants and giving an impetus to fraud. The success of the fleet system in protecting the Crown's silver was its undoing. Ultimately, the cost of defense, which was for the most part borne by Spanish merchants, consumed the trade it was designed to protect. The recourse of the merchant was fraud.

While fraud was always a problem in the Indies trade, its dimensions

---

[18] Ibid., p. 163.

were beyond control by the 1630s. For example, the *almorjarifazgo* was an ad valorem customs duty collected at Spanish and colonial ports. In the colonies, the tax was administered by the treasury officials, and in Seville by the customs officers of the port on behalf of either the Crown or tax farmers.[14] The tax on goods from Spain was 15.5%. Goods imported from the New World were taxed at the rate of 17.5%. Appraisal was made without unpacking or opening the goods for inspection. The officials were bound by custom to accept the oath of the merchants that the value of their goods was identical to that written in the register. A system of fraud was, consequently, institutionalized in which merchants underestimated the value of their goods. As silver confiscations became more common, merchants took refuge in avoiding the registration of silver altogether. Some imports had particularly heavy duties. By 1616, cochineal was taxed at more than a third of its value. Registered imports of cochineal plummeted accordingly, from 7673 arrobas (1 arroba equals 25 pounds) in 1607 to a mere 859 in 1615, although in this last year it was well-known that at least 4000 arrobas had left New Spain.[15] The Indies trade could adjust to unrealistic taxation, but it did so by circumventing the legal channels that upheld the monopoly system. During the first decades of the seventeenth century, in terms of ships, sailors, and cargo, the Indies fleet began to take on the appearance of an international venture rather than a Spanish monopoly.

Between 1630 and 1650, the Indies trade experienced a severe depression. Spanish-controlled trade with the Indies did not surpass its peak levels (1580–1620) until the *flota* system was abandoned by the Bourbons. The volume of trade, in terms of both tonnage and ships, declined by over 50%. Table 1 and 2 provide some appreciation for the dimensions of the decline.[16]

TABLE 1

Years	Total treasury imports of Silver [a]	Registered private silver [a]
1591–1595	35.1	25.1
1601–1605	24.4	17.8
1631–1635	17.1	12.3
1646–1650	1.6	10.1
1656–1660	.7	2.7

[a] Measured in millions of pesos.

[14] Haring, *Trade and Navigation*, p. 88.
[15] Lynch, *Spain under the Hapsburgs*, vol. 2, p. 164.
[16] Earl J. Hamilton, *American Treasure and the Price Revolution in Spain 1501–1650* (Cambridge, Mass., 1934; reprint ed., New York, 1965), p. 34, Table 1. This table

TABLE 2

Years	Number of fleet vessels	Tonnage
1606–1610	965	273,560
1646–1650	366	121,308

By the mid-seventeenth century, the Spanish monopoly system was in a shambles. The trade was not, however, wiped out. Fleets continued to sail for another century, and merchants in both Spain and the Indies still made profits. Still, the concept of a Spanish monopoly on trade with the Indies was a dead letter. Spain had become one trading partner among many, and if we can judge from the level of contraband, perhaps a lesser partner at that. The commercial links between Spain and the New World were tenuous in the last years of Hapsburg rule. The colonies became detached from the monopoly system. Intercolonial trade and contraband trade expanded to meet the needs of colonial markets.

Thus far, we have stressed those factors that weakened the Spanish commercial system and were rooted, roughly speaking, on the Spanish side of the Atlantic. The destruction of the Spanish carrying trade with Northern Europe, the defeat of the Armada, the growing reliance on foreign ships, sailors, and merchants, the continued foreign conflicts that increased pressure on the fleets, the mounting defense costs, unrealistic tax structures, and rampant fraud and silver confiscations—all these factors damaged Spanish commerce. In addition, the gaps that developed in the colonies weakened the monopoly system. Other European powers began to supply the colonies directly and probably received greater shares of silver than Spain herself. Moreover, the nature of the colonial economy had shifted by the seventeenth century. It was more self-sufficient and less dependent upon Spanish products. The production of silver is especially important in this regard, since the decline in the Indies trade is often attributed to an economic depression in America caused by the decline in silver production. At stake is the relative interdependence of the Spanish and colonial economies. A colonial economy that shows relatively little economic integration with that of its mother country would be a strange "colonial" system indeed. Let us first, however, turn to the organization of contraband trade and the holes it opened up in the Seville monopoly.

contains figures for public (Crown), private, and total treasure imports for the period 1506–1660 by 5-year intervals. The tonnage and fleet sailings compilations are from Lynch, *Spain under the Hapsburgs*, vol. 2, p. 184.

GAPS IN THE MONOPOLY SYSTEM

The Dutch were the first to establish a thriving contraband trade in the New World. This trade centered on the Caribbean islands and the continental north coast of South America, especially Venezuela. These were marginal areas of the Spanish empire, distant from the silver mines of New Spain and Peru, and virtually outside the commercial networks of the Indies trade. The arrest of Dutch shipping in the Iberian peninsula (1595, 1598) by the Spanish Crown created a shortage of salt in the Netherlands that threatened the herring industry.[17] The Dutch turned to the salt pans of Venezuela as a replacement for Iberian deposits. Dutch ships did not come empty to the New World. They traded heavily, exchanging merchandise for pearls, tobacco, sugar, and hides. The hide trade with Cuba and Hispaniola was said to employ 20 ships of 200 tons each in 1606 and to be valued at 800,000 florins.[18] The Dutch obtained tobacco along the Venezuelan coast. In 1603, the Dutch received some 30,000 pounds of tobacco from the region around Cumaná alone.[19] The Spanish military offensive in the region succeeded in driving out the Dutch (1605–1611). But the conditions that fed the contraband remained. The home government could not provide adequate shipping to meet the demands of the region. The Seville monopoly could not provide sufficient goods at reasonable prices. The Dutch provided a market for an area not serviced by the fleet system. When Spain restored her economic control in Venezuela, stagnation returned, since the region lost the outlet for its products. But when hostilities were renewed with Spain in 1621, the Dutch West India Company was able to reestablish her commercial ties along the north coast of Venezuela with comparative ease. Contraband trade had willing allies in the *cabildos*, since the *alcaldes* were often the worst smugglers in the community.[20]

Using the island of Curaçao as a base, the Dutch became the major suppliers of slaves to the continental north coast (Venezuela, Columbia). Slaves were exchanged for hides, tobacco, cacao, and wood. The Spanish colonists participated wholeheartedly in the illegal traffic.[21] Eventually, cacao replaced tobacco as the most important product of the Venezuelan

---

[17] Engel Sluiter, "Dutch–Spanish Rivalry in the Caribbean Area, 1594–1609," *Hispanic American Historical Review* **28** (1948): 176.

[18] Ibid., p. 184.

[19] Ibid., p. 182.

[20] Ibid., pp. 184–193.

[21] Cornelius Goslinga, *The Dutch in the Caribbean 1580–1680* (Amsterdam, 1971), p. 355.

coast. In 1630, there were half a million trees under cultivation. The principal market for cacao was not just the international market via the Dutch but also the domestic market of New Spain. Between 1620 and 1650, Venezuela exported well over 35,000 fanegas of cacao to New Spain (1 fanega equals 116 pounds). This jumped to 322,264 fanegas between 1651 and 1700.[22] In the last decade of the seventeenth century, cacao exports to New Spain were valued at over one million pesos. Exports to Spain carried on the fleets were only a tenth of this. The Seville-Cadiz system did not profit from intercolonial trade. Mexican silver was channeled to Venezuela where it found its way into the pockets of the Dutch in exchange for slaves. The Portuguese carried on a brisk trade with Potosí by way if Brazil that may have accounted for a quarter of Potosí's silver production during much of the seventeenth century.[23] The Portuguese were supplied with merchandise by other European nations, especially the Dutch. In the eighteenth century, the British traded with the La Plata region through the Portuguese in Brazil.

The British also penetrated Spanish defenses. Jamaica was seized in 1655 and quickly became a center for the contraband trade with New Spain. The British sold manufactured goods and slaves to the Spaniards, receiving in turn a steady supply of silver that "enriched England and provided her continental colonies with most of their hard money." [24] The use of slave labor expanded during the seventeenth century. Slaves were in demand for the production of cacao, tobacco, and sugar. The average annual importation of slaves jumped from about 810 (1551–1595) to about 2880 (1595–1640), reaching an average of around 3880 during the rest of the century. These figures are based on the number of ships licensed by Spanish authorities to carry slaves to the Indies.[25] Plantation agriculture was spreading, and its demands for labor could not be met by the declining Indian population. It is not known to what extent slave labor was carried to the Indies illegally, bypassing the Spanish system of direct contract, or *asiento*. But both the Dutch and the British received significant amounts of bullion via the slave trade.

At the end of the seventeenth century, the value of the Jamaican trade

---

[22] Eduardo Arcila Farías, *Comercio entre Venezuela y Mexico en los siglos xvi y xvii* (Mexico, 1950), p. 53.

[23] Lynch, *Spain under the Hapsburgs*, vol. 2, p. 227. This trade continued to be important throughout the eighteenth century. See H.E.S. Fisher, "Anglo–Portuguese Trade, 1700–1770," *Economic History Review* 16 (1963): 219–233.

[24] Curtis Nettels, "England and the Spanish American Trade 1680–1715," *Journal of Modern History* 3 (March, 1931): 1.

[25] Philip Curtin, *The Atlantic Slave Trade* (Madison, 1969), p. 25.

in exported Spanish bullion was appraised at £200,000 annually, making a substantial contribution to the trade of the British East India Company, whose annual exportation of bullion to the Far East amounted to £400,000.[26] As the contraband traffic intensified, the *flota* system designed to control the flow of silver to Spain and to reap the harvest of silver by dominating the supply of merchandise, became progressively irrelevant to the movement of ever larger amounts of silver. The fleets became but one supplier in an economy that met its needs through intercolonial trade and illegal trade with foreigners.

Let us examine the contraband process more closely by looking at the Acapulco trade with Manila.[27] This was a trade that involved Spanish merchants and ships and, one would think, a trade that could more easily be controlled by the mother country. As early as 1573, the first shipment of Chinese silks, satins, china, porcelain, and spices from the East arrived at Acapulco. This initiated over two and a half centuries of transpacific trade between the Philippines and New Spain. Peruvian merchants met the Manila fleet at Acapulco, where they bought the largest part of the cargo and transported it to Lima for resale. The Peruvian merchant marine employed some 52 vessels, plying the Pacific from Chile to Mexico and participating in the Acapulco trade. By the 1590s, the value of the Lima–Acapulco trade must have involved 2–3 million silver pesos a year. In 1597, the bullion shipped from Acapulco, much of it bound for China, reached the enormous sum of 12 million pesos. The *cabildo* of Mexico City estimated that, during the first years of the seventeenth century, the silver lost to the Philippine trade was 5 million pesos annually. The sums involved approached the value of all the registered silver imported into Seville during the same period (1601–1605). This was not a leak in the monopoly system. It was a veritable chasm.

Contraband Trade and the Bureaucracy

Peruvian capital gravitated to the Philippine trade. Chinese silks were very cheap, selling for perhaps a ninth of the price of Spanish cloth in Peru. Although no *flota* arrived in 1593, shops in Lima were still stocked with unsold Spanish goods. The Philippine trade was not only more profitable but less risky, since the sea lanes were relatively free of privateers and

---

[26] Nettels, "Spanish American Trade," p. 8.

[27] Woodrow Borah, *Early Colonial Trade and Navigation between Mexico and Peru* (Berkeley, 1954), pp. 116–124 (Ibero–Americana 38).

the route less prone to natural disasters. The Seville merchants and the Crown were quite aware of the unfavorable competition. The trade between Acapulco and Peru was forbidden, in fact, several times. In 1593, the shipment of Chinese goods to colonies other than New Spain was prohibited. The trade between the Philippines and New Spain was limited to two vessels of 300 tons each. Still, the value of the trade reached unprecedented heights after this date. As the Marqués de Cañete, Viceroy of Peru (1590–1596), had warned the king, any prohibition on the importation or sale of Chinese goods could almost certainly not be enforced. He was, or course, correct. Luis de Velasco, in spite of more vigorous attempts to implement the cedulas (1596–1604), also proved unsuccessful. Without the support of the *audiencia* or the treasury, the hands of the viceroy were tied. The *oidores* of the Audiencia of Lima steadfastly resisted enforcement. A vast array of smuggling networks blossomed in Peru with the connivance of royal officials. In New Spain, the purchase of Chinese goods at Acapulco and their consignment to vessels bound for Peru continued with the collusion of port officials, the Audiencia of Mexico City, and the viceroy. Even religious authorities were involved. Viceroy Velasco claimed that the worst loophole was the Inquisition, whose cargo was immune from search. In 1615, "the clergy of the Indies were charged to cease assisting in the smuggling of goods and furnishing hiding places in their homes and convents."[28]

The Hapsburg bureaucracy tended to view laws as statements of ideals that might not necessarily be achieved. Everyone, from the viceroy down, was likely to make some adjustments between the ideals and the exigencies of particular situations. We have examined this process before. But it is worth observing that cedulas restricting economic activity, from the regulation of commerce to the prohibitions against the planting of vineyards, were especially prone to this process of adjustment. On one level, the Crown was simply not strong enough. Heavily committed in Europe, Spain could not afford a permanent fleet in the Indies to patrol the Atlantic and Pacific coasts. Even the British, who were more disposed to undertake such a task, found it impossible to eradicate smuggling in their continental colonies. Spain did not dispatch troops to burn vineyards, olive groves, or *obrajes*. Instead, she tended to legitimize illegal activities for a fee. Foreigners purchased the right to participate in the Indies trade, and the farming of the *asiento* (the right to deliver a specified number of slaves to the Indies) allowed the Crown to profit from an activity it could not control.

---

[28] Ibid., p. 126, 120–127.

On another level, however, illegal economic activity had yet to attain the status of an unforgivable crime against the state. The Spanish could be harsh with foreigners, especially the English and the Dutch. But they were the declared enemy and heretics as well. To her own subjects, leniency was the rule. When the Dutch trade with Venezuela was squelched (1605–1611), the new governor made it clear to the inhabitants, who almost to the man had been engaged in smuggling, that "past sins would be forgotten, provided there were no new infractions of the rules." [29] On the other hand, riots and civil disorders directed against the representatives of royal authority were offenses of a different magnitude. These sent men to the gallows. So did heresy. But these activities represented assaults on the normative order of Christ and King. Maintaining illegal *obrajes* or engaging in illicit commerce were violations of a utilitarian nature that reflected human weakness rather than entrenched perfidy. Royal officials found guilty of pecuniary offenses by a visitor-general paid fines, were demoted, or lost their jobs. They rarely went to prison. From our standpoint, the Council of the Indies, in such instances, appears mild. But to the Hapsburgs of the seventeenth century, the Indies represented more than a source of exploitation. The bureaucracy was entrusted with the maintenance of a moral order. Seen in this light, we are better able to understand the actions of a bureaucratic structure that fined smugglers but sent religious deviants to the stake. The English were quite different. Religious dissenters became national heroes. Smugglers were sent to the gallows.

In the case of the intercolonial trade between New Spain and Peru, royal prohibitions were ineffective. Although all intercolonial traffic was outlawed in 1631, loopholes were soon found. Chinese goods were transported to Nicaragua, where Peruvian merchants still carried on a legal trade. Transactions were also made at sea. The value of this illegal trade was probably in the neighborhood of 10 million pesos annually.[30] Peruvian ecclesiastics argued that the laws were unjust and not binding. Trade was not heresy.

The success of contraband trade was linked to the nature of the bureaucracy, since adjustments made to the inadequacies of the fleet system involved both royal officials and powerful local interests. The bureaucracy did not enforce trade regulations but, as in the case of Indian labor, it sought an accommodation between the law and existing social conditions. With their roots deep in Creole society, *oidores* were reluctant to press

---

[29] Sluiter, "Dutch–Spanish Rivalry," pp. 192-193.
[30] Lynch, *Spain under the Hapsburgs*, vol. 2, p. 226.

for the vigorous implementation of cedulas that ran contrary to their own self-interest and to that of their Creole associates. The division of power among roughly equal authorities made decisive action difficult, since a consensus was not easily reached. Especially stringent measures were appealed to the Council of the Indies. The result was delay and evasion. The sale of public offices, especially treasury offices, reduced accountability to the Crown and made the influence of local power strong and direct. The bureaucracy pursued a number of goals, and commercial regulation was but one. For all these reasons, the bureaucracy was ill-fitted to suppress contraband trade. Furthermore, the growth of contraband trade, illicit intercolonial trade, and domestic economic activity all occurred within a larger international arena in which the military and economic strength of Spain was declining in relation to her chief competitors. A global economy was emerging in which Spain was progressively being pushed to the periphery. The balance of power was shifting both internationally and within the Hispanic world. The Spanish monopoly system simply could not meet the needs of her colonies. Contraband trade was the symptom of this basic incapacity.

SILVER PRODUCTION AND THE INDIES TRADE

Total silver remittances to Seville dropped moderately in the decade 1620–1630. Thereafter, the drop was more precipitous and irreversible. It was accompanied by a growing depression in the Indies trade. To what extent does this decline indicate economic contraction in America? Can the drop in silver imports be attributed to a depression in the colonial silver industry? Was the sharp decline in the trade with New Spain symptomatic of a fall in consumer demand caused by low levels of silver production?

In New Spain, silver production is not correlated with a drop in demand for European products. Production remained steady and possibly increased precisely when imports were falling.[31] It was not until well into the 1630s that silver production appreciably declined. The Indies trade had entered a period of contraction by 1620. While silver production remained high until 1635, the importation of registered silver declined. What happened to the difference? The decline in the share of the royal treasury was prob-

---

[31] Peter J. Bakewell, Silver Mining and Society in Colonial Mexico: Zacatecas, 1546–1700 (Cambridge, England, 1971), pp. 228–229.

ably due to increased defense expenditures in the colonies, a cost paid out of the exchequer in Mexico City. As historians are beginning to recognize, "it was as much defense expenditures in America as the failure of mining that caused decreasing returns of Crown bullion to Spain in the seventeenth century." [32] But how do we account for the drop in the remittances of private silver? Certainly, fraud may have been involved. During this period, many contraband outlets for the silver of New Spain existed. But the Creoles of New Spain simply were not buying European goods shipped from Spain in the same quantity as before. This was due not only to growing contraband trade, but also to the fact that New Spain was producing substitutes for products previously imported from Europe. Growing economic self-sufficiency was creating a situation of economic independence in which the "colonial" economy of New Spain was capable of withstanding the effects of economic depression in the mother country.[33] The progressive diversification of Mexican agriculture, for example, is reflected in the character of her exports. While, in 1594, precious metals had accounted for 95.6% of American exports, by 1609, nontreasure exports from New Spain alone had increased in volume to 35% of her total exports to Spain.[34]

It has been suggested that severe economic contraction occurred in New Spain as a result of the drop in the Indian population, especially after the great epidemic of 1576–1579.[35] Certainly this led to short-run scarcity. But in the long run, *repartimiento* and debt peonage appear to have been adequate and reasonably efficient responses to a contracting labor supply. An insufficiency of agricultural produce was certainly not the rule in the century after 1576. Agricultural imports from Spain were declining by the last decades of the sixteenth century. The contraction of the Indies trade is simply not synchronized with the decline of the Indian population. The response to depopulation, as discussed previously, led to the creation of a new economy in which the Indian population was engaged in an agricultural structure based on European models and dominated by Creole entrepreneurs producing, by and large, for a domestic market.[36] The growth of the great estate during the late sixteenth and early seventeenth centuries is not symbolic of economic retrenchment. It is more likely that the great investment in land was an outlet for surplus capital that could no longer be

---

[32] Ibid., p. 233.

[33] Ibid., p. 235.

[34] Lynch, *Spain under the Hapsburgs*, vol. 2, p. 185.

[35] Woodrow Borah, *New Spain's Century of Depression* (Berkeley, 1951), pp. 22–28 (Ibero–Americana 35).

[36] See Bakewell, *Silver Mining and Society*, p. 225.

as profitably employed in the Indies trade. The mining industry was experiencing a boom during the early seventeenth century (1600–1635) and the fortunes accumulated were recycled into the security of landed estates. The great estate produced sugar, hides, wool, meat, indigo, and grain. Sugar production required heavy capital investment, especially in equipment for refining. Indigo was an important export commodity. The great *hacienda*, typical of the semiarid region of the North, followed the mining frontier. While it aimed at self-sufficiency, it generated further economic activity. Hides were a good export commodity and an important raw material in the furniture industry.[37] Wool supplied the *obrajes* of Mexico City. The *hacienda* itself was an importer of consumer goods and the focus of an extensive trade network between North and South. New Spain was rapidly developing an economy shaped by, and responding to, its own domestic needs. In sum, neither the decline of the indigenous population nor the growth of the *hacienda* coincided with the great drop in the Indies trade. Moreover, both of these processes occurred during a boom in the mining industry.

Still, the mining industry of New Spain contracted after 1635 and did not attain its former levels of production until the 1670s. The second great expansion of the Mexican mining industry did not get underway until the eighteenth century. This decline was not due to a labor shortage, as Borah supposed, but to a drop in the supply of mercury. After 1630, mercury (the principal ingredient in the amalgamation of silver) from Almadén, the major source of supply for New Spain, was diverted to Peru. Almadén production dropped by 50% after 1640. While Peru was supplied with mercury from the mines of Huancavalica, there was not a surplus for shipment to New Spain.[38] In addition, the Crown undermined the capitalization of the industry when, in 1634, it refused to sell mercury on credit (mercury was a Crown monopoly) and demanded payment of outstanding debts. In Zacatecas—the most important mining district in New Spain— the fall in production can be attributed to "variations in the supply of mercury [and to] administrative decisions to exercise stringency with miners [with regard to credit] where leniency had previously been the rule."[39]

But how disastrous was the fall in silver production? It was by no means as catastrophic as the figures on silver imports into Seville has led historians to believe. The production of silver at Zacatecas dropped substantially dur-

---

[37] Lynch, *Spain under the Hapsburgs*, volume 2, pp. 210–212.

[38] D. A. Brading and Harry E. Cross, "Colonial Silver Mining: Mexico and Peru," *Hispanic American Historical Review* 52 (November, 1972): 573–574.

[39] Bakewell, *Silver Mining and Society*, p. 234.

ing 1635–1670, as compared to the boom years of 1600–1634. Yet, production during these depression years was still comparable to the output of the late sixteenth century, a period that sustained a high volume of both external trade and silver remittances to Seville.[40] This was not a boom and bust situation but a boom followed by reduced but still substantial production. By the 1670s, silver production in the Zacatecas district began to pick up and did not fall to the levels of 1635–1670 during the colonial period. This renewed production was independent of credit extended by the Crown. It was now the native capital of New Spain that supported the mining industry, further evidence of sustained economic growth and self-sufficiency.

Silver remittances to the central treasury in Mexico City did not fall substantially during the period 1635–1670. The *alcabala*, an index of internal trade, remained relatively steady. There is "a strong presumption in favor of sustained economic activity" during these years.[41] Less silver was remitted to Spain because Mexico retained more public revenues for its own use. If there was an economic depression in New Spain after 1635, it was not severe and it did not reverse the long-term trend toward the growing independence of the economy from the links with Spain.

In Peru, the search for a significant depression in the silver industry that could account for the fall in silver returns to Seville has proved abortive. D. A. Brading and Harry E. Cross have generated a series of estimates for the production of amalgamated silver during the seventeenth century based on a known fixed ratio between mercury consumed in the refining process and silver output (110 marks or 935 pesos per quintal of mercury).[42] The estimates are conservative, but they indicate the continuous high levels of precious metal production sustained through most of the seventeenth century. Although output in New Spain may have contracted, Peruvian production continued at record levels, reaching an overall peak between 1625–1640. Peruvian silver production did not seriously decline until the end of the seventeenth century. It was precisely at this point that silver production in New Spain began to expand. By the 1630s, Peru had become the primary producer of silver and had overtaken New Spain as a market for the Indies fleet. Yet, although a greater proportion of the Indies trade now went to the Viceroyalty of Peru, this occurred within a general cycle of overall decline in transatlantic shipping.

How can we account for the difference between the silver refined in Peru

---

[40] Ibid., p. 259, Graph 1.
[41] Lynch, *Spain under the Hapsburgs*, vol. 2, p. 212.
[42] Brading and Cross, "Colonial Silver Mining," p. 579, Table 1. See also pp. 568–576.

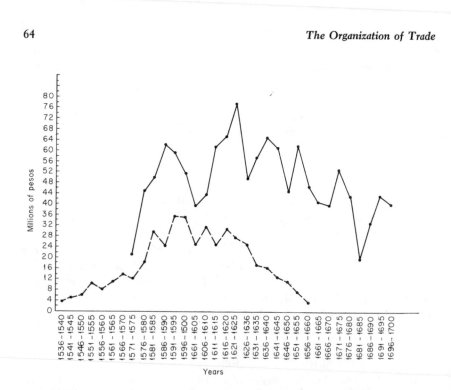

Figure 3.1 Total American bullion production compared to bullion imports received in Seville. Broken line (- - -) represents the total treasure imports into Seville, both public (Crown) and private [Source: Earl J. Hamilton, *American Treasure and the Price Revolution in Spain, 1501–1650* (Cambridge, Mass., 1934: Reprint ed., New York, 1965), p. 34]. Solid line(—) represents the total estimated bullion production [Source: D. A. Brading and Harry E. Cross, "Colonial Silver Mining: Mexico and Peru," *Hispanic American Historical Review* **52** (November, 1972): 579.

and the small proportion that reached Seville? The pattern is similar to New Spain. A greater share of public revenue was being spent in the viceroyalty, especially on defense, including naval construction and fortifications. Between 1651 and 1739, the income of the Lima treasury, some 179 million pesos, was allocated as follows—30% was spent on the defense of the viceroyalty and its dependencies, 49.4% was absorbed by administration, including salaries, pensions, grants, and the purchase of mercury for sale at Potosí; only 20.6% was remitted to the Royal treasury in Madrid.[43] As for private silver, we have already examined one important outlet. The Peruvian merchants, who supplied Potosí, were investing in the trade with the Philippines to the detriment of the Indies trade. The volume of illegal

---

[43] Lynch, *Spain under the Hapsburgs*, vol. 2, pp. 223–224.

traffic with Potosí via Brazil and the Río de la Plata had reached epidemic proportions by the seventeenth century. Perhaps one of the most interesting outlets for Peruvian silver was provided by the infamous *Peruleros.* They first appeared in Seville in 1609. The *Peruleros* were representatives of Creole capitalists. They made purchases directly in Spain or other parts of Europe, bypassing the Spanish middleman. In 1623, Seville interests complained to the king's minister Olivares about these "drones in the hive of Spanish commerce" who "assemble all the silver from Peru, silver which ought to be employed in purchasing from the fleet at Portobello.[44] The *Peruleros* were symptomatic of the growing strength of Creole interests and the shift in economic relationships between Spain and her overseas kingdoms. American silver avoided the net of the Indies trade.

Although the Peruvian economy was probably less diversified than that of New Spain, it produced important products besides silver. Wine was second in importance to silver and it was exported to Chile, New Granada, Venezuela, Central America, and Mexico.[45] Sugar, grown extensively on Jesuit estates, had both an export and a domestic market. The *obrajes,* employing Indian labor, supplied the domestic market with woolen and cotton cloth. Trade with New Spain, although overshadowed by the Philippine trade, continued. It included such items as leather goods, jewelry, clothing, and household goods manufactured in New Spain. The growth of the Peruvian economy was impressive. Indeed, as early as the end of the sixteenth century, the viceroy could inform the king that "the colony was virtually self-sufficient in foodstuffs, including wine and sugar and in coarser textiles, while the Philippine trade supplied it with silks and linens—all this to the detriment of Spanish trade."[46]

The disengagement of the colonial world from economic dependence on Seville was a general phenomenon. In the 1640s, the shipyards of Havana were supplying at least 40% of the vessels engaged in transatlantic trade.[47] The slave trade between New Spain and Jamaica was carried in ships of colonial construction.[48] The intercolonial trade between New Spain and Peru depended on the shipbuilding industry of Guayaquil that also produced galleons for the transpacific trade. Maracaibo produced suitable vessels for coastal navigation in the Caribbean.[49] The collapse of the fleet

[44] Ibid., p. 196.
[45] Ibid., p. 219. Generally, see pp. 212–224.
[46] Borah, *Early Colonial Trade and Navigation,* p. 124.
[47] Lynch, *Spain under the Hapsburgs,* vol. 2, p. 197.
[48] Nettels, "Spanish American Trade," pp. 13–14.
[49] Lynch, *Spain under the Hapsburgs,* vol. 2, pp. 197–199.

system was symbolic of a new distribution of wealth within the Hispanic world. The growing independence of the New World economy had created a situation in which Spain was more dependent on colonial silver than the colonies were on Spanish products. Consequently, the colonies continued to prosper during the seventeenth century while the Spanish economy contracted.

The seventeenth century belies most of our common assumptions about the Spanish empire in America. Creoles exerted strong pressure on bureaucratic administration. The proof of the vitality of that power is that the economic interests and needs of the colonists in the long run determined the nature of the economy. Whether it was the regulation of Indian labor, the restrictions on intercolonial trade, the prohibitions against the contraband traffic, or the limitations on vineyards and olive groves, the initiative of the monarchy had, at best, mixed results. Our image of colonial Spanish America as a stagnant morass capable only of silver production is false. So is our assumption of remorseless Spanish exploitation that deprived the New World of all its silver in exchange for a rigid political theocracy that imposed the will of Madrid. In the seventeenth century, the colonists of the New World retained the greatest share of silver for their own use, investing it in the domestic economy or employing it to purchase foreign goods through either the Indies fleet or contraband channels. They built ships, carried on trade, developed plantation agriculture oriented toward tropical products, and invested in mining and *obrajes*. The merchants of Lima were no less resourceful than those of Boston, and their influence was often extensive. "Mercantilism" does not aptly describe the economic relationship between Spain and her kingdoms in America. Not only did commercial theories face bureaucratic practices that could reshape official policy, but the Council of the Indies, treating each *audiencia* as a separate entity, was capable of pursuing contradictory economic policies in neighboring *audiencias*. While Manila could trade with New Spain, direct trade with Peru was forbidden. The bureaucratic organization of the Spanish empire was inconsistent with the kind of centralized economic control implied by the theory of mercantilism.

The American colonies always returned a profit to the Crown. But at root, the integration between mother country and colony was not fundamentally an economic integration, particularly during the seventeenth century. It was more on the order of a spiritual integration cemented by an institutional church and an institutionalized kingship. Spain in America was the accomplishment of a pre-Reformation society. The economic drift of Spain from America did not produce a political separation. Certainly, a colonial system in which political networks and economic networks were asymmetrical presents us with somewhat of an anomaly. The eighteenth century was to alter this situation. The Bourbon kings, as agents of the Enlightenment, produced a new conception of "empire" that was to disrupt the delicate political synthesis that joined together the kingdoms of Castile and those of America.

Map 2 Political divisions in the Spanish Empire (1800).

IV

The Bourbon Reforms

THE BACKGROUND TO REFORM

The death of Charles II (1665–1700) caused a crisis in Western Europe. Childless, he was the last Hapsburg king of Spain. Both the Austrian Hapsburgs and the French Bourbons, related by marriage to the Spanish royal house, claimed the throne. In the last year of his reign, Charles II left his Spanish dominions undivided to the grandson of the French king. In February of 1701, Philip V (1701–1746) became the first Bourbon king of Spain. The prospect of an expanded Bourbon dynasty stretching from France and Spain to Quebec and the Indies upset the balance of power in Europe. The rest of Europe, led by the English, Dutch, and Austrians, fought to prevent the consolidation of the French and Spanish thrones.

The war graphically underscored the weakness of the Spanish. The superiority of British naval strength further reduced the capacity of the *flota* system to deliver merchandise to the New World. There were only five fleet sailings from Spain during the war: in 1706, 1708, 1710, and 1712. Spain was unable to provide her fleets with sufficient defense. This task was performed by her ally, the French. Spain also found it necessary to license French naval expeditions in the Caribbean against enemy marauders. The disruption of the fleet system and the privileges enjoyed by French vessels brought interloping to unprecedented heights. Enjoying unrestricted entry into American ports, the French used the alliance to achieve a position of dominance in the Indies trade. During the first 5 years of the war, over 130 French vessels were listed as having called at American ports. They all engaged in trade.[1] When, in 1706, a Spanish fleet finally arrived in the Indies, there was no demand for goods, "so thoroughly had the French done their job of glutting the market with contraband."[2] In addition, Spain made extensive purchases of war materials in France and subsidized the French defense of the Spanish Netherlands. It is estimated that the French government probably received a greater share of the registered shipments of treasury silver from the Indies than the Spanish. This, of course, does not even include the enormous profits made by the French interlopers.[3] The deterioration of the Indies trade during the war was blamed on the French, and contributed substantially to the impairment of diplomatic cooperation.

The Peace of Utrecht (1713) brought the War of Spanish Succession to a close. It was an English peace. England's great seventeenth-century rivals, the Dutch, were seriously weakened by the war; they failed to regain their former commercial strength. At Utrecht, Spain lost most of her dynastic holdings in Europe. She ceded Naples, Sicily, Milan, and the Spanish Netherlands to the Austrian Hapsburgs. She was compelled to relinquish the commercial privilege of supplying the Indies with slaves—the *asiento*—to the English. The *asiento* provided a cover for British contraband operations, which increased during the next half century. Throughout the eighteenth century, England posed the most serious threat to the Spanish empire. The growing menace of English military and commercial strength provides the background to the Spanish response—a program of economic, bureaucratic, and military revival referred to as the "Bourbon reforms."

BOURBON REFORM IN SPAIN

The revolts of Catalonia, Aragon, and Valencia against the new Bourbon monarchy were crushed during the War of Spanish Succession. The ancient *fueros* (rights) enjoyed by these provinces were suppressed. The

---

[1] Henry Kamen, *The War of Spanish Succession 1700–1715* (London, 1969), pp. 140–150.
[2] Ibid., p. 148.
[3] Ibid., p. 193.

first Bourbon, Philip V (1701-1746), extended uniform administrative units—intendancies—throughout the Spanish peninsula. Modeled on the French system, the intendancies provided a stronger link between central and local government. Gradually, they acquired full fiscal control in the provinces, replacing the *corregidores*. Individual ministries began to replace the old Hapsburg councils. Economic reform began. Internal customs barriers were abolished; model factories were established with the technological assistance of foreigners, and a period of protection began for Spanish industry. These reforms received their greatest impetus from Charles III (1759-1788).

Charles curbed the power of the *mesta*. Exportation of raw wool was discouraged in favor of ensuring a plentiful supply for domestic industries.[4] The growth of applied science was encouraged. The curriculum of the universities was revised. Scholastic philosophy was deemphasized in favor of physics, mathematics, and the "new philosophy" of Descartes and Leibnitz.[5] Progressive elements founded economic societies, such as the *Amigos del País*, dedicated to the advancement of agriculture, commerce, and industry. These *"luces"* (lights) looked to the enlightened government of Charles III as the appropriate authority to implement reform. The Spanish Enlightenment was predominantly an orthodox movement that accepted the two pillars of insitutional life—the Church and the monarchy. Charles III did not find it inconsistent to support both the advancement of learning and the Inquisition. Physiocrats were welcome, but not Locke or Rosseau. In her attempt to catch up with the rest of the West, Spain was willing to borrow from the administrative and economic reforms that she felt supported the prosperity of other state systems. But she would borrow on her own terms so as not to disrupt traditional institutions. The Inquisition was the intellectual watchdog. New techniques were to be adopted, but without the contamination of foreign ideas. Spain was involved in a process of selective modernization.

To institute these reforms, Charles continued to build a more efficient state bureaucracy. He extended the powers of the ministries, and limited the role of the Council of the Indies. The authority of the Ministry of the Indies, under José de Galvez, became predominant. The ministers began to meet regularly in a *Junta del Estado* (Council of State) to outline overall policy. Decision-making, previously dispersed among several councils where lengthy debate, delay, and procedural formality were the rule,

---

[4] Richard Herr, *The Eighteenth-Century Revolution in Spain* (Princeton, 1958), p. 127.

[5] Ibid., pp. 163-183.

became more centralized, specialized, and efficient as authority was re-located at the center. A more streamlined state apparatus had been formed. When Charles III began his major reforms in America, "he had a central agency, at once more efficient and manageable, that afforded far greater possibilities of control over colonial affairs than had ever been available to the Hapsburgs."[6]

The vigorous government of the Bourbons received strong support in Spain from progressives. They hoped a strong state would implement reforms to aid and protect the growth of Spanish industry and agriculture. However, the state could reform society only if additional resources could be placed in the hands of centralized, bureaucratic institutions controlled by the Crown. Such resources were tied to local institutions and groups, reluctant to relinquish their customary rights to the state. In Spain, the monarchy moved cautiously, displaying acute sensitivity to the growing alienation of the privileged classes that formed the traditional base of its support. Less discretion was displayed in America.

The Bourbon program of administrative centralization, fiscal reform, and economic reorganization, aggressively pursued in the colonial world, disrupted the social order. In America, the Bourbon monarchy replaced Creole *corregidores* with Spanish intendants. It endeavored to make tax collections more efficient, and it reorganized the colonial treasury to reduce corruption. The sale of public offices were limited. Such a program was a direct challenge to systems of local control, whether that control was exercised by Creoles or Peninsular Spaniards. A new understanding of bureaucratic control that placed a greater emphasis on utilitarian goals and the strict adherence to royal commands superseded the old Hapsburg order. The effectiveness of the royal bureaucracy was to be counted in the treasury and not measured in heaven: Pesos usurped salvation. In America, Bourbon reform became Bourbon despotism. Bourbon policy represented the assertion of centralized state power against the forces of regionalism and local identity. It was an attempt to build a more unified system to replace the independent layers and separate kingdoms of the Hapsburgs. This assertion of control over the colonial system was the cornerstone of Bourbon policy. Its object was the renewal of Spanish economic power and the reconstruction of her military stature. A strong colonial system was essential if Spain was to sustain a direct confrontation with Great Britain. Such a confrontation appeared inevitable, since the Indies trade was crucial to the commercial systems of both powers.

---

[6] John Lynch, *Spanish Colonial Administration, 1782–1810; The Intendancy System in the Viceroyalty of the Rio de la Plata* (New York, 1958), p. 7.

BRITISH COMMERCIAL LINKS
WITH THE INDIES

Charles III was convinced that Britain owed her commercial dominance to favorable treaties permitting her to trade with the Indies. Spain hoped to annul these treaties and to limit British incursions. If Spain recaptured the Indies trade, she could create a greater demand for her own products and thus stimulate her own industry.[7] But Britain continued to use the treaty system to her own advantage. The South Sea Company legally held the *asiento* but transported illicit merchandise to the Indies not only in the "permission" ships approved by treaty but in the slave ships as well. The illegal traffic in the company's slave ships amounted to £5,000,000 during the years 1730–1739.[8] The South Sea Company flooded the Spanish-American colonies with British contraband goods to such an extent that *flota* merchandise in 1737 could not be sold at the fairs until the supply of British goods were exhausted.[9] The escalated contraband trade not only deprived the royal treasury of customs duties; it also caused a severe drop in market prices. Markets formerly dependent on the Spanish *flota* system, like Portobello and Veracruz, were now supplied by British merchants. A dangerous competitive system had been created in the heart of the Spanish empire.[10] The response of the Spanish government was to step up the activities of coastguard vessels and to insist upon the right to inspect the *asiento* ships. The *asiento* trade and the attempts of the Spanish government to limit its scope were major causes of the Anglo–Spanish War of 1739.[11] This conflict soon merged with the larger War of Austrian Succession. The Peace of Aix-La-Chapelle in 1748 returned the Caribbean to the *status quo ante*.

Jamaican trade with the Spanish Caribbean also continued to grow. Although the bulk of this trade was carried on Spanish colonial vessels in direct violation of the British Navigation Acts, the trade was so crucial that it received the sanction of the British government. In 1759, British contraband trade was estimated at 6 million pesos a year, and most of this

---

[7] Allan Christelow, "Great Britain and the Trades from Cadiz and Lisbon to Spanish America and Brazil, 1759–1783," *Hispanic American Historical Review* 27 (1947): 9.

[8] George H. Nelson, "Contraband Trade under the Asiento 1730–1739," *American Historical Review* 51 (October, 1945): 63–65.

[9] Ibid., pp. 65–67. See also Vera Lee Brown, "The South Sea Company and Contraband Trade," *American Historical Review* 31 (July, 1926): 662–677.

[10] Nelson, "Contraband Trade," p. 66.

[11] Walter L. Dorn, *Competition for Empire, 1740–1763* (1940: New York, 1963), pp. 122–130.

trade passed through Jamaica.[12] The English colonists of North America were major participants in the Jamaican circuit. The trade provided specie for circulation in North America and supported the colonial purchase of British goods. The Spanish Indies were an essential link in the British system of world trade. They provided raw materials (leather and dye-woods) vital to the British textile industry.[13] Tobacco, cochineal, and indigo were also important. But it was the bullion of the Indies that lubricated the entire system.

Britain was also linked to the Indies via Spain herself. Foreigners had investments in the *flotas* that often surpassed that of Spanish merchants By 1760, the British probably reaped the greatest profit from the Cadiz trade. They either sold British products on credit to Spanish merchants or participated directly in the trade through Spanish cover men. Bullion returns were smuggled out of Spain on British naval vessels, which enjoyed the right of free entry in Spanish ports.[14] Since Britain's treaty privileges were a facade masking an enormous smuggling operation, it is no wonder that Charles III wanted to abrogate them. In 1761, Spain, allied with France, declared war on England. But the war was a disaster. The treaties were renewed at the Peace of Paris in 1763. In addition, France ceded Quebec to England, eliminating a major source of pressure on the British empire. The threat of British power in America loomed ominous.

BOURBON COMMERCIAL REFORM

Bourbon commercial reform was designed to meet the maritime challenge of Great Britain by creating more direct commercial links between Spanish and American ports. Reorganization began in earnest. In 1765, the policy of restricted ports of clearance from Spain and limited entrance to the Indies was modified. Additional ports in both Spain and the West Indies were open to direct commerce or *comercio libre*. This system of free trade was gradually extended to the rest of the empire. By 1778, it applied to all of Spanish America with the exception of New Spain and Venezuela. They were included by 1789. The American trade gradually became "free" trade in the sense that it was open to all important Hispanic seaports and to all Spanish subjects. In 1772, customs duties were reduced and even-

---

[12] Allan Christelow, "Contraband Trade between Jamaica and the Spanish Main and the Free Port Act of 1766," *Hispanic American Historical Review* 22 (May, 1942): 313.

[13] Ibid., pp. 309–313.

[14] Christelow, "Great Britain and the Trades," pp. 3–5.

tually many articles became duty-free. If Spain could not abrogate her treaties with Britain, she could perhaps minimize them with a more efficient and competitive commercial system. The fleet organization, with its ponderous tax structure, restrictive licensing, antiquated methods, burdensome formalities, and interminable delays, only succeeded in raising the prices of Spanish goods in the Indies. Transporting Spanish textiles to Cadiz for reexportation to the Indies, for example, created additional costs that reduced the competitiveness of Spanish products. The unreliability of the *flotas* that sailed sporadically from Cadiz did not provide a suitable outlet for American products. Spain had finally accepted the fact that the key to the Indies trade was supply and that, as long as she was unable to provide either an outlet for colonial produce or an adequate supply of merchandise, the prohibition against contraband would be ineffective. Commercial reform was also consistent with the reality of economic life in the peninsula. For it was in the coastal periphery, the provinces of Galicia, Asturias, Vizcaya, Catalonia, and Valencia, that commercial revival was centered. The opening of this periphery to direct trade with the Indies stimulated economic growth. The coastal ports of Barcelona, La Coruña, Bilbao, and Valencia soon rivaled the old Andalucian centers of Cadiz and Seville.

The result of these reforms was a rather remarkable increase in trade between Spain and her colonies. The Cuban trade with Spain, which in 1760 engaged only 6 ships, required over 200 ships in 1778. The exportation of hides from Buenos Aires rose from 150,000 in 1778 to 800,000 per year in 1783.[15] Between 1778 and 1788, the value of the entire trade with Spanish America is estimated to have multiplied by 700%.[16] The revival of Spanish industry, especially the Catalan cotton industry, helped to support the new trade pattern. In 1792, the Catalan textile industry employed 80,000 workers and exported 16 million pesos worth of merchandise to the Indies. Catalonia ranked second only to the English midlands in the production of cotton cloth.[17] The Basque hardware industry also expanded. In 1790, 4000 tons of finished iron products were exported to the New World.[18] While the British still sold merchandise to Spain to be resold in the Indies, the proportion of Spanish goods carried in the trade was growing. At the end of the seventeenth century, only about 15% of

---

[15] Lynch, *Spanish Colonial Administration*, p. 169.
[16] Clarence H. Haring, *The Spanish Empire in America* (New York, 1947), p. 342. See also Jaime Vicens Vives, *An Economic History of Spain*, trans. Frances López–Morillas (Princeton, 1969), pp. 579–580.
[17] Herr, *Revolution in Spain*, p. 141.
[18] Ibid., p. 136.

the products shipped to America were Spanish. By 1798, the figure was closer to 50%.[19] The proportion of Spanish national goods imported into New Spain continued to rise. In 1804, the consulado of Veracruz recorded the value of imported Spanish goods at 10,412,000 pesos, while foreign products imported through Spanish middlemen had dropped to 4,493,000 pesos.[20] Still, competition from British goods—especially cotton textiles—was strong. Her position was based not so much on treaty privileges as it was on superior capital, financial, and technological resources.[21] In a true "free trade" system, many Spanish products would not have been competitive with British goods.

British merchants did not resist *comercio libre*, for they became progressively less interested in penetrating the old system of limited fleets. Rather than trading on their own behalf through undercover men, they preferred to sell their products directly to Spanish merchants or to trade directly with the Indies. In spite of the demise of the fleet system, British merchants were confident that their manufactures "would not want a vent as they could clandestinely find their way to the coasts of America."[22] Spanish products required protection, British products did not. While the Spanish government sought to strengthen control over its colonies, the British government actively conspired to break such control. British agents in Spain were instructed to gather military intelligence concerning "the strengths and weaknesses of the Spanish dominions in South America . . . [and the] amount of discontent that was supposed to prevail there."[23] In 1783, the British were reported to be "sending out spies, stirring up dissatisfaction and landing rifles in Latin America."[24]

THE EFFECTS OF COMERCIO LIBRE ON THE AMERICAN ECONOMIES

We have surveyed the effects of *comercio libre* on the Spanish economy and the reaction of Spain's adversary, the British. But what was the impact of free trade on the colonial economy and the structure of mercantile interests?

---

[19] Ibid., p. 147.

[20] Brian Hamnet, *Politics and Trade in Southern Mexico, 1750–1821* (Cambridge, England, 1971), p. 114.

[21] Christelow, "Great Britain and the Trades," p. 9, 18.

[22] Ibid., p. 28.

[23] Ibid., p. 24.

[24] Ibid., p. 27.

Before *comercio libre* was extended to New Spain in 1789, the great merchants (*almaceneros*) who monopolized the Cadiz trade were Peninsular Spaniards, predominantly Basques and Montañeses from the north of Spain. They commanded sufficient capital to buy out the fleet at Veracruz. Since the Cadiz merchants were prohibited from selling their products inland on their own behalf, and because undue delays were costly, the merchants of Mexico City enjoyed the advantages in the setting of prices. The goods were transported to warehouses in Mexico City, where the *almaceneros* released their stock at intervals to lesser merchants under favorable market conditions. They also resold part of their wares at the Jalapa fair to provincial merchants—many of them Creoles—on credit terms as high as two-thirds the value of the goods.

The great merchants financed commercial agriculture, especially cochineal. Credit was extended to municipal officials, such as the *corregidor*, who in turn issued credit to Indian laborers. The credit was redeemed in agricultural produce, in this case cochineal, that was exported to Spain. In addition, the merchants provided the *corregidor* with such items as mules, bulls, and cloth that were sold to the Indians, often under duress and at great profits.[25] Mining provided an outlet for capital as well. Credit or cash was extended to refiners so that they could purchase raw materials used in the refining process. The credit operations of the great *almaceneros* touched many levels of society. They became a focus of envy and a symbol of Peninsular dominance.

The abolition of the monopoly system in New Spain undercut the economic base of the *almaceneros*. The influx of European goods kept the market well-supplied. Merchandise was cheap and profits low. The Crown also attacked the forced distribution of goods to Indians by *corregidores*, a business largely financed by the merchants. The price of cochineal fell substantially during the same period. The overall result was a dramatic change in commercial networks and investment patterns. Veracruz began to replace Mexico City as the entrepôt for European goods. Products were sold on credit, allowing the merchants of Veracruz to buy directly from Spanish shippers instead of from the *almaceneros*. Additional *consulados* were established in Veracruz and Guadalajara in competition with that of Mexico City. Shrinking profits and increasing competition drove the *almaceneros* to seek more profitable outlets for their capital. They turned to mining and commercial agriculture. The role of new capital in the mining industry of Mexico provided the basis for the continued growth

---

[25] D. A. Brading, *Miners and Merchants in Bourbon Mexico 1763–1810* (Cambridge, 1971), p. 99.

of silver production in the 1780s and 1790s.[26] Commercial activity was passing into the hands of a new breed of merchants, predominantly Creoles, who were not dependent on the monopoly system of artificially high prices. They invested smaller sums and were content with smaller profits.[27]

The period of *comercio libre* was an era of fundamental reorganization. Established merchants found it difficult to break with the engrained habits of the old system. During the last decades of the century there were numerous bankruptcies. Whereas, before, it was only necessary "to import infrequently enough and the high prices would follow," it was now necessary to have an accute sense of timing "to make the proper kind of importations at the right time."[28] The policy of *comercio libre* changed the location of European Spaniards in the economic structure of New Spain. Their capital investments shifted from commerce to landholding and mining. The restructuring of mercantile interests heightened the hostility between Creoles and Peninsular Spaniards. Free trade attacked the monopolistic base of the Peninsular merchants, who found they faced a serious commercial challenge from the Creole merchants of Veracruz and Gudalajara. The movement of Peninsular capital into landholding increased the price of land to the detriment of Creoles. In New Spain, Bourbon commercial reform mobilized Creoles and European Spaniards against each other. This tension was intensified by bureaucratic reforms initiated from Madrid that reduced the number and significance of Creole officeholders while enlarging the administrative role played by European Spaniards.

In Guatemala, the policy of *comercio libre* did not unseat a commercial monopoly "comprised of a phalanx of Creoles and Peninsulares, closely knit by ties of marriage, blood and commercial interest." [29] The Guatemalan merchants controlled both foreign and domestic trade. The principal export was indigo. Some 24 million pounds were produced during the last quarter of the eighteenth century. The center of production was El Salvador, followed by Guatemala, Honduras, and Nicaragua. Produce was brought to the annual indigo fair in Guatemala City where merchants and planters bargained over grades and prices. Planters then selected domestic supplies and foreign goods from the merchants' stores and re-

---

[26] Ibid., pp. 114–116.

[27] Herbert Ingram Priestly, *José de Gálvez, Visitor General of New Spain 1765–1771* (Berkeley, 1916), p. 385.

[28] Ibid.

[29] Floyd S. Troy, "The Guatemalan Merchants, the Government and the Provincianos 1750–1800," *Hispanic American Historical Review* **41** (February, 1961): 90.

ceived advances for the next year.[30] The merchants controlled prices, the distribution of goods, and the extension of credit. They played the same role vis-à-vis the cattle industry. Provincial cattlemen and indigo planters held common attitudes of resentment and hostility toward the merchants of Guatamala City. As more land was converted to indigo production, the cost of food rose, cutting into the profits of planters and increasing their debts to merchants. The crisis in the indigo industry was due to the underproduction of foodstuffs, but irate planters blamed the merchants. The continued expansion of indigo production also reduced the supply of cattle. "More cattle were needed for food, more oxen for transportation on the indigo haciendas, and more hides for zurrones in which to pack indigo."[31] In this situation of scarcity, the Spanish government attempted to fix a "just" price for beef that was not in concert with economic realities and favored the merchants who purchased the cattle. No doubt the outraged Creole ranchers and planters took little comfort in the fact that many of the merchants were also Creoles. *Comercio libre*, in spite of the efforts of the Spanish government, had little effect on the monopoly of the Guatemalan merchants.

The economic potential of the La Plata region (Argentina) expanded tremendously under *comercio libre*. The colony could now receive European goods more directly and cheaply. The livestock industry responded to the steady demand of new markets. Before 1778, the annual export of hides was 150,000. This had increased to 1,400,000 by 1783.[32] Cattle were slaughtered not only for hides but for fats and the exportation of salted beef.[33] Revenues collected at the customhouse rose from 54,000 pesos in 1778 to 400,000 during the years 1791–1795. In 1804, close to a million pesos were collected. The population of Buenos Aires also grew from 25,000 inhabitants in 1779 to 40,000 by 1801. Commercial expansion involved the emergence of a Creole merchant community centered in Buenos Aires.

Madrid viewed the policy of *comercio libre* as an intelligent, rational shift in economic policy. In many areas of America, however, it generated several decades of abrupt economic change that altered the relationship between important social groups. The dynamics of this change varied, since the impact of *comercio libre* on economic interests was by no means uniform. This was the consequence not only of dissimilar economic structures, but must also be attributed to variations in the control of these structures.

---

[30] Ibid., p. 100.
[31] Ibid., p. 105.
[32] Lynch, *Spanish Colonial Administration*, p. 169.
[33] Ibid., pp. 33–34.

In Guatemala, the Creole elite and Peninsular Spaniards were bound together by economic and social ties. *Comercio libre* had little impact on the organization of the merchant community. Their control of trade was a joint effort. This solidarity determined the structure of Guatemalan independence. It was an aristocratic movement that declared independence "to prevent the consequences that would be fearful in the event that the people should proclaim it."[34]

The ties between Creoles and European Spaniards in different areas of the New World were key factors in determining how independence was achieved. It is important to know in which regions segments of these groups were allied or mutually hostile, and how these relationships shifted in response to the Bourbon reforms.

In New Spain, Creoles and European Spaniards were arrayed against one another in virtually every important colonial institution. The conflict between monopolistic and free-trade merchants was also a conflict between *Peninsulares* and Creoles. The great *almaceneros* of Mexico City, who benefited from the old monopoly system, were almost exclusively Peninsular Spaniards. This Peninsular dominance was perpetuated by the semihereditary and endogamous character of the Peninsular merchant community.[35] Since commerce was a very personal activity in New Spain, it required a high degree of trust. Merchants trusted relatives and men from the same village or town in Spain. When they took on assistants, they brought in relatives or *paisanos* from Spain. While they preferred to educate their sons for professions of high social standing, they often married their daughters to trusted assistants. Thus, the family business was kept in the hands of European Spaniards. From about midcentury (1750), Basques and Montañeses dominated the *consulado* of Mexico City and rotated the major offices among themselves.[36] Group solidarity was further reinforced by religious *cofradías* (confraternities) dedicated to specific religious patrons. Creoles were, consequently, excluded from the ranks of the *almaceneros*—a situation that increased Creole resentment. *Comercio libre*, since it undercut the Peninsular merchants and offered new opportunities to smaller Creole merchants, set in motion an economic struggle that was still going on when the Napoleonic Wars disrupted the Spanish empire. The road to independence in New Spain began as a bureaucratic coup directed against the Creole community. The Peninsular merchants of Mexico City and their allies in the *audiencia* took the first step that led

---

[34] R. A. Humphreys and John Lynch, Eds., *The Origins of the Latin American Revolutions 1808–1826* (New York, 1965), p. 25.

[35] Brading, *Miners and Merchants*, p. 113.

[36] Ibid., p. 107.

to civil war and independence. The viceroy had the support of the Creoles who dominated the *cabildo* of Mexico City. In a quick coup, the *Peninsulares* removed the viceroy and his Creole supporters.[37]

In the La Plata region, the nonmonopolistic merchants and the landowner-cattlebreeders were the great beneficiaries of *comercio libre*. They displaced the merchant monopolists who controlled the traditional overland commerce between Buenos Aires and Peru. This expensive provisioning was no longer competitive. By 1800, the economic expansion of Buenos Aires and its hinterland had outpaced Spain's capacity to absorb colonial production and to satisfy the growing demand for manufactured goods at reasonable prices. Spain had positioned herself between Buenos Aires and lucrative foreign markets. England was the colony's major market and the principal source of the commodities it needed. But *comercio libre* forced Buenos Aires to trade with Britain through Spain, "robbing the colony of nearly all the benefits flowing from international commerce." [38] Merchants and catttlemen, especially after 1800, became advocates of free international trade. The demand for economic autonomy rapidly became a movement for political autonomy.

Comercio libre brought economic hardships to the interior provinces of La Plata, provinces that had achieved a considerable degree of economic integration and self-sufficiency. They were transit points in the trade between Peru and Buenos Aires. The textile industries of Cordoba, Catamarca, and Corrientes supplied local needs and produced a surplus for export. Sugar was produced in Tucumán. Mendoza made wine and brandy. Given the technology of the industries, however, they could not withstand foreign competition "either with regard to cost or quality of production".[39] While the merchants and cattle interests supported free trade, the interior provinces were in favor of restrictions that would protect their industries.

Comercio libre not only changed the internal relations among economic interests, but it also began to alter the nature of the relations between local economies and world markets. The old monopoly system, by restricting supply, created conditions favorable to colonial industry. Substantial evidence points to the growth of colonial industry during the seventeenth century and through much of the eighteenth century. But after a period of steady expansion, colonial industry began to decline. In a period of about three decades, from 1780 to 1810, the economic system that protected domestic industry gave way. The textile industry of La Plata could not with-

---

[37] Hamnett, *Politics and Trade*, pp. 121–122.

[38] Miron Burgin, *The Economic Aspects of Argentine Federalism 1820–1852* (Cambridge, 1946), p. 12.

[39] Ibid., p. 15.

stand the competition of Spanish and British merchandise imported through Buenos Aires.[40] In the Audiencia of Quito, the *obrajes* that exported goods to Chile, Buenos Aires, and Venezuela were in decay by 1790. Production in the Mexican manufacturing center of Puebla, famous for its chinaware, dropped disastrously between 1793 and 1802.[41] The textile industry of New Spain, however, held firm in the face of Spanish competition. In Oaxaca, the number of looms increased from 500 to 800 between 1793 and 1796. But while the best colonial industry could withstand Spanish competition, it could not compete against the unlimited influx of foreign manufacturers, especially British, that occurred with the introduction of free trade in the Independence Period. In 1823, the number of textile looms in Oaxaca had fallen to 50, "due to the import of foreign machine-produced cottons, which, while of good quality, sold for a lower price than the local product." [42] Investment patterns also shifted. Domestic capital, whether Creole or Peninsular, supported mining and commercial agriculture during the eighteenth century. But foreign capital, especially British, financed the expansion of export-oriented, agricultural economies in the nineteenth century.[43]

The Bourbon reforms accelerated the growth of colonial economies that exchanged primary products for manufactured goods. The tremendous expansion of Cuban sugar production, for example, occurred during this period, increasing from 50,000 quintales at midcentury (1 quintal equals 100 pounds) to 650,000 quintales by 1800.[44] The Caracas company in Venezuela stimulated the growth of cacao.[45] Coffee production was introduced, and the sugar industry spread along the Gulf of Mexico. The slave trade also intensified, in response to a growing demand for labor in plantation agriculture.[46] Stock-raising in Argentina, as we have already noted, multiplied several times over. While trade increased, the demand was for the primary products of commercial agriculture and stock-raising. An expansion of exports was accompanied by the contraction of internal trade and domestic industry. But the problem was not simply *comercio libre*. Latin America was part of a larger world economy prepared to supply

---

[40] Ricardo Levene, *A History of Argentina*, trans. William Spence Robertson (Chapel Hill, 1937: New York, 1963), p. 123.

[41] Benjamin Keen, Ed., *Readings in Latin American Civilization* (Boston, 1955), p. 157.

[42] Hamnett, *Politics and Trade*, p. 187.

[43] R. A. Humphreys, *Tradition and Revolt in Latin America* (London, 1969), pp. 106–109.

[44] Vicens Vives, *Economic History of Spain*, p. 545.

[45] See R. D. Hussey, *The Caracas Company, 1728–1784* (Cambridge, Mass., 1934).

[46] Philip Curtin, *The Atlantic Slave Trade* (Madison, 1969), pp. 24–29.

cheap manufactured goods while demanding agricultural products and bullion. In this international system, the future of colonial industry was bleak.

Free trade changed basic economic and social patterns. Restricted trade had favored the viceregal capitals of Lima and Mexico City. But *comercio libre* favored the growth of new commercial centers like Veracruz and Buenos Aires. The creation of new viceroyalties—New Granada in 1739 and La Plata in 1776—reduced the political significance of the old viceregal centers. Provincial towns began to challenge the hegemony of the capital. The *consulados* of Veracruz and Guadalajara fought successfully against the pretensions of the older and more prestigious *consulado* of Mexico City. The rebellion against a Peninsular-dominated bureaucracy in New Spain began in the Bajío, a region whose recent prosperity "had liberated it from the financial control of Mexico City".[47]

In Guatemala, the expansion of commercial agriculture created hostility between provincial planters and urban merchants. Similarly, as Buenos Aires became more commercial and European-oriented, friction with surrounding provinces based on social attitudes and economic interests increased. The growing alienation between center and periphery characteristic of the post-Independence Period received its impetus from the program of the Bourbon reformers. The task of containing the new economic forces set in motion by *comercio libre* fell to the bureaucracy. But bureaucratic organization itself was the object of an aggressive reform program, which altered its relation to society, undermining its legitimacy as the guardian of a universal moral order. The bureaucracy, transformed by the Spanish Bourbons, could not cope with the sharpened divisions in colonial society.

BUREAUCRATIC AND FISCAL REFORM UNDER THE BOURBONS

Comercio libre was only one part of a broad imperial reorganization. The rebuilding of Spain's military potential and the strengthening of colonial defense continued unabated. After the Peace of Paris in 1763, Spain and France were soon linked together in a new alliance, the famous Family Compact. Based on the assumption of the inevitable resumption of hostilities with Britain, the compact was the keynote of French foreign policy. Although Spain was by far the junior partner, France hoped that a reju-

---

[47] Brading, *Miners and Merchants*, p. 343.

venated Spain would tip the balance of power in favor of the Bourbon alliance. There was no more ardent supporter of Bourbon reform in America than the French Minister of War, the Duc de Choiseul.[48] Bourbon reform in America was essentially fiscal reform. The rebuilding of military strength required the expanding of financial resources. Reform aimed to increase returns to the royal treasury.

Royal officials (*vistadores*) were dispatched to the empire to assess the situation, the most famous being the visitation of José de Galvez to New Spain (1765–1771) and that of José Antonio de Areche to Peru and La Plata (1777–1782). They reached identical conclusions. The bureaucracy was dominated by Creoles who pursued their own self-interest rather than that of the Crown. Both discovered that Creoles held a majority of seats on the highest tribunals, the *audiencias*.[49] The organization of the treasury no longer served the financial interests of the Crown. The selling of treasury offices had created a situation in which "posts were filled by men still trying to pay off the interest on the purchase price of their office and resorting to treasury funds to do it."[50] Taxes, such as the *alcabala* and Indian tribute, were still farmed out to individuals and institutions who profited from their collection. Areche decried not only abuses that were recognized as such but also "those that custom has come to regard as legitimate practices."[51] Moreover, offices at almost all levels, but in particular at local levels, were deeply enmeshed in family ties and factional politics. Areche, who attempted to win over Viceroy Guirior to the cause of reform, quickly discovered how powerful was the influence of his Creole and Peninsular opponents. Copies of Areche's secret instructions, which he had entrusted to the viceroy in the strictest confidence, were soon being read in the cafes of Lima.[52]

Bourbon Reform in New Spain

The Spanish plan to reform the bureaucracy was pursued zealously by the new Minister of the Indies, José de Galvez, fresh from his visitation to New Spain. The initial focus of reform was in New Spain. Two principles

---

[48] Allan Christelow, "French Interest in the Spanish Empire during the Ministry of the Duc de Choiseul, 1759–1771," *Hispanic American Historical Review* 21 (1941): 515–537. See also Arthur S. Aiton, "Spanish Colonial Reorganization under the Family Compact," *Hispanic American Historical Review* 12 (1932): 269–280.

[49] Brading, *Miners and Merchants*, pp. 35–36.

[50] Lynch, *Spanish Colonial Administration*, p. 117.

[51] Eunice Joiner Gates, "Don José Antonio de Areche: His Own Defense," *Hispanic American Historical Review* 8 (February, 1928): 21.

[52] Ibid., p. 28.

were involved. First of all, control over the sources of revenue must be placed firmly in the hands of the Crown. This required the creation of new institutions manned by disinterested, trustworthy officials. Secondly, since Creoles were, almost by definition, partial and self-interested, the new wardens of royal government were to be Peninsular Spaniards. In 1776, the practice of farming out excise taxes was terminated in the major towns of New Spain. Salaried excise directors supervised by a director-general resident in Mexico City now directly controlled the collection of the al-cabala—a 6% sales tax—and the tax on pulque, an alcoholic beverage. The majority of these new officials were Peninsular Spaniards anxious to demonstrate ability. Total receipts increased from 1,488,690 pesos in 1775 to 2,360,252 pesos in 1779 and to a later average of almost 3 million pesos. The pulque duty advanced as well, from 468,888 pesos in 1775 to 814,755 by 1779.[53] The new fiscal system was demonstrating its value.

The Crown tightened its regulation of the tobacco industry and silver production. The royal monopoly on tobacco production was a monopoly in name only until its reorganization under Galvez. With a capitalization of some 600,000 pesos and the power to appoint new administrators recruited from the peninsula, visitor Galvez reestablished the monopoly on firm foundations.[54] The Crown now effectively licensed production, purchased the tobacco at fixed prices, and established factories that manufactured cigars and cigarettes. By the early 1770s, the factories established in Mexico City, Puebla, Oaxaca, and Orizaba employed some 12,000 workers. In 1801, net profits were nearly 4 million pesos. From its establishment in 1765 until 1809, profits have been estimated at some 177 million pesos.[55]

Silver production quadrupled during the eighteenth century in New Spain. In the 1770s alone, production jumped from 12 to 18 million pesos and reached annual levels of over 25 million pesos in later decades. The royal treasury profited accordingly. Unlike Upper Peru, where the control of the mint and the silver treasury was in disarray, in New Spain the Crown successfully monitored the movement of silver from the mines and refineries to the mint in Mexico City. In 1729, the Crown had terminated the leasing of the mint to private individuals. It appointed salaried officials and set up a revolving fund to purchase silver at the mint, undercutting the business of the silver merchants. The Crown cut 69 reales from each silver mark and returned the legal price of 65 reales to the owner. The

---

[53] Brading, *Miners and Merchants*, p. 52.
[54] See Priestly, *José de Gálvez*, pp. 135–171.
[55] Ibid., p. 154.

Crown monopolized the distribution and sale of mercury, the crucial ingredient in the amalgamation of silver. Galvez ended the farming of the gunpowder monopoly (gunpowder was essential in the mining industry) and installed salaried officials to supervise its production and sale. All silver, after it was refined, had to be presented at the nearest treasury where the royal tax of 10% (diezmo) was deducted. The Crown made a profit on every phase of the industry: on the raw materials it supplied often on credit, on the amount of silver refined, and on the minting of silver into specie. During the late eighteenth century, the Crown granted tax reliefs to the mining industry to help increase production. Miners were exempt from paying the alcabala on their raw materials. Galvez reduced both the price of mercury—by almost 50%—and the price of gunpowder. Bourbon policy was also willing to support capital risks. Galvez granted the famous miner, José de la Borda, an exemption from the silver tithe until the cost of the restoration of the Quebradilla mine of Zacatecas was recovered.[56] In this way, the Crown granted subsidies to the industry to help restore older mines to productivity. The prudent policies of the Crown, a plentiful supply of mercury, and the decisive flow of merchant capital into mining following the implementation of comercio libre, all combined to support rising productivity in the mining industry. In 1789, a typical year, royal revenue from Mexican mining was over 5 million pesos.[57] While Peninsular Spaniards did not dominate the industry, they were on equal footing with Creoles. If Peninsulares did not actually invest capital in the mining operation itself, as suppliers of raw material and credit, they did help to support expansion. They made good their investment by purchasing silver from the miners at a discount.[58]

The Bourbon reorganization of finance was a huge success in New Spain. Even Indian tribute rose from an average of 596,220 pesos in the 1760s to 955, 813 pesos in 1779. The overall revenue yielded by New Spain multiplied by a factor of three: from 6 million pesos in 1765 to about 19 million in 1782.[59] But the Creoles of New Spain did not share in the benefits of the newly created fiscal positions. Indeed, they were displaced from the traditional offices they held. By a decree of 1776, Creoles were restricted to not more than a third of all posts in American audiencias and cathedral chapters.[60] In the decade after 1769, the Audiencia of Mexico City was transformed from a Creole stronghold to an institution with a clear major-

---

[56] Brading, Miners and Merchants, p. 143.

[57] Ibid., p. 145, table 9.

[58] Ibid., pp. 149–152.

[59] Ibid., p. 53.

[60] Ibid., p. 37.

ity of Spaniards. The Creoles of New Spain not only paid more taxes, but their taxes supported a burgeoning bureaucracy staffed by Peninsular Spaniards. They paid the salaries of the men who picked their pockets. Yet, the most momentous change was yet to come.

Intendancy Reform in New Spain

In 1786, the ordinances for the establishment of the intendancies were finally promulgated. They constituted a full-scale attack on the bureaucratic structure of the empire, a structure inherited from the Hapsburgs and considered to be compromised at every level, inefficient and incapable of exercising that purity of disinterestedness required of a reforming instrument. The purpose of the reform was to reduce the jurisdiction of Hapsburg institutions by concentrating power in a uniquely Bourbon institution —the intendancy. The reform touched every level of the bureaucracy. General responsibility for the treasury was taken out of the hands of the viceroy and placed under the supervision of a superintendant free from the viceroy's interference. The *corregidor*, whose duties, prerogatives, and overall jurisdiction varied considerably, was replaced by a more uniform system of intendants. The well-known abuses of the *corregidores*, like the forced distribution of merchandise to Indians, were to be suppressed. The intendants were to be salaried officials and experienced bureaucrats from the peninsula who would bring efficiency and honesty to a level of administration characterized by illegal commercial activities and the sale of offices. They would also, of course, supervise the collection of revenue and thereby increase remittances to the Crown. The intendants were, first and foremost, revenue collectors and, in this capacity, subject only to the superintendant. The judicial scope of the intendants was enlarged as well as their authority to oversee general administrative reform. The intendancy replaced the quilt-like *corregimientos* with true provinces, and the intendant became an "omnicompetent provincial governor."[61] While he was subject to the *audiencia* in his capacity as a judge and to the viceroy as a military official and general administrator, still, the effect of the reform was to create provincial capitals where the lines of authority converged. Previously, the multitudinous *corregidores* were under the direct authority of the *audiencia*. Each *corregimiento* was independent of the other. But now, *corregimientos* were joined together into larger units under the centralized jurisdiction of the provincial capital. The intendant chose subdelegates to administer the towns and localities under his jurisdiction.

---

[61] Ibid., p. 64.

Furthermore, the Bourbons concentrated functions rather than dividing them between competing institutions. Clear lines of authority were at last evident. But the touchstone, as always, was revenue. In suppressing the office of *corregidor*, the object was "not so much to better the conditions of the Indians, as to limit the power of (local) officials, to establish closer supervision, and to eliminate those abuses which cut down the revenue so much desired by the Crown."[62]

What to the Bourbons was an attempt to "improve the structure of government" and "to restore integrity and respect for law," the Creoles saw as a rather blatant power play geared to deprive them of lucrative offices and the control of revenue and administration.[63] Every precaution was taken to maintain the purity of the Crown's brainchild from the contamination of Creole intrigue and corruption. The appointments of intendants rested exclusively with the Crown. Only in the case of a sudden vacancy could the viceroy appoint a successor—a clear break with the control viceroys often exercised over the appointment of *corregidores*. Salaries were substantial, both to bolster the incumbent against temptation and to underscore the status of the office. The intendancy was created for the new Bourbon bureaucrat whose mode of thinking was considered to be at once "pure, sincere and impartial," qualities evidently lacking in the Creole, and whose competence and institutional loyalty had been tested in Spain.[64]

The New World was being reconquered by the Bourbons. Bureaucratic authority emphasizing a clearly defined hierarchy of offices, spheres of competence, fixed salaries, technical qualifications, systematic discipline, promotions, and careers, had finally penetrated to the sphere of local government.[65] The reorganization of the Spanish state system allowed Charles III to attempt to initiate what had eluded his Hapsburg predecessors—the extension of firm royal control from the great cities to the small towns and hinterland. The old balancing act of the Hapsburg bureaucracy, which placed wide discretionary powers in the hands of officials—considered to be more accurate judges of local conditions—gave way to a new conception of bureaucracy stressing a more disciplined adherence to central authority. The demands of the new Ministry of the Indies emphasized performance, displaying less patience with delays and the modifi-

---

[62] Gates, "Don José Antonio de Areche," p. 17.

[63] John Fisher, "The Intendant System and the Cabildos of Peru, 1784–1810," *Hispanic American Historical Review* 49 (August, 1969): 430–453.

[64] Lynch, *Spanish Colonial Administration*, p. 79.

[65] See Max Weber, *The Theory of Social and Economic Organization* (New York, 1947), pp. 333–335.

cation of directives. The Bourbon bureaucracy demanded results, especially those that could be counted in the royal treasury. The patrimonial concept of office as personal property, a custom that predominated on the local level and was maintained by the sale of offices and official patronage, was to be terminated. The intendancy envisioned a new bureaucratic order of disciplined, well-trained, and salaried officials who would protect the interests of the Crown, especially its financial interests, from Creole corruption. In Peru, where the oppression of Indian subjects under the graft of *corregidores* was a notorious abuse, it was hoped that the creation of intendancies would improve conditions. The Hapsburg concern to place the Indian population under its more direct supervision was revived. The goal was to eliminate or reduce centers of power, including the old Hapsburg institutions, that did not support the new bureaucratic order.

The expulsion of the Jesuit order in 1767 can be seen in this light, for it eliminated an influential religious order less subject to royal control and under suspicion for its alleged disloyalty and ultramontanism (a doctrine that favored papal rather than royal control over the church). The confiscation of Jesuit property also brought considerable sums to the royal treasury.[66] The expulsion was, moreover, symptomatic of a shift in emphasis. The Bourbons relied less on ecclesiastical institutions to maintain royal control. They restricted clerical privileges and legal immunities, a tendency that reduced the authority and prestige of the church.[67] Cooperation between the church in America and the new Bourbon state gave way to antagonism.

In New Spain, a token military force numbering about 3000 in 1758 increased to over 29,000 by 1800. While Creoles entered the expanding military ranks, advancement was limited. There were less than 200 Creole officers in 1800.[68] The new military units functioned virtually beyond the jurisdiction of traditional bureaucratic structures. Officers enjoyed the complete *fuero militar*. They were subject to trial by their military superiors and not to the judges of the *cabildo* or the *audiencia*. Military tribunals linked directly to Madrid came to exercise increasing authority in New Spain. Even the part-time soldier of the militia enjoyed special exemptions and rights under the *fuero*.[69] By 1784, some 16,766 enlisted men possessed the criminal *fuero*. While the growth of the army was predicated on the

---

[66] Humphreys and Lynch, *Latin American Revolutions*, pp. 55–59.

[67] N. M. Farriss, *Crown and Clergy in Colonial Mexico, 1759–1821* (London, 1968), pp. 1–12.

[68] Brading, *Miners and Merchants*, p. 213.

[69] Lyle N. McAlister, *The Fuero Militar in New Spain 1764–1800* (Gainesville, 1957), p. 11. See also pp. 93 and 98 tables 1 and 5.

need to maintain a force sufficient to repulse an English invasion, it also served as a new institution of integration. The army was "the Crown's favored institution for securing the loyalty of its colonial subjects."[70] The new missionaries were Spanish soldiers. Whereas the Crown attacked clerical privileges, it extended military *fueros*.

The Bourbon reforms constituted a total program of fiscal, military, commercial, and administrative reform. Unprecedented as they were in scope and pervasiveness, they evoked a reaction that severely undermined bureaucratic authority at a crucial moment in colonial history. The Bourbon reforms split the bureaucracy. Older Hapsburg institutions, notably the viceroy and the *audiencia*, resisted the diminution of their power with every resource at their command. They especially resented the establishment of intendancies. In practically every instance, the viceroy and the superintendant immediately clashed over the control of the exchequer. In New Spain, this experimental division of authority lasted only 9 months. The separate office of superintendant was abolished. The viceroy resumed his authority in exchequer affairs and became the intendant of the viceregal capital district. But peace was not restored between viceregal government and the intendants of outlying districts, or between the *audiencia* and the intendants.

With the demise of the superintendant's authority over exchequer affairs, the most important attribute of the intendancy system reverted to the *Junta Superior de Real Hacienda* (Superior Junta of the Royal Treasury)—an institution dominated by officials from the old institutions who "regarded the entire scheme with grave suspicion if not enmity."[71] On the local level, intendants found it almost impossible to implement the directives of the intendancy ordinance. They enjoyed little support from the local *audiencia* or the junta. They had difficulty in asserting their authority over municipalities in their districts. The towns appealed to the junta or the *audiencia* where they were often upheld against the decisions of the intendant. Local power and the established Hapsburg institutions joined together against the Bourbon upstart.

Intendants, having jurisdiction over more extensive areas than the old *corregimientos*, needed a large number of subdelegates (*tenientes*) to assist them. The subdelegates had full authority in native districts where they replaced the old *corregidores*. But they were prohibited from distributing goods to the Indians. Their support came from a 5% commission on Indian tribute. In districts with Spanish towns, the subdelegate had less juris-

---

[70] Brading, *Miners and Merchants*, pp. 27–28.
[71] Ibid., p. 67.

diction. He did not preside over the *cabildo*, and the collection of Indian tribute was left in the hands of the municipal council. In such a case, the financial status of the office was precarious indeed. The intendants were unsuccessful in dislodging tribute collection from the *cabildos*. Inadequately financed, the position of subdelegate was unattractive to most Spaniards. It became a Creole office, sought in many instances because of the status it conferred upon the holder. Since the Crown did not finance the subdelegate, standards were difficult to enforce. "Subdelegate" tended to become a new name for "*corregidor*." Many could not support themselves from tribute collection alone and began to engage in commerce. In 1794, the junta suspended the prohibitions against the *repartimiento de comercio* (forced distribution of goods), arguing that they were prejudicial to the welfare of the Indians and led to the impoverishment of subdelegates. Merchandise could once again be sold on credit to the natives.[72]

Many important goals of the intendancy reform were subverted, but at the price of bureaucratic turmoil. The cost of the Bourbon reform program was high because it alienated every important segment of colonial society. The bureaucracy was divided between the reformers and the conservative defendants of ancient institutions, a rift that was widened by the antagonism between Creoles and *Peninsulares*. The church was beset by attacks upon its status as a distinct corporation. The clergy became subject to the secular court in a disturbing number of criminal and secular cases.[73] By the end of the colonial period, the Mexican church no longer provided a dependable basis of support for the Crown. Municipalities clashed continually with military authorities over the *fueros* of militia men. Creoles were discontented over their growing displacement from old institutions and their exclusion from new ones. The efficiency of financial institutions controlled by *Peninsulares* extended the hand of royal government into the pockets of Creoles and Indians as never before. The reforms created opposition that at times led to violent confrontation. As early as 1767, the expulsion of the Jesuits, following on the heals of new taxes, Crown monopolies, and riots against the militia, sparked open rebellion. Galvez ruthlessly suppressed the movement. The rebellion was not resolved through endless litigation in the *audiencia* or the Council of the Indies. It was solved by regular troops; 85 persons were hanged, 73 flogged, 117 banished, and 674 imprisoned.[74]

The Bourbon reforms emphasized the role of central power. Local

---

[72] Ibid., pp. 80–87.
[73] Farriss, *Crown and Clergy*, p. 10.
[74] Brading, *Miners and Merchants*, p. 27.

authorities could still ambush the reform movement, as they did in the case of the intendancy. But central authority, previously diffused throughout an amorphous Hapsburg structure, stood out boldly under the Bourbons. The problem was no longer an overzealous viceroy who could eventually be tamed by the *audiencia* or the archbishop. The challenge came from Madrid, and was supported by its army of bureaucrats.

The Spanish Bourbons were involved in the process of constructing a new administrative framework, in both Spain and America, that would support a stronger state system. The crux of the problem was to detach resources from the control of local power structures that could then be applied toward the general expansion of the state bureaucracy. The Spanish state, as an extractive apparatus, was limited by the economic organization and productivity of the Hispanic world. With its free-trade policy, it endeavored to expand productivity to generate new sources of taxation and to exploit more efficiently traditional sources of revenue. During the eighteenth century, taxation was a difficult process even given a good administration.[75] Financial reform in New Spain was most successful and provoked least resistance when it applied to expanding economic activities concentrated in one setting. The great increase in revenue that accompanied the expansion of the mining industry and the processing of tobacco are outstanding in this regard. These activities were relatively easy to monitor and their control by the Crown did not represent so direct a loss to local interests. But the renewed effort to control the collection of revenues previously monopolized by local groups, such as the *alcabala* (sales tax) and Indian tribute, was met with adamant opposition. Treasury officials often recycled these local revenues back into the community. The old system of tax farming often supported a complex network of credit that financed local agriculture and industry.[76] These practices were, of course, forbidden by the Laws of the Indies. The reorganization of the exchequer and the creation of intendancies were reforms designed to sever the ties that bound together treasury funds and local interests. Fiscal reform in the old *corregimientos* frequently provoked serious conflict between the financial needs and interests of the community and those of the state defended by the new Bourbon bureaucracy. In Peru, less advanced and economically productive than New Spain, fiscal reform placed a greater financial burden on local interests, and tax resistance occurred more frequently and with greater violence. Fiscal reform was not simply a matter of replacing

---

[75] Gabriel Ardant, "Financial Policy and Economic Infrastructures of Modern States and Nations," in *The Formation of National States in Western Europe*, ed. Charles Tilly (Princeton, in press).

[76] Hamnett, *Politics and Trade*, pp. 6–8.

untrustworthy officials. Reform was likely to change the entire power structure of the community.

Bourbon Reform in Upper Peru and La Plata

The scope and intent of royal policy in other parts of America was similar to that of New Spain. But the pace of reform was frequently different. The advent of the intendancy program in New Spain followed two decades of persistent reform, especially in the treasury. In Peru and La Plata, reform began later. The Areche visitation (1777–1782) occurred 10 years after the Galvez initiative in New Spain. The installation of a strong viceregal center in Buenos Aires was based on strategic considerations. Only a strong Spanish presence in the La Plata estuary could halt Portuguese penetration. Furthermore, Potosí silver escaped from the treasury via La Plata and Brazil. In 1777, the largest Spanish armada ever sent to America, consisting of 116 ships and 19,000 men, arrived to destroy Portuguese bases along the Plata.[77] With the La Plata estuary now secure, and with Upper Peru (Bolivia) detached from the corrupt administration of Lima and placed under the jurisdiction of the viceroy in Buenos Aires, it was hoped that reform could begin.

The visitor Areche arrived in Peru under orders to increase the *alcabala* from 4% to 6%, to repress smuggling, to regulate the accounts in all branches of government, to collect past debts, and to make new tribute lists of the Indian population.[78] His efforts to put the new tax rate into effect led to riots in La Paz, Arequipa, Cochabamba, and Cuzco. But the duties were nonetheless imposed. Tribute collection was restructured. General tribute quotas were no longer farmed out to *caciques*. A more accurate list of tribute payers was drawn up, including men of mixed blood formerly exempt. By 1778, tribute collection had jumped a million pesos annually.[79] The Inca rebellion of Tupac Amaru (1780–1783) was rooted in a past anterior to Areche's "reforms," but still the rhetoric of the revolt was aimed primarily at European Spaniards. Both Creoles and Indians found themselves at odds with the Bourbon government. Tupac Amaru attacked the *alcabalas*, internal customs duties, and tribute exactions—in short, the Bourbon financial program.[80] Initially, Creole opposition to Bourbon

[77] Dauril Alden, "The Undeclared War of 1773–1777: Climax of Luso–Spanish Platine Rivalry," *Hispanic American Historical Review* 41 (February, 1961): 68.
[78] Gates, "Don José Antonio de Areche," p. 24.
[79] Lillian Estelle Fisher, *The Last Inca Revolt 1780–1783* (Norman, Ok., 1966), p. 19.
[80] Humphreys and Lynch, *Latin American Revolutions*, p. 17.

measures disposed them to support the Inca cautiously, hoping the revolt would create circumstances in which they could nullify the reforms. Lampoons, critical of royal policies, were displayed in several towns:

> Here we are waiting until these customhouses, monopolies and new impositions of fifths and other robberies shall be removed, since it is not fitting that we shall endure such impudence. If they are not taken away, it will not be long until the heads of the thieves will be hanging. Long live the King of Spain, and may the thieves die! If it goes on thus, we shall defend Tupac Amaru, the Inca, as our Inca King and monarch. [81]

> This is to let . . . the treasury officials, governors, the receivers and the director of monopolies know that now our supplication demands that the dues, which have been collected violently in our province, must not be collected from us, or we shall place ourselves under the banner of Tupac Amaru, who has written us about the union of his crown. [82]

This situation did not last very long. As the rebellion became more serious, the Creoles quickly aligned themselves with the Crown. As Areche testified: "When I called them to my side, they turned with courage and unselfishness against the Indians." [83] The spectre of social revolution drove Creoles to the royalist cause. Nonetheless, the last great Inca revolt was tied to the unrest created by the reform movement.

The *comunero* revolt in the Viceroyalty of New Granada (1781) was clearly touched off by the Bourbon reforms. The delicate balance of interests maintained by the Hapsburg bureaucracy was upset by the fiscal, administrative, and political reforms of Charles III. The aggressive manner in which they were introduced alienated every important social group in New Granada.[84] The result was a multiracial coalition of Creoles, Blacks, Mestizos, and Indians that climaxed in the occupation of Bogota. They demanded that the new tax on tobacco be abolished, that the *alcabala* be lowered to 2%, and that Indian tributes be reduced. They insisted that the royal *visitador* be expelled from the kingdom, "who tried to squeeze blood out of stones and destroy us with his despotic rule until the people of this kingdom . . . were made desperate by the growing extortions." [85] Finally, they commanded that "the natives of America shall be privileged and preferred over Europeans."[86] The viceroy, an astute politician, made some concessions and destroyed the coalition by playing Creoles against the *castas*.

---

[81] Ibid., p. 100.

[82] Ibid., p. 101.

[83] Gates, "Don José Antonio de Areche," p. 29.

[84] A full account of this revolt will soon be available in John L. Phelan's forthcoming book, *The Comunero Revolution in New Granada in 1781*.

[85] Keen, *Readings in Latin American Civilization*, p. 177.

[86] Ibid.

From the perspective of the seventeenth century, the *comunero* revolt would certainly have appeared grotesque. The role of the bureaucracy was to mediate. The Council of the Indies might have reprimanded officials who provoked such massive opposition. The mandate of the Bourbon bureaucracy was counter to this spirit. It was assumed that the Creoles would resist the reforms. The role of the bureaucracy was to overcome that opposition. The *comunero* revolt represented the attempt of traditional groups, especially Creoles, to preserve their influence over royal policy. They attacked not the center of power but specific individuals, such as the *visitador*, for their "arbitrary conduct." In brief, royal officials had pursued policies detrimental to the interests of the *comuneros* and had acted without due respect for the traditional and customary rights of the groups concerned. The revolt challenged the disciplined bureaucratic order of the Bourbons. The next generation of *comuneros*—led by Bolívar—would directly attack the link with Spain that sustained the Bourbon order.

Intendancy Reform in Upper Peru and La Plata

The disorder created by the revolt of Tupac Amaru and the *communeros*, an event that would have caused the Hapsburgs to redirect their policy, only convinced the Bourbons of the need to regulate closely local affairs. While Creoles attributed the Inca revolt to the reforms of Areche, the Crown blamed corrupt officeholders, especially *corregidores*. Fiscal and administrative reform was intensified as the intendancy system was extended to Upper Peru (Bolivia). Linked as it was to the intendancy reform, fiscal rehabilitation was less impressive in Upper Peru than in New Spain.

Control over the mining industry remained weak. Although treasuries were ordered to keep cash on hand to purchase silver directly from miners, the contraband export of Potosí silver continued unabated. The contribution of Potosí to the total silver production of the Andean region continued to decline in the late eighteenth century. In 1774, Potosí accounted for about 40% of the overall Andean production of 6.5 million pesos.[87] A more dispersed mining pattern based on wage labor was replacing the old Toledan system of forced labor (*mita*) with its concentration on a few rich deposits. The major increase in the revenue of the Potosí intendancy came from customs revenue and not from mining. Revenue rose about 200,000 pesos between 1782 and 1787. While other modest increases occurred, the intendants of Upper Peru were generally unable to displace

---

[87] D. A. Brading and Harry E. Cross, "Colonial Silver Mining: Mexico and Peru," *Hispanic American Historical Review* **52** (November, 1972): 577–579.

an entrenched class of treasury officials who traditionally profited from revenue collection.[88] In some provinces, the new machinery brought no improvement. *Alcabala* revenue actually fell in La Paz, and the treasury was constantly in debt. The financial failure of the intendancy reform in Upper Peru was predictable. Although the administration of the treasury was unified and procedures standardized, the intendancy was simply a new bureaucratic stratum imposed on an unregenerate layer of treasury officials.

The subdelegates were crucial links between the intendant and local treasuries. To work, the system required subdelegates of exceptional honesty and ability. But subdelegates were never granted a dependable salary and the intendant lost control over their appointment. While, in theory, subdelegates were to be exclusively Peninsular Spaniards, in practice, the unattractiveness of the position made it necessary to employ Creoles. Poorly financed, the standards of the office declined. The subdelegate reverted to type. Supported by a commission on Indian tribute, subdelegates were soon accused of all the abuses that had characterized the *corregidor*.

Control of subdelegates and exchequer officials constituted but one aspect of the obstacles faced by the intendant. As in New Spain, he encountered the opposition of more established bureaucratic structures. Particularly caustic was the continuous hostility between the intendants of Upper Peru and the Audiencia of Charcas. The tribunal resented the challenge to its prerogatives posed by its subordination to the new Viceroyalty of La Plata. But the most serious challenge to the authority of the *audiencia* came from the creation of the intendancy system which cut into its jurisdiction over the exchequer. The *audiencia* attacked the intendants at every opportunity. It succeeded in removing and discrediting the Creole intendant Flores, a move that combined the dislike of the intendancy system with the overt anti-Creole sympathy of the tribunal. Virtually every intendant in Upper Peru experienced the venom and intrigue of the *audiencia*. The consequence of this conflict was a running battle that continued into the revolutionary period. The introduction of the intendancy in Upper Peru provoked a kind of bureaucratic genocide that "completely shattered the united front of Spanish government in this part of the empire, and created a tension that contributed in no small part to the undermining of the colonial regime in Upper Peru."[89]

Only in the Audiencia of Buenos Aires could the tie between the tribunal and the intendancies be described as cooperative. But both institu-

---

[88] Lynch, *Spanish Colonial Administration*, p. 142.
[89] Ibid., p. 241.

tions were newly created and the powers of the intendant were not viewed as an encroachment on established traditional authority. In Cordoba and Mendoza, revenues increased substantially.[90] In Argentina, the intendants faced neither a corrupt class of officials nor the hostility of older institutions. In many cases, the intendants provided the first real framework of royal government in the area. *Cabildos* were created or rejuvenated, and a steady stream of flattering testimonials flowed from the *cabildo* to Buenos Aires. But harmonious cooperation turned to distrust by the end of the century. Having galvanized a new interest in town government, the intendants were soon challenged by a local power center that resented any intervention in its electoral affairs and sought to extend its control over local finances.[91] Even where the intendancy reform was "successful," it stimulated the mobilization of dormant groups against the control of the center.

Although the intendancy reform program initially enjoyed the vigorous support of the Crown, that energy was soon spent. The strong sense of direction characteristic of the Ministry of the Indies under Galvez failed to continue after his death in 1787, Charles III, who managed to retain the support of both conservative and reform-minded factions in Spain, died on the eve of the French Revolution. Preoccupied with events in Europe and beset by the growing hostility between liberal and conservative factions in Spain, the Spanish government lost control of the colonial bureaucracy. The struggle that engulfed the bureaucracy over the intendancy question was symptomatic of the mounting crisis in Spain after 1789. The bureaucracy began to drift, and Madrid could no longer impose strict discipline over its agents. The success of the intendancy program required an unprecedented unity of purpose and a single-minded concentration of bureaucratic energy. Neither was provided. The deterioration of the international situation made additional revenue expenditures on reform programs unlikely. In Upper Peru, the Crown did not establish a salaried treasury service as it had in New Spain. The office of subdelegate, so important for the success of the intendancy system, was never given a strong salaried base. The reform movement faltered. The Spanish government was unable to follow through on those reforms begun in the 1780s. The reforms went far enough to alienate established groups, including other bureaucratic agencies, but they were not pursued far enough to yield much of a return. In the two decades following 1789, the Spanish colonial system degenerated from within and was attacked from without.

---

[90] Ibid., p. 132.
[91] Ibid., pp. 230–231.

The Bourbon reforms jeopardized Spanish administration in America. A modernized bureaucracy attacked the traditional role of privileged groups. Administration was a royal monopoly and the fruits of that monopoly were to be enjoyed by the trusted servants of the Crown, the European Spaniards. The Creoles were losing ground under the Bourbons at precisely the time when British colonists were challenging their mother country. By the 1790s, Creoles in New Spain occupied fewer and less prominent positions in the bureaucracy than previous generations. This phenomenon certainly played an important role in the mobilization of Creole groups against central power. If the Crown was to put forth its exclusive claims to control the polity, it required the graceful exit of corporate groups that controlled important resources and wielded immense influence under the Hapsburgs and the first Bourbons.

The traditional role of the church, the control of resources by local interests, the prerogatives of economic and civil corporations, all were seen as obstacles blocking the implementation of an intelligent state policy. By removing the barriers, the Crown also reduced its support. The intendancy reform even mobilized the bureaucracy against itself. Treasury officials played the *audiencia* against the intendant; the church supported the intendant against the viceroy; *cabildos* resisted the new fiscal policies; and the corporations in the capitals fought against the growing pretensions of the provinces. Ultimately, bureaucratic channels could not contain the heavy load of conflict. Everyone was mobilized.

Spain did not lose her American colonies simply because of the Napoleonic invasion, but because the political and economic transformations that occurred under the Bourbons were synchronized with events in Europe. During the War of Spanish Succession (1701–1713), Spain was occupied by invading armies; Madrid was captured; colonial commerce came to a standstill; and the throne was claimed by both the Hapsburgs and the Bourbons. These events failed to provoke a crisis in America. But a century later, Napoleon's invasion of Spain precipitated the collapse of the empire. The *reconquista* of the Bourbons set the stage for the counterrevolution of the colonies. The revolution was a response to four decades of colonial reform.

The crisis provoked by Napoleon's seizure of the Spanish throne shattered a bureaucratic structure that was already weakened. The response of Spanish officials to the interim government established by the Junta of Seville was vacillating and self-contradictory. In the La Plata region, the *oidores* of the Audiencia of Charcas, the intendants, and the viceroy were immediately at odds. The open struggle of Creole against Spaniard was usually preceded by desperate bureaucratic infighting organized in terms of the divisions created during the reforms. As the bureaucracy hesitated, the conflict surfaced, spilling beyond the confines of traditional institutions. The result was a series of revolutions whose nature reflected the unique political configurations of individual *cabildos* and provinces.

Independence proceeded, *cabildo* by *cabildo*, following the organization of a system that concentrated everything in towns. There was no united opposition to imperial taxation, no Continental Congress. The revolution was the creature of local politics, nurtured in relation to a bureaucratic structure. When this structure collapsed, the familiar organization of power disintegrated as well. Adversaries now faced each other directly, without reference to a bureaucratic center. There were no colonial institutions analogous to the assembly of the English colonies that could provide a coherent framework for the ordering of conflict. The independence movement rapidly assumed the character of a civil war.

II
ENGLAND IN AMERICA

The Spanish Crown sent its bureaucracy to uphold royal authority in America. The flota system protected silver shipments and Spanish commerce. The wealth of the Indies—diverted to Spain by the bureaucracy and the fleets—supported Spain's position in Europe during the sixteenth century. But Spain's ability to control America's resources faltered during the seventeenth century. Tied as it was to colonial interests, the bureaucracy was not the obedient instrument of the state. Only in the eighteenth century did the Bourbon state, having centralized its control in Spain, assert its claims to taxes, offices, and economic privileges controlled by colonial merchants, officeholders, and local corporations.

The Spanish section of this study examined the shifting character of Spain's authority in America and the impact this had on economic and political patterns in the colonies. It considered the commercial and bureaucratic arrangements that joined Spain to the Indies, and how these were modified: by competition from other state systems, by the internal problems of the parent state, and by the growth of competing centers of power in the colonies.

The same problems are considered in the English section. What part did the Crown play in colonial society? To what extent was royal power conditioned by the customs and practices colonists brought to America? What kind of commercial and political ties bound England to her plantations, and how did these change? What resources—money, labor, crops, goods, organizations, loyalty—did the parent state seek to regulate in America? What patterns of resistance did the colonists present to the authority of the mother country?

The English Crown did not actively participate in the early settlement of the New World. Political and economic patterns designed by colonists in the early seventeenth century later presented obstacles to royal control. This is the subject of the initial chapters. Subsequent chapters examine royal attempts to regulate commercial and political life, how these initiatives were shaped by events in England and how the colonies responded.

The colonial systems of Spain and England took shape during different phases of the economic and political reorganization of Europe. Their em-

pires reflect differences in bureaucratic and commercial perspectives. While the questions raised in both sections are similar, the answers are often dramatically different. In the conclusion, we will compare the answers more directly.

V

The Beginnings: Virgina

The English penetration of the Americas occurred within the context of
an international struggle against the Spanish empire. The French, Dutch,
and English attempted to break Spanish power in Europe while challenging the commercial dominance of Spain in the New World. The symbol
of England in America during the sixteenth century is that of pirate and
privateer, pillaging a Spanish town and attacking Spanish shipping. The
archetypal heroes of this epic are the Elizabethan "sea dogs"—the buccaneers, men like Sir Francis Drake and John Hawkins, who sustained a floating guerilla war directed against Spanish commerce and coastal ports. Such
men were masters of the sneak attack, of bold, aggressive raids undertaken
for the immediate tangible reward of Spanish bullion. They were adventurers, caught up in the cold-war psychology of Elizabethan England that
pitted the rebellious young gods of Protestantism against the ancient God
of Medieval Catholicism. It was both economic warfare and a battle of the
gods.

The Elizabethan war with Spain (1585–1604), which witnessed the defeat of the Armada, was preceded by two decades of undeclared naval war-

Map 3 Counties of Tidewater Virginia (1750).

fare fought in the Caribbean between English privateers and Spanish squadrons. Conflict occurred in an atmosphere of "no peace beyond the line."[1] The Caribbean during much of the sixteenth and seventeenth centuries was, from a diplomatic standpoint, beyond the territorial limits of European treaties. In a very real sense, it was an area out of control. Warfare was not governed by the social conventions of Europe. Treachery and extermination, a state of undeclared war, existed. The English, as well as the French and the Dutch, tried to break open the Spanish monopoly. They used every possible means to accomplish this objective. The Spanish tenaciously resisted, annihilating any foreign settlements established in the New World. The Spanish attack on the French Huguenot settlement of Fort Caroline in 1565 was not unique. The fort, located on the St. Johns River (near the present site of Jacksonville, Florida) posed a threat to the homeward voyage of the great *flotas*. Except for a few who professed Catholicism, the French were put to the sword.[2] In 1568, John Hawkins, under the pretense of being a peaceful trader, entered the Caribbean with a flotilla of seven well-armed ships. He convinced the inhabitants of Río de la Hacha to trade with him, but only after he had burnt half the town and raided the treasury. No less honorable, the viceroy of New Spain, under the pretense of coming to a peaceful understanding with Hawkins, treacherously seized him and attacked his ships.[3] The exploits of Drake are legendary from the English point of view for their boldness, and from the Spanish point of view for their destructiveness and barbarity. In 1572, he pillaged Nombre de Dios on the Isthmus of Panama, and seized the silver convoy. Such was the atmosphere within which initial English contact with America occurred. The buccaneering, sea dog tradition is the oldest tradition of England in the New World.

Throughout the seventeenth century, the practice of maintaining a base for buccaneering operations remained an important aspect of English policy directed against Spain. But the buccaneer was not a colonizer. Sir Francis Drake or John Hawkins never tried to establish colonies. They were adventurers for whom profit, patriotism, and religious zeal could be combined in a sea war against the Spanish empire. Living and fighting beyond the line, the buccaneer represented a way of life that was severed from the social controls of European life. In many respects, the colonial societies established by England in the Caribbean, such as Jamaica, Barbados, and

---

[1] Richard S. Dunn, *Sugar and Slaves* (Chapel Hill, 1972), pp. 3–45. See also Carl and Roberta Bridenbaugh, *No Peace Beyond the Line* (Oxford, 1972), pp. 3–5.

[2] Wesley Frank Craven, *The Southern Colonies in the Seventeenth Century* (Baton Rouge, 1949), pp. 11–12.

[3] John B. Black, *The Reign of Elizabeth, 1558–1603* (2d ed., Oxford, 1959), pp. 124–125.

St. Kitts, would reflect the influence of the buccaneering spirit. Still, English colonization was not to occur under the aegis of the buccaneer. The whole tenor and organization of the buccaneering enterprise, with its emphasis on mobility and speed, quick profits, and good fortune, could not easily be turned to that more mundane task of endurance and patience required by colonization.

If Sir Francis Drake, lying in wait for a Spanish convoy, is an integral part of the spirit of England in America, so also is John Winthrop, first governor of Massachusetts, thoughtfully delivering a sermon to his fellow Puritans aboard the Arabella during their transatlantic passage to America. England in America was to engender tremendous diversity. Massachusetts was settled by a religious community preoccupied with establishing a "city upon a hill" that would embody a new social order of faith and justice. Virginia, the first permanent English colony, was established by a commercial company motivated by the anticipation of future profits. Buccaneers, Puritans, merchants, and incipient capitalists all came to the Americas during the first half century of colonization. But who was to regulate this scenario? To a much greater extent than was characteristic of Spanish America, the English Crown left responsibility for the construction of institutional life in the hands of its colonists. It did not send an army of professional bureaucrats to America so that royal institutions could oversee the process of building new societies. But why was this the case? Why did the English Crown not exercise greater control over colonization?

The existence of important precedents minimized direct royal involvement in English colonization. The great trading company, chartered by the Crown, served as the institutional model for colonization. The same customs and practices that sustained English commercial enterprise provided the vehicle for coordinating and directing that human effort and those resources required for colonization. By 1600, the organization of the trading company and the buccaneering expedition had already taken definite shape. Since buccaneering, trading, and colonization were seen as part of the same basic process—the extension of English commercial strength—it is not surprising that techniques characteristic of these activities were extended to colonization. This extension had both its assets and liabilities. The use of a commercial form of organization meant that the Crown would probably play a minor role in the activities of the company, including that of colonization. On the other hand, colonization was subsumed under the general heading of a business enterprise expected to yield tangible profits to investors. But colonization was not the kind of venture that yielded a quick profit. Investors were easily discouraged and it proved to be extremely difficult to sustain high levels of investment over a long period of time. Yet, this was precisely the kind of financial base required to establish a colony, since virtually everything, from the food supply to tools and domesticated animals, had to be provided. Failure to appreciate the unique type of effort required to establish a self-sufficient colony led to many abortive attempts to set up colonies in America. Although the Crown granted a charter of colonization as early as 1578, it was almost three decades before the Virginia Company finally succeeded in establishing a permanent, if precarious, colony at Jamestown in 1607.

There were two general types of chartered companies. Regulated companies were associations of merchants who traded on their own behalf but in accordance with chartered regulations and procedures. The Merchant Adventurers was the great prototype of the regulated company during the sixteenth century. It dominated the carrying of cloth to the Netherlands and West Germany. The officials of the company, consisting of a governor and 24 assistants, were elected by the members. It was a large company numbering between 3000 and 4000 members at the beginning of the seventeenth century.[4] The joint stock company accumulated capital to support its commercial activities by selling shares to interested parties. Individual merchants did not trade on their own behalf. The selling of goods was carried out by the officials of the company. Joint stock companies were especially important for carrying on trade with distant ports. The Moscovy Company, chartered in 1553, sought to develop trade with Russia and to discover a new route to the spice lands of Asia; the Levant Company (1581) traded with Turkey; and the East India Company (1599) traded with Asia. Men like Sir Francis Drake organized short-term joint stock ventures to support the buccaneering business. Queen Elizabeth was a heavy investor in such enterprises.[5] The expeditions of Drake and Hawkins received the general approval of the queen. But they were not acting under her specific orders or instructions.

Privateering established an important precedent. It legitimized the harnessing of private self-interest in the pursuit of the national welfare. Personal profit and the public good were capable of being combined. Adam Smith was born "beyond the line." The chartered companies and the joint stock syndicates of Drake attracted heavy investment not only from the merchants but from the nobility and gentry as well. The welfare of the trading company became a concern that touched many levels of English society. Commerce became an affair of state. Indeed, it was the strength

---

[4] Wallace Notestein, *The English People on the Eve of Colonization* (New York, 1954), pp. 250–251. See also J. Holland Rose, A. P. Newton, and E. A. Benians, Eds., *The Cambridge History of the British Empire*, 8 vols. (Cambridge, Eng., 1929–1936), vol. 1, *The Old Empire*, pp. 2, 38–39.

[5] *Encyclopaedia of the Social Sciences*, S. V. "chartered companies." See also Notestein, *Eve of Colonization*, pp. 251–253.

of the state and its willingness to back mercantile operations that made long-term investment in joint stock companies secure. As the seventeenth century progressed, the English state became more suitably organized to support the structure of commerce.

The chartered company conformed to the pattern of a private group licensed to promote the common welfare. The East India Company was chartered as a self-governing enterprise. Control was vested in officials chosen by the General Court (an assembly of all the members) of the company. It had a monopoly of all trade in the Indian and Pacific Oceans. The company was given the power to purchase land and to make on that land any reasonable laws not contrary to the laws of England.[6] Companies were licensed as self-governing agents of the Crown. Once chartered, trading companies controlled their own activities. They provided an important institutional experience in self-government.[7] As merchants, adventurers, and men of wealth became interested in the establishment of overseas colonies in America, they naturally turned to those familiar institutions that had proven to be effective instruments in other commercial activities. They turned to the trading company with its joint stock operations. The Crown played the same role relative to the planting of overseas colonies that it did vis-à-vis the establishment of a new trading network. It licensed private companies and issued patents and charters. But it did not attempt to control the operations of the company. Consequently, the initial institutional framework of English colonization in America was provided by the chartered company and not by the English Crown. Jamestown was the child of free enterprise. English America was a business.

VIRGINIA: FROM BUSINESS ENTERPRISE
TO SOCIETY

Not only did colonization develop along the lines of a chartered commercial organization guided by the profit motive, but such activities occurred during a period of international commercial rivalry. The establishment of English enclaves in America was the final phase of the Elizabethan struggle with Spain.[8] Some of the earliest attempts to establish English "colonies," such as that of Sir Humphrey Gilbert in 1578, were

---

[6] *Encyclopaedia of the Social Sciences*, p. 349.

[7] Rose *et al.*, *Cambridge History*, pp. 2–3.

[8] A. P. Newton, *The Colonizing Activities of the English Puritans* (1914: Yale, 1966), p. 326.

efforts to set up self-sufficient military outposts from which more vigorous attacks on the Spanish empire could be launched.[9]

The Hakluyts, throughout the reign of Elizabeth, urged colonization on both their fellow countrymen and the queen. The younger Hakluyt was especially persuasive as a pamphleteer. His program had an important influence on the men who organized the first colonial expeditions in English history. He argued that Spanish power in Europe was based on the resources of important tropical products—notably dyes, oils, sugar cane, oranges, lemons, hides, figs, and almonds—and that English access to the Far Eastern spice trade was potentially blocked by Dutch and Portuguese competition. Under these circumstances, the vitality of English commerce, and hence the national interest, was tied to the establishment of colonies or plantations in America that could produce a variety of tropical products.[10] These could be used at home and exported to other countries in Europe. The plantations would also provide a new market for English goods. This advantageous situation would free England from dependence on Spanish colonial products, while the demand for English products in America would help diversify English exports excessively dependent on the wool trade with Northern Europe.[11] The heart of the Hakluyt program was commercial. Mercantile interests and the national interest happily coincided. The merchant and the privateer, by seeking their own profit, served the national good. Productive English plantations could undercut the Spanish colonial venture in America, thus weakening Spain in Europe. The point is that, in terms of both motivation and organization, the structure of trade, commercial warfare, and the establishment of overseas plantations were linked together.

The image of "good Queen Bess" investing in one of Drake's buccaneering expeditions is suggestive. The queen is permitting Drake to undertake commercial warfare as he sees fit. The result will be to the mutual advantage of all concerned. It was not then such a great departure from the practices of the time for the monarchy to authorize the establishment of commercial companies that would plant colonies. The company was free to devise its own policies and methods. This arrangement simply was not viewed as a threat to the royal prerogative. It was the logical extension of a mutually acceptable commercial practice to colonization, an activity viewed as essentially commercial. Virginia was the ill-bred offspring of a

---

[9] David Hawke, *The Colonial Experience* (New York, 1966), p. 33.

[10] The English settlements in America were called "plantations" by contemporaries, but the word did not necessarily imply a specific type of agricultural organization. Eighteenth-century documents usually called English possessions in America "colonies."

[11] Craven, *Southern Colonies*, pp. 34–43.

business venure. The involvement of the English Crown in the initial development of American institutional life was minimal. This is especially
striking when we recall the dominant role played by the Spanish Crown
in colonial social life. The cultural patterns of societies in English America
are found in the more mundane folkways of chartered companies, associations of dissenters and foreign immigrants. In terms of its intensely local
institutions, colonial English America reflected its diverse social origins.
This diversity contrasted with the serial forms of Spanish culture ordained
by a royal and ecclesiastical establishment.

In 1606, James I (1603–1625) approved the incorporation of two chartered companies established for the purpose of planting colonies in North
America. The Virginia Company of London undertook what became the
first permanent English settlement in America. The company represented
the interests of London merchants whose capital largely financed the expedition. The company experienced a number of reorganizations during
its troubled history. In 1609, it became a joint stock company owned by
56 London firms and 659 individuals. The final form of the charter (1612)
placed the selection of company officials in the hands of a general court of
all shareholders.[12] The company was also authorized to exercise legislative
and judicial authority in Virginia. The charter stated, for example, that
the company "shall and may have full Power and Authority to ordain
and make such Laws and Ordinances, for the Good and Welfare of the
said Plantation, as to them from Time to Time, shall be thought requisite
and meet: So always as the same be not contrary to the Laws and Statutes
of this our Realm of England."[13] Furthermore, the Crown expressed its
willingness "to give Furtherance unto all good Means that may advance
the Benefit of the said company" and gave assurance that "the happy Success of the said Plantation" was in effect equivalent to the "General Weal
of human Society" and the "Good of our own Estates and Kingdom."[14]
The Crown had delegated the task of colonization to free enterprise.

The plantation of Virginia was an unsuccessful business venture. Stockholders did not receive a favorable return on their investment. It became
extremely difficult, after initial enthusiasm waned, for company officials
to raise enough capital to keep the company afloat. Only about 60 colonists,
a small fraction of those who had arrived in the colony since 1607, survived the winter "starving time" of 1609–1610.

---

[12] John E. Pomfret, *Founding the American Colonies, 1583–1660* (New York, 1970),
pp. 31–32.

[13] Jack P. Greene, Ed., *Great Britain and the American Colonies 1606–1763* (Columbia, 1970), p. 15.

[14] Ibid., p. 13.

In accounting for the early difficulties of the Jamestown settlement, the tendency has been to create an image of the expedition as fundamentally unsound from the beginning. But the efforts and expectations of the company were more realistic than is sometimes supposed. The search for mineral resources was not confined to gold. Iron and copper deposits were also the object of an intensive exploration. An attempt was made to determine the prospects for certain extractive industries. Exports in the manufacture of glass, pitch, tar, and soap ashes were hired by the company for this purpose. In addition, tests were made to determine the suitability of Virginia for the production of a variety of West Indian agricultural products such as olives, sugar cane, hemp, currants, tobacco, cotton, and hops.[15] Generally, the company seems to have had an intelligent plan of action that reflected the writings of the Hakluyts and the earlier experiences of Sir Walter Raleigh at Roanoke (1585–1587). Still, the expectations of the company, as balanced and reasonable as they appear, proved to be illusory in the context of early Virginia.

Virginia did not yield either a valuable mineral or an important tropical product. It was well over a decade before tobacco was developed as an important cash crop. The promise of quick profit could not be fulfilled. The instrument of colonization, the company, proved to be a major obstacle blocking the success of the plantation. The joint stock company was set up to be a successful trading organization. Establishing a viable colony proved to be a task with a set of demands quite different from building a trading network or financing a buccaneer. The Virginia Company of London had great difficulty making the adjustment. While an investor might be willing to wait a couple of years for a return on his capital, would he be willing to wait 10 years, or 20? The company also faced substantial internal dilemmas. It had great difficulty enforcing its authority. The company was, after all, only a business organization. Its directives did not carry the authority of a royal decree or divine grace. The company did not embody a moral order. Its officials represented the self-interest of stockholders, a concern often at odds with the inclinations of its employees. Inadequate leadership, an uncertain basis of authority, and a labor force committed to its own ends rather than to the welfare of the company created a situation of considerable instability.

Under these circumstances, the company asserted its control over the enterprise by imposing a rigid, disciplined, coercive order upon the colonists. For almost a decade (1610–1619), Virginia was subject to the military regimen of the company's governor, Sir Thomas Dale. But discipline

---

[15] Craven, *Southern Colonies,* pp. 67–71.

did not solve Virginia's most pressing problem, the need to attract a labor supply. Indeed, it damaged the company's reputation. Virginia became identified with "severe discipline, sharp laws, a hard life and much labor."[16] The employees of the company had little land of their own. They were obliged to work on company lands. As reports filtered back to England, the attractiveness of Virginia to potential emigrants sharply declined. So did investments. The company could not be a profitable venture unless it could increase the labor supply and thereby help to raise the value of company lands. Virginia had to attract skilled labor and investments. The image of Virginia had to be changed.

The plantation was radically reorganized in 1619. The new policy formally instituted the headright system. Any person who came to Virginia at his own expense received 50 acres of land in the colony. Anyone who paid the passage of immigrants received 50 acres per head. All persons who came to Virginia at company expense were to receive 50 acres of land after they had completed 7 years of labor for the company. Land was the lodestone that attracted immigrants to Virginia during the seventeenth century. The company also initiated a concerted effort to bring women to Virginia. In addition, martial law was terminated. Authority was partially vested in an assembly of elected representatives from each district in Virginia. The company's representative, the governor, had the right to veto enactments of the assembly. Decisions of the assembly were also subject to the review of the company's General Court in London.[17] In other words, the political organization of the joint stock company was extended to Virginia. The assembly was to provide a common political framework to represent the divergent interests of the plantation. The new blueprint also called for a variety of land utilization schemes. In each of four boroughs, 3000 acres were to be set apart as the company's land. It would be cultivated by tenants on a half-share basis. The company also hoped to attract groups of associated adventurers who might establish large estates and support the transportation of immigrants to labor on their behalf (the patent system). Individuals, under the terms of the headright system, would own varying amounts of land.[18] The introduction of these new proprietary ventures "brought a diversity of interest and a dispersal of settlement unknown in the primitive and relatively compact community of earlier years."[19] The company tried to counteract the forces of dispersion

---

[16] Sigmund Diamond, "From Organization to Society: Virginia in the Seventeenth Century," *American Journal of Sociology* 63 (March, 1958): 120.

[17] Ibid., pp. 126–128.

[18] Craven, *Southern Colonies*, pp. 129–130.

[19] Ibid., pp. 134–135.

it had set in motion by establishing an assembly. Representative government was to balance the requirements "of local particularism and the necessities of an essential union."[20]

It would be difficult to overemphasize the importance of the pattern that was being established. The self-interest of the company was to be assured by giving a free rein to the economic self-interest of individual colonists and groups of colonists. The resulting threat to the overall unity of the enterprise posed by the unfettered pursuit of personal and corporate profit was to be minimized by the assembly, an organization that would seek to balance private interest and the public welfare. Such a conception of social organization did not spring randomly from the head of Zeus. It derived from the experience of the joint stock company, an experience demonstrating that economic self-interest could be harnessed in support of larger social goals, the advancement of English commerce.

The reforms of 1619 were designed to enhance the attractiveness of Virginia to prospective settlers, and to induce their willing cooperation. In adopting the headright system, the company had embraced the "doctrine of allurements," a doctrine that "was supposed to involve the free play of economic opportunity within the context of an industrious society."[21] Moreover, it was argued that such freedom was not inconsistent with overall social development. Bluntly stated, "Virginia had been founded upon the premise that profit was the spring of action."[22] It was this motivation that provided the framework for the peculiar social order that was Virginia.

There is in practically every society a tension between overall social goals, or the general welfare, and the peculiar self-interest of individuals. The organization of Medieval society tended to subject the individual to a series of social, economic, and religious controls that bound him to the social goals of the community. Medieval society weighted social organization in favor of the community. Ideally, such a society would resemble More's Utopia, in which hierarchically arranged layers of institutions constrain individual behavior and direct it into channels that serve the common welfare of all citizens.[23] Virginia was not Utopia. The pattern established by the company in seventeenth-century Virginia was weighted in favor of self-interest and economic freedom. People were free to organize their economic activities without the interference of political or religious institutions. The predominant influence in the early history of Virginia was not the Anglican vestry, royal councils, or the social ethos of the Eng-

---

[20] Ibid.
[21] David Bertelson, *The Lazy South* (New York, 1967), p. 29.
[22] Ibid., p. 33.
[23] Sir Thomas More, *Utopia*, trans. Peter K. Marshall (New York, 1965), pp. 42–63.

lish gentry. The institutions that provided the ordered framework of social life in England were not transferred to Virginia with the thoroughness characterizing the efforts of the Spanish government to impose an ecclesiastical and royal hierarchy on the New World. The English colonist in Virginia was faced with the necessity of conquering the land, and the emergence of a local aristocracy was the product of several generations. In contrast, the rise of the *encomendero* class in Spanish America was the immediate product of the conquest. Its social position was based on the control of Indian labor. In Virginia, the growth of an enduring social hierarchy, characterized by a distinctive way of life, was more gradual. Only in the eighteenth century was there a fully developed class of great planters whose social position was based on a plantation economy, dependent on slave labor and oriented to a world market. And even then, the great Virginia planter was not a carbon copy of the English landed gentry.

The company did attempt to define some general social goals. The blueprint it had established in 1619 sought to diversify agriculture and provide for religious life, schools and orderly settlement. But its plan was thwarted because the colony was concentrating on a particular product that commanded a high price on the English market and was easy to produce. For by 1619, tobacco influenced many of the conditions of Virginia life. It was estimated that the labor of one man, with hoe cultivation, could produce 100 bushels of corn, 20 bushels of beans and peas, and from 800 to 1000 pounds of tobacco.[24] In 1627, Virginia produced over 500,000 pounds of tobacco.[25] Artisans, if they did not abandon their trades, were usually part-time planters.[26] Access to water frontage for transportation purposes became an important consideration for farms that were thus strung out along the James River estuary. Unlike New England, the town never became an important focus for political organization in Virginia. Indeed, in the eyes of contemporaries, Virginia was a social monstrosity—a society organized for the production of a socially useless commodity ("that stinking weed," as the king called it), a society so "dispersedly and promiscuously planted" that it even lacked towns.[27]

In England, the management of the company came under increasing criticism. Its charter was revoked in 1624. Ostensibly, Virginia became a royal colony. But no significant changes in the administration of Virginia occurred. The instructions given to royal governors generally duplicated

---

[24] Lewis Cecil Gray, *History of Agriculture in the Southern United States to 1860* (Washington, 1932), p. 27.

[25] Ibid., p. 22.

[26] Bertelson, *The Lazy South*, p. 27.

[27] Ibid., p. 28. In addition, see pp. 19–46.

those that the company had drawn up to guide its own officials.[28] Only in 1641 was a final decision made to confirm Virginia as a royal colony rather than to return it to the jurisdiction of the company. By then, royal government had the firm support of the settlers. It had accepted the headright system, the assembly, and the general pattern of political organization based on the county that was established over the previous decades. The Crown confirmed the settlers in their estates and in their rights. It accepted a society whose growth, direction, and orientation was dictated by the exigencies of local needs, local conditions, and local institutions. If the Crown intended to play a greater role in Virginia, it was distracted by the explosive political situation at home. By 1640, Parliament and the king were engaged in a constitutional battle that precipitated civil war in 1642.

Many institutions that gave direction to social life in England were transformed or absent in early Virginia. The Anglican Church, an institution that exercised such an important influence on the course of political events in England, had little impact on the development of early Virginia. In 1662, there were only 10 clergymen to serve the needs of 45 to 48 parishes.[29] Virginia never had a resident bishop. A system of diocesan control of parish organization did not develop. Since Anglican authorities in England failed to assume responsibility for ecclesiastical organization, the Virginia Assembly assumed responsibility for ecclesiastical organization and became the primary determinant of ecclesiastical policy.[30] Parish life was dominated not by the clergymen but by lay officials (vestrymen) who regulated the temporal affairs of the church. They selected the minister and determined his salary. If a clergyman was not available, it was not uncommon for a service to be conducted by a layman. In England, the priest, supported by the productivity of parish lands, had great financial independence. But in Virginia, land was useless without labor. The minister had to be supported by an annual parish grant. The laity exercised financial control over the Anglican ministry. Parish organization reflected the decentralization of Virginia's political life. Parishes tended to be autonomous units rather than end points of a heirarchical order, just as the county court became an independent, self-contained focus of local political life. Both vestry and county court became centers of local power representing the interests of the most affluent planters. Since such a weakened form of the Anglican Church took shape in Virginia, it is not surprising that other aspects of religious authority were also much reduced. The functions of

---

[28] Craven, *Southern Colonies*, p. 154.

[29] William H. Seiler, "The Anglican Parish in Virginia," in *Seventeenth-Century America*, ed. James Morton Smith (Chapel Hill, 1959), p. 129.

[30] Ibid., p. 125.

the church court, for example, were gradually absorbed by the county court. The secular court began to hear divorce and adultery cases. It granted marriage licenses and kept vital statistics.

The Virginia colonists did not construct institutions *de novo*. Generally, they tried to reconstruct what they had known at home. But without the strong pressure of royal and ecclesiastical bureaucrats, social institutions when reconstructed tended to reflect the concerns of local planters. Beyond the local level, the most important source of social authority was the Virginia Assembly. It combined, until 1663, the appointed councilors of the governor as well as the elected representatives of the planters. It was the assembly and the extension of its authority at the local level—the county court—that provided the initial framework of government within Virginia. These crucial institutions were not administered externally from the English side of the Atlantic but locally, by planters in Virginia. Who were these Virginia planters?

The men who presided over the political life of Virginia in the three decades following the dissolution of the company (1624–1654) were not drawn from the nobility and the gentry. They were skilled workers and yeoman farmers. They stepped into the political void created by the demise of the company. But this new leadership had no legitimate claim to the exercise of authority. Their position "rested on their ability to wring material gain from the wilderness." [31] The political development of early Virginia was "out of control" or "chaotic" only in the sense that it was directed by men whose political behavior was not governed by the cultural patterns that characterized the background of the nobility and gentry. The planter competed for political leadership just as he competed for wealth; it was not externally conferred. The early institutional development of Virginia was a vulgar enterprise in the original sense of the word, i.e., "of, belonging to, or common to the great mass of people in general; common; popular." [32] The consequence was to reinforce the pattern of economic self-interest as the mainspring of social life. In Virginia, planters were free to organize their economic and social life with little reference to the constraints of church, court, and social hierarchy which structured the activities of farmers and tradesmen at home.

> The private interests of this group, which had assumed control of public office by virtue not of inherited status but of newly achieved and strenuously maintained economic eminence, were pursued with little interference from the traditional

---

[31] Bernard Bailyn, "Politics and Social Structure in Virginia," in *Seventeenth-Century America*, ed. James Morton Smith (Chapel Hill, 1959), p. 94.
[32] *Webster's New World Dictionary*, College Edition, 1966.

restraints imposed on a responsible ruling class. Engaged in an effort to establish themselves in the land, they sought as specific ends: autonomous local jurisdiction, an aggressive expansion of settlement and trading enterprises, unrestricted access to land, and, at every stage, the legal endorsement of acquisitions. [33]

The struggling planters who assumed control in the first generation were not able to pass on political power to their descendants. By the 1660s and 1670s, a new ruling group was being formed. It would succeed in maintaining its social predominance into the eighteenth century, establishing the basis for the celebrated Virginia aristocracy. The great wave of immigration that flooded Virginia for over two decades (1650–1675) and the new aggressive policies of the restored Stuart monarchy (1660–1688) precipitated a social transformation in Virginia. But the legacy of the initial patterns set during the first half century would remain. Local power continued to be strong, entrenched in the assembly and in the political organization of the county. Institutional development remained more the product of internal forces than the result of imported royal policies. Profit, but especially the profit of the rising planter class, persisted as the overriding social goal. The organization of economic life would continue to be generated by the free play of economic opportunity unrestrained by any economic blueprint directed toward the general good.

Social life in Virginia during the seventeenth century changed from an initial social fluidity to a structure of social relationships ordered and defined by a ruling class of great planters. This social transformation was linked to the formation of the great plantation, an economic unit tied to the system of indentured servitude. In Virginia, where land was plentiful but labor scarce, large economic units could be productive only if they were able to secure an adequate supply of labor. While it was slavery that sustained commercial agriculture during the eighteenth century, slavery did not create the plantation system. During the latter half of the seventeenth century, Virginia became the destination of an unprecedented stream of immigration from the mother country. The majority of these immigrants came as workers contracted to the men who paid their passage. The plantation system was made possible by the contractual, voluntary labor of indentured servants. Slavery did not transform the institutional life of Virginia. Instead, it helped to perpetuate distinctive characteristics that had already emerged in the frequently abusive system of indentured servitude, a system that tended to reduce the servant from the socially respectable category of apprentice to that of a profitable commodity to be bought and sold.[34]

---

[33] Bailyn, "Politics," p. 96.
[34] Bertelson, *The Lazy South*, pp. 101–105.

For the most part, American colonists succeeded in treating their indentured servants as private property. They bought and sold them, sued each other for possession of them and set up engines of law for their protection of rights in them. . . . To be sure, the servant had rights, but while he was in servitude these rarely conflicted with the conception of him as property. [35]

Such a development was consistent with the organization of economic life in Virginia free from the control of external institutions. The free play of economic opportunity in the context of Virginia meant the unrestrained interests of planters. The long-term effect of such "free play" was the creation of a labor force totally controlled by the planter. In later years, slavery replaced indentured servitude as the new vehicle of economic opportunity. Between 1650 and the end of the century, close to 70,000 immigrants came to Virginia, a truly impressive figure since the base population of Virginia in 1650 was probably not greater than 15,000.[36] (See Table 1.) The greatest concentration—in excess of 27,000—

TABLE 1

White Immigration to Virginia: 1640–1699
(by five-year periods)[a]

Year	Number of immigrants
1640–1644	2,785
1645–1649	1,984
1650–1654	10,910
1655–1659	7,926
1660–1664	7,979
1665–1669	10,390
1670–1674	9,376
1675–1679	3,991
1680–1684	5,927
1685–1689	4,424
1690–1694	5,138
1695–1699	4,270
Total	75,680

[a] From Wesley Frank Craven, *White, Red* and *Black: The Seventeenth-Century Virginian* (Charlottesville, 1971), pp. 15–16.

[35] Abbot E. Smith, *Colonists in Bondage* (Chapel Hill, 1947), pp. 278–279.
[36] Wesley Frank Craven, *White, Red and Black: The Seventeenth-Century Virginian* (Charlottesville, 1971), p. 25.

occurred in the 15-year period 1660–1674. As many as three-fourths of
these immigrants came to America as indentured servants.[37] Immigration
was big business, and the indentured servant was a prized cargo. Frequently, merchants acted as entrepreneurs in the servant trade. They
spent £4 to £10 transporting a servant to America. He could be sold for
anywhere from £6 to £30, depending on market conditions, his age, skills,
and health. Typically, a servant was exchanged for colonial produce, especially tobacco.[38] The traffic in servants was a basic element in the commercial links between England and the Chesapeake. The capacity of the
plantation economy to absorb such an influx of labor and the ability of
English merchants to raise cargoes of servants and organize their distribution in Virginia facilitated the eventual importation of slave labor. The
society that could create procedures to transport, sell, or otherwise distribute some 18,000 servants in 12 years (1663–1664) was institutionally
equipped to import over 50,000 slaves between 1710 and 1769.[39]

The indentured servant was not usually drawn from the bottom ranks
of English society. Laborers were a distinct minority. The majority were
artisans, tradesmen, yeomen (freeholders of the class below the gentry
who worked their own land), and husbandmen (tenant farmers).[40]
Whatever may have been the hardships endured by servants in America,
the attractiveness of indenture remained strong in England. The practice
of "service and services in return for land, training, protection, in short,
for social and economic security—was an idea basic to medieval thinking
and practice and one that had by no means disappeared."[41] The status
of the indentured servant was a respectable one in the scheme of English
social life and it was viewed as an extension of the apprenticeship system.
The promoters of emigration especially stressed the opportunities for
advancement. Service lasted 4 to 5 years. Indentured servants tended to
be unmarried women and men from 18 to 24 years old. The individual
in question signed a formal contract that specified the terms of his
indenture. At the completion of the term of service, the indentured
servant was entitled to claim "freedom dues." These were fixed by custom
or law in each colony. In Virginia, the freed servant was entitled by law
to the sum of £3, 10s in current money.[42] No doubt this was often re-

---

[37] Smith, *Colonists in Bondage*, p. 298.

[38] Ibid., p. 39.

[39] Philip D. Curtin, *The Atlantic Slave Trade* (Madison, 1969), p. 143.

[40] Mildred Campbell, "Social Origins of Some Early Americans," in *Seventeenth-
Century America*, ed. James Morton Smith (Chapel Hill, 1959), p. 71.

[41] Ibid., pp. 69–70.

[42] Smith, *Colonists in Bondage*, p. 239.

deemed in goods or produce. In Virginia, after the company died out, there was no legal provision for a grant of land to freed servants. Promoters often promised "fifty acres according to the custom of the country" but this proved to be a deception.[43] Under the headright system, the bounty of 50 acres per immigrant went to the person who paid the servant's passage. Still, in the continental colonies, wages were high enough that the freed servant could reasonably expect to eventually purchase land.

In 1666, perhaps 30% to 40% of the landholders in Virginia had been indentured servants. But when we consider that probably 75% of all immigrants came to Virginia as indentured servants, the figure is less impressive.[44] Although Virginia may have offered many servants opportunities that were not available to them in England, the majority either died during their servitude, returned to England, or entered the ranks of poor whites. Only a minority eventually acquired their own land, settled down as artisans, or perhaps became overseers on a large estate. Virginia developed a reputation as a land of opportunity, but only because the more typical experience of failure and disappointment was overshadowed by a sufficient sprinkling of success stories.

While the apprenticeship system in England provided the original model for indenture, the institution was often transformed in the colonies. A servant might enter into a contract that resembled English apprenticeship. However, as it worked out in Virginia, indenture frequently meant exploitation and excessively hard labor under the direction of an overseer. The most frequent complaint of servants, in addition to insufficient food and clothing, concerned cruel and abusive treatment.[45] The institution was doubled-edged. It could be quite similar to the more personal and protective relationship of master and apprentice. On the other hand, many of its characteristics pointed to the future, toward the impersonal planter-dominated system of slave labor. The servant's labor facilitated the rise of the great plantation and the development of a stable class of wealthy planters. The great names of eighteenth-century Virginia begin to appear for the first time during the third quarter of the seventeenth century. This was precisely the period in which the great flood of immigration entered Virginia.[46] Virginia was a land of opportunity for the younger sons of merchants and the gentry who brought capital of their

---

[43] Ibid., p. 43.
[44] Ibid., p. 298.
[45] Ibid., p. 247.
[46] Bailyn, "Politics," p. 98.

own to invest, who inherited estates or came to redeem earlier investments made by their families in the company. They are able to purchase
or gain title to land that was, in many instances, already cleared. In
addition, they could draw on the growing numbers of indentured servants
to make their land productive.

In the last decade of the seventeenth century, a marked increase in
the importation of slave labor into Virginia occurred. While the absolute
number involved was relatively small compared to the number of white
immigrants who entered Virginia during the same period, still the trend
was significant. A definite drop in the high levels of white immigration
was counteracted by an increase in the use of slave labor. The eighteenth
century beheld a total transformation in the relationship between indentured and slave labor. White migration reduced to a trickle, while
the importation of slave labor attained the proportions of a deluge. By
1750, half the counties of Tidewater Virginia (roughly the area bordering
on and between the Potomac and James Rivers below the fall line) had
a population that was composed of from 40% to 60% slaves.[47] What
factors enabled and facilitated such a fundamental alteration in the social
composition of Virginia?

The economic institution that could advantageously utilize slave labor,
the plantation, had already developed during the seventeenth century.
The institutional climate of Virginia, supporting as it did the free play of
economic interests, responded to the needs of the planters. Just as such
an atmosphere had contributed to the growth of a harsh and severe ver-
sion of apprenticeship, it placed no restraints on the use of slave labor.[48]
Slaves had been imported into Virginia in small but increasing numbers
since 1660. But slavery did not originate in Virginia. In terms of English
America, the slave system had its beginnings in the English West Indies,
specifically in Barbados. By midcentury (1650), Barbados was already a
slave society. Probably most of the slaves who came to Virginia during the
greater part of the seventeenth century were brought from Barbados.[49]
While there was some early confusion about the status of black men in
Virginia, after 1640 it seems clear that they were treated as slaves.[50] The
definition of slavery as perpetual servitude was transplanted to Virginia

---

[47] Robert E. and Katherine B. Brown, *Virginia, 1705–1786: Democracy or Aristocracy?*
(East Lansing, 1964), p. 73, table 1.

[48] See Stanley M. Elkins, *Slavery* (Chicago, 1959), pp. 27–80. Richard S. Dunn,
Sugar and Slaves (Chapel Hill, 1972), especially pp. 3–45 and 335–341. Frank Tannenbaum, *Citizen and Slave* (New York, 1947).

[49] Craven, *White, Red and Black*, pp. 93–94.

[50] Winthrop D. Jordan, *White Over Black* (Chapel Hill, 1968), p. 73.

from Barbados. As a legally defined status, the law generally lagged behind actual social conditions. Slavery, as hereditary lifetime service, was written into Virginia law in 1660. The transition to slave labor was eased by the fact that it was already clearly established as a definite condition both legally and as a familiar social practice before the great slave importation began. But why did such large importations begin in the first place and what underlies the specific timing, the fact that the plantation system turned to slave labor between 1690–1720?

One line of argument has been to emphasize the economic advantages inherent in a slave labor system.[51] While the initial capital outlay for a slave was greater than that required to purchase an indentured servant, the slave served for life, the indentured servant for a relatively short period of time. There was a constant turnover of indentured servants. Not only the slave but his descendants as well were bound perpetually. Slave labor, consequently, offered a more secure, stable, and, in the long run, cheaper, labor supply than that of indentured servants. In colonial Virginia, such considerations were absolute. They were not subject to the veto of other social institutions acting in the name of society at large. In addition, the supply of indentured servants was beginning to decline. The absence of free land in Tidewater Virginia made it increasingly difficult for the freed servant to obtain holdings anywhere but on the remote frontier.[52] The flow of immigrants to the Chesapeake was progressively diverted to the middle colonies, especially Pennsylvania.

Virginia was becoming less attractive to immigrants during the last quarter of the seventeenth century. But the expansion of tobacco production continued. Chesapeake production doubled from 15 million pounds in 1669 to about 30 million pounds in 1699.[53] Demand for labor was increasing at precisely the time when immigration was beginning to taper off. The decrease in white immigration after 1680 in the face of continued agricultural expansion certainly gave an impetus to the use of slave labor. Fewer white servants meant a greater reliance on black slaves. This, in turn, made Virginia less attractive to potential immigrants. All of these factors—the institutional atmosphere of Virginia, the rise of the plantation system under indentured servitude, the model of slave systems in the West Indies, the economic advantages of slavery, a decline in white

---

[51] Gray, *History of Agriculture*, p. 350. See also Richard B. Morris, *Government and Labor in Early America* (New York, 1946), p. 314.

[52] Gray, *History of Agriculture*, p. 348.

[53] Jacob M. Price, "The Economic Growth of the Chesapeake and the European Market, 1697–1775," *Journal of Economic History* 24 (1964): 497.

immigration, and yet a continued expansion of the demand for tobacco—were conducive to the emergence of a slave system.

If predominantly internal factors supported the gradual transition to slave labor during the 40-year period from 1680 to 1720, the tremendous expansion of the European tobacco market between 1725 and 1775 provided an extraordinary momentum to the growth of the slave system. If Virginia inched into slavery before 1720, the victim of the so-called "unthinking decision," it plunged into slavery without hesitation during the next half-century.[54] Tobacco exports in the Chesapeake Bay region increased from 50 million lbs in the years between 1738 and 1742 to 70 million lbs between 1752 and 1756, reaching 100 million lbs on the eve of the Revolution (1771–1775).[55] The slave population increased by an even greater margin. Virginia had a slave population of about 23,000 in 1715. This figure had almost doubled by 1743. In 1756, the slave population exceeded 120,000, reaching 200,000 by 1774.[56] The extension of the slave labor system in eighteenth-century Virginia was inextricably linked to the international tobacco market.

The slave system provided a secure base for the plantation system, and a stable economic foundation for the Virginia aristocracy. After the initial social confusion and instability of the preceding century, the tendency to identify social and political leadership, the predisposition of the age, became more firmly established in Virginia. An "establishment" had emerged. The introduction of slave labor did not affect just the top of the social pyramid. It had important consequences for the economic position of the small freehold farmer. The establishment of the slave system in Tidewater Virginia was accompanied by an exodus of independent small planters to the frontier or to other colonies, especially Delaware and Pennsylvania. Survival in what at times was a highly volatile international market favored the large producer who could sustain himself in spite of falling tobacco prices. Only by increasing the volume of producton was it possible to maintain a viable margin of profit. Virginia tobacco did manage to capture the lion's share of the European market. But it did so by underselling its competitors. Tobacco had been a high-priced luxury item that could yield an attractive profit to even the small producer. But in the 1670s, the price of tobacco began to fall considerably. It was becoming a low-priced basic commodity—the poor man's drug.

---

[54] For a discussion of the "unthinking decision," see Jordan, *White Over Black*, pp. 44–98.

[55] Price, "Economic Growth," p. 497.

[56] Arthur Pierce Middleton, *Tobacco Coast: A Maritime History of Chesapeake Bay in the Colonial Era* (Newport News, 1953), p. 455.

Tobacco became a profitable commercial crop mostly for the large planters. The smallest farms were driven to the wall. The discontent of the small planter and his opposition to the increasing dominance of an affluent class of large planters was a major undercurrent in Bacon's Rebellion (1676).[57] But the rebellion did not materially alter the plight of many poor farmers. The small planter voted with his feet. In the 1680s, the process of thinning out the hundreds of small farmers who cultivated the soil of Tidewater Virginia began to gain momentum. The migration became serious enough in the 1690s to alarm the English government. The major social contours of Tidewater Virginia were formed during the last half of the seventeenth century.

Even in the late seventeenth century, perhaps 65% of all landowners in Tidewater Virginia possessed neither servants nor slaves.[58] An investigation of the 1675 tax rolls revealed "hundreds of little farmers, many of them trusting entirely to their own exertions for the cultivation of the soil, others having but one or two servants, and a bare handful of well-to-do men each having from five to ten or in rare cases twenty or thirty servants and slaves."[59] But in the eighteenth century, this "bare handful of well-to-do men" underwent considerable expansion. Most counties came to have a substantial number of large estates. In Lancaster County, of some 167 slaveowners, 48 owned five slaves or more in 1745. About 66% of all family heads owned slaves.[60] Still, the typical planter in Tidewater Virginia, even in the eighteenth century, was not a great planter. Most planters owned from 100 to 200 acres of land and possessed from one to three slaves. But the "hundreds of little farmers trusting entirely to their own exertions" no longer predominated. While the class of independent farmers characteristic of seventeenth-century Virginia did not disappear, their influence certainly waned The trend was for the great plantation to control a greater share of the most valuable resources in the Tidewater region—land and labor. In Norfolk County, for example, 35% of the landowners controlled 75% of the land in 1771, while 30% of the slaveholders held over 50% of the slaves.[61] Land and labor were gathered in by the large estates.

The great planters did not eliminate the small freeholders. The latter

---

[57] Thomas Jefferson Wertenbaker, *Torchbearer of the Revolution* (Princeton, 1940), Chapter 1.

[58] Thomas Jefferson Wertenbaker, *The Planters of Colonial Virginia* (Princeton, 1922), p. 59.

[59] Ibid., p. 57.

[60] Brown and Brown, p. 75, table 3.

[61] Ibid., p. 13, table A; p. 75, table 3.

survived as an important class throughout the colonial period, but they tended to follow the great planters' lead. The small freeholder was also predominantly a slaveholder even if, as was often the case, he could afford only one. Consequently, the antagonism that could have developed between the small freeholder and the great plantation owner was mitigated by the fact that both embraced the slave system. The small freeholder shared the social goals of the great planter; he did not define a competing system of social values. The great planter had arrived. The small planter hoped he was on his way.

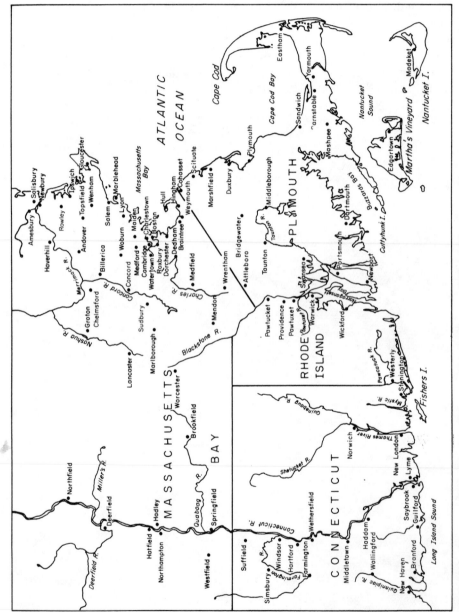

Map 4. Puritan Areas (1650)

VI

The Beginnings: Massachusetts

PURITAN NEW ENGLAND: THE BACKGROUND

The settlement of Virginia was but one of a series of English colonial ventures that extended from New England to the tropical battleground of the Caribbean. The organization of different colonial enterprises, as in Virginia, mirrored the variety of goals and social values of the respective colonizing groups. Behind these operations, there was no single unified vision of England in America. The Crown chartered trading companies, buccaneers, and landed proprietors. The net result was that colonization absorbed the energies of a bewildering collection of Englishmen. The diversity of the colonies faithfully reflected the complex, politically charged atmosphere of seventeenth-century England.

The relationship between Parliament and the Crown, strained during the reign of James I (1603–1625), deteriorated steadily under his successor, Charles I (1625–1649), leading to civil war in the 1640s. The Crown had fostered the growth of trading companies. Now it was challenged by the representatives of a new economic order—merchants and gentry who opposed the restrictions of royal authority. Politically, the conflict centered in Parliament. But the tension between the Court and Parliament pervaded the society at large. The challenge to established authority also took the form of attacks on religious hierarchy. The Crown upheld the Church of England and became progressively more hostile to those who attacked the hierarchical structure of religious control—the Puritans. The Crown saw Puritanism as the religious expression of the opposition. John Pym, deeply involved in mercantile activities, was a leading member of Parliament, an opponent of the king, and a staunch Puritan. He was not unique in this combination of attributes. Still, Puritanism was not synonymous or inherently concordant with the economic aspirations of merchants. The Puritan was not a disguised capitalist. Puritanism was to some extent a response to a rapidly changing social order characterized by unprecedented social mobility and urban expansion. The Puritan sought to order a disordered universe. He began by imposing order upon himself. But Puritanism was, parodoxically, both a way of ordering one's life in the face of rapid social change and a significant factor in the acceleration of that change. The assault on ecclesiastical hierarchy certainly helped to loosen the bonds that attached Englishmen to the institutional authority of the Crown. The Puritan search for religious and social stability helped to underwrite revolution.

Seventeenth-century England was a crucible of economic change, religious tension, and constitutional deadlock. The royal persecution of the Puritan faction within the state church turned some Puritans against the Crown. Such harassment also led to a mass exodus—the Great Puritan Migration. A major destination of this migration was Massachusetts. New England was the project of men profoundly alienated from their own society. Massachusetts was the embodiment of dissent. It was the religious experiment of the most radical element within the Puritan movement. New England was peopled by the opponents of royal and ecclesiastical power. Preoccupied by events at home, the Crown was unable to act decisively in the New World.

The New England Puritan was a radical according to the primary meaning of the term: "of or from the root or roots; going to the center, foundation or source of something; fundamental; basic." [1] The center of Puritanism was salvation. The classic image of the Puritan is John Bunyan's pilgrim making his way to the heavenly city through the disorder and evil of the world around him. The experience of a disordered world was fundamental to the Puritan vision. The Puritans

> saw war and disorder as the natural state of fallen men out of which they had been drawn by God's command and by the painful effort of their own regenerate

---

[1] *Webster's New World Dictionary*, College Edition, 1966.

wills. But they lived always on the very brink of chaos, maintaining their conviction only through a constant vigilance and, indeed, a constant warfare against
their own natural inclinations and against the devil and his worldliness.[2]

At the heart of Puritanism was a penetrating, moving, religious experience
in which men and women found themselves called out of a disordered,
confusing world by God's saving grace. They became new people, re-
generate, saved, visible saints, justified not by virtue of any merit of their
own but only because of God's freely bestowed gift of grace. Salvation
was not conferred by an institutional church. It could not be earned
through good works or by participation in the sacramental rituals performed by the clergy. People were awakened individually by God's grace.
This was an encounter between person and God without the mediation
of a hierarchical religious structure.

The religious structure of Puritanism was comprised of an association
of visible saints. They joined together to support each other through
life's pilgrimage. The transformed person was self-confident and free of
the anxiety, guilt, and doubt that had characterized his or her unregenerate self.[3] Their religious world now ordered through faith in Christ,
the Puritans faced the disarray of the material universe with renewed
self-assurance. They approached the dangerous stuff of this life with a
rigid self-discipline and control. Puritan politics was the skillful and wise
handling of worldly affairs. Its end was the creation of a controlled,
ordered social environment that would reinforce rather than undermine
godliness. As a political orientation to this world, the Puritan emphasis
on discipline, method, and order was in vivid contrast to the aristocratic
ostentation and extravagance that characterized the English Renaissance
Court.[4] The life style of the Puritan was at odds with basic aspects of
English social life.

Not all men reacted to the social climate of seventeenth-century England by entering the godly ranks of Puritanism. There were many "gentlemen and citizens who certainly enjoyed the new freedoms of mobility,
extravagance, individuality and wit" afforded by the changing social values
of the era. They "eagerly sought entrance to the Renaissance Court." [5] Certainly, large numbers of English men and women, tucked away in the more
traditional agricultural sectors of society, were insulated from the economic and social changes that engulfed the urban areas. To a large extent,

---

[2] Michael Walzer, "Puritanism as a Revolutionary Ideology," *History and Theory* 3
(1963): 24.
[3] Ibid., p. 29.
[4] Ibid., p. 29–31.
[5] Ibid., p. 29.

Puritanism was the religious experience of the middle sectors of society. It affected grocers, clothiers, attorneys, tailors, merchants, professors, clergymen, skilled workers, and yeoman farmers, especially those located in urban areas. But even within the rising middle class, Puritanism was by no means universal. There were, moreover, many shades of Puritanism. It was not a monolithic, well-defined perspective. Had Massachusetts been settled by a systematic random selection of Englishmen drawn from the intermediate ranks of society, the sample would undoubtedly have included a healthy sprinkling of Puritans with varying degrees of religious commitment. But such a collection of Englishmen would certainly not have been motivated to cross the ocean for the sake of embarking on a godly experiment. The settlement of Massachusetts, like most social processes, was not random. The Massachusetts Bay Company was chartered to establish a colony in New England. The company was dominated by Puritans of a particularly dedicated and serious variety.

The Massachusetts Bay Company was chartered as a trading corporation and enjoyed certain powers of government over a specified area. Typically, charters provided for regular meetings of the company in question, and designated a particular city in which such meetings or General Courts were to be held. But the charter of the Bay Company did not explicitly state where the meetings of the company were to occur. The Puritans took advantage of this omission by proposing that the company's meeting place be moved to the colony itself. Consequently, the man chosen governor of the company would also be, in effect, the governor of the colony, and the General Court of the company could become the legislative body of the colony.[6] By moving the control structure of the company to New England, the Puritans effectively withdrew their enterprise from royal surveillance. The proposal had the backing of the dominant Puritan faction. It was approved by the company. John Winthrop, a leading Puritan who had recently decided to emigrate to New England, was chosen by the General Court as first governor. To the Puritans facing renewed persecution at home, the advantages of moving the company to New England were obvious. The company would become

> a self-governing commonwealth, with the charter a blank check justifying everything it did. It would thus be able to enforce the laws of God and win divine favor. It could create in New England the kind of society that God demanded of all his servants but that none had yet given Him. [7]

---

[6] Edmund S. Morgan, *The Puritan Dilemma: The Story of John Winthrop* (Boston, 1958), pp. 45–46.

[7] Ibid., pp. 46–47.

Massachusetts was settled by the most radical faction of English Puritanism, by men and women who had experienced a basic, fundamental change in the direction of their lives, men and women who had been transformed by God's saving grace, who were visible saints and who had the self-assurance to forsake the past to face an uncertain future. Massachusetts was the religious undertaking of a self-selected minority of Englishmen who were primarily concerned with salvation and godliness. The silent majority stayed at home.

The social climate of New England was molded by a religious community. It was not the work of profit-minded adventurers. The Puritans weighted social organization in favor of the social goals of the community. No doctrine would have appeared more absurd to the Puritan than the notion that men, permitted to pursue their own economic self-interests unhindered by traditional institutions, would secure the general welfare of society. For them the civil man, the man who at least outwardly conformed to the behavioral standards of the community, was the product of an overlapping system of institutional controls. Separating themselves from the confusion and disorder of the Old World, the New England Puritans sought to construct a society of ordered relationships. In economic and social terms, New England Puritanism was a philosophy of social stratification.[8] The exercise of authority was the prerogative of the properly qualified—the educated gentleman.

In stressing the hierarchical nature of the social order, the Puritans reflected the beliefs and practices of most Englishmen. But the rationale behind that structure of authority was the need to constrain men to act justly and righteously. Man's nature was a fallen one. It was corrupted by original sin. Constant vigilance was necessary to prevent the eruption of man's distorted and evil nature. Authority was to be exercised on behalf of the community against the unbridled liberties of individuals. Governor John Winthrop addressed the assembly (General Court) of the colony on precisely this matter in 1645. He warned against the error of thinking that liberty consisted in permitting men to do as they wanted, to choose evil as well as good.[9] Such liberty was incompatible with the welfare of society and was at odds with the authentic function of authority. The end and object of authority was the preservation of liberty, but a certain kind of liberty, "the liberty to do only that which is good, just and honest."[10] What was good usually served the overall needs of the

---

[8] Perry Miller and Thomas H. Johnson, Eds., *The Puritans: A Sourcebook of Their Writings*, 2 vols. (New York, 1963), vol. 1, p. 19.

[9] Ibid., p. 106.

[10] Ibid., p. 207.

community. The individual was not at liberty to pursue his own personal profit at the expense of his brothers. The health of the entire body politic was always more important than the welfare of any single member. To this end the Puritans controlled prices, wages, and profits, inspected the quality of goods, and made sure that proper weights and measures were used by shopkeepers. The Puritan ideal was neither economic success nor the social mobility of individuals. Worldly ambition was forever the enemy of a well-ordered society. Puritans were urged by a vigilant ministry to humbly accept their stations in life. The following from a sermon aptly expresses this sentiment.

> This intends that we keep within the line and place that providence has set us. . . . We must not without God's call quit our post, thrust ourselves into another's province, with a conceit that there we may serve best, and promote the good of the world. But herein observe the will of God by keeping to the service that belongs to our station, which providence has made our peculiar business. Thus every man is to serve his generation by moving in his own orb; and discharging those offices that belong to that order the government of heaven has assigned him to. [11]

The New England Puritan envisioned a relatively static and ordered social existence. Puritan society in America was not constructed to provide a new setting for social change. It was not to be a land of economic opportunity in which the lowborn could improve their social standing. The Puritan was not an advocate of "progress." To be a Puritan meant to participate in overlapping networks of economic and social relations. Good Puritans knew their places and stayed there. The good society, once established, would stay in place as well. The Puritans were radicals who rooted their existence in a stable, unchanging order that they would vigilantly defend against the onslaught of worldly temptation. But they built their world in the eye of a hurricane. The society envisioned, and to a surprising degree implemented, by the first generation of Puritans was progressively undermined. The artificial tranquility of the center disintegrated. The Puritans then faced the full fury of the storm. The increasing dissension in the Bible commonwealth was generated to a considerable extent by contradictions at the heart of Puritanism itself.

THE GODLY COMMONWEALTH BESIEGED

The Puritans affirmed the importance of hierarchical authority. They believed that "the essence of the social order lay in the superiority of hus-

---

[11] Ibid., p. 19.

band over wife, parents over children, masters over servants in the family, ministers and elders over congregations in the church, rulers over subjects in the state."[12] At the same time, the Puritans upheld the primacy of an inner, personal, religious experience: the presence of God's saving grace within the individual soul. Salvation was based on a conversion experience. It was not predicated on the institutional authority of the Anglican state church. The covenant of grace that bound together Christ and His chosen saints took precedence over the hierarchical authority of a clerical establishment. The Puritans had repudiated the authority of what they considered to be an unregenerate Anglican clergy. What was to prevent the same process from repeating itself in Massachusetts? How could one congregation of saints be prevented from deciding that the rest of Massachusetts was in error? Men and women who had refused to tolerate the evils of Anglicanism would undoubtedly possess the personal strength required to separate themselves from heretical communities in New England. The doctrine of the "inner light" was dangerous indeed. The Puritans who made their way to New England brought with them strong separatist impulses. This situation created an immediate and pressing dilemma—the fact that rebels, to put their vision into effect, must prevent rebellion.[13] Separatism had made the "city upon a hill" possible, but its survival hinged upon containing the same forces that had given it life. Was there a place in this Godly commonwealth for those whose inner light put them at odds with civil and religious authorities? There was not. Massachusetts was soon exporting dissenters to the rest of New England.

If the implication of certain ideas in Puritanism can be seen as facilitating separatism, this tendency was further encouraged in its congregations. The Massachusetts Puritans, free to experiment with church organization, put into practice the most extreme theories advocated by English Puritans. They became congregationalists. Membership in a congregation was restricted to visible saints, to people who could prove that they had experienced God's saving grace. Each congregation exercised complete local autonomy. Each minister and congregation was sufficient unto itself. The people of Massachusetts had undertaken an almost impossible task. "They had accepted a mission that required them to follow a specific body of religious principles; but among those principles was one that encouraged the development of schism (inner light) and another (congregationalism) which denied them the means of preventing it." [14] John Winthrop devoted

---

[12] Edmund S. Morgan, *The Puritan Family* (New York, 1966), p. 19.
[13] Morgan, *The Puritan Dilemma*, pp. ix, 73–76.
[14] Ibid., p. 80.

much of his energy to dampening the flames of separatism. But he was not always successful. Roger Williams and Anne Hutchinson had to be expelled from the colony to preserve doctrinal purity.

But Puritanism was not a monolithic body of doctrines. Congregational independence could foster diversity without calling attention to itself. Within certain limits, the congregational structure permitted individual localities to develop their own particular theological tendencies without creating the threat of separatism.[15] To some extent, the congregational structure probably helped to reduce doctrinal confrontations, since no specific institution was given the task of ferreting out the potential heretic. However, when religious controversies did emerge, they shook the colony to its very roots. There was no way to enforce a majority decision on a recalcitrant minority of stubborn congregationalists. Permanent schism could result. This is, in fact, what occurred.

The enthusiasm, sacrifice, and commitment of a radical generation of Puritans had created "that one and only polity that Christ has outlined in scripture." It was generated out of their sainthood, their confidence, and their determination. They were the builders and the founders, intoxicated and driven by the boldness of their own vision. But could they pass on such zeal to the next generation? Could they transmit the excitement of the "revolutionary situation" to their descendants? They faced the problem that confronts the leadership of every revolutionary generation. How does one maintain the impetus of revolution?

The religious fervor of Puritan New England could not be sustained. Symbolic of the waning of intense religious experience was the decline in the number of visible saints. Conversion and personal transformation became less characteristic of New England Puritanism. The inner light was growing dim. The Halfway Covenant (1657) opened church membership and baptism to the children of saints who, while exhibiting godly behavior and professing their faith, could not bear witness to an intense personal experience of God's saving grace in their lives. Not all congregations were willing to accept such a deviation from the original purity of a church of visible saints. New England was clearly split over the issue. But while some churches fought a rearguard action to maintain adherence to original principles, the long-run trend was evident. Expanding the base of church membership and thus preserving some semblance of religious unity was viewed as more important than rigid orthodoxy. The radical church of the 1630s and 1640s was becoming the establishment of the 1660s and 1670s.

---

[15] Edmund S. Morgan, "New England Puritanism: Another Approach," *William and Mary Quarterly* **18** (1961): 236–242.

The problem in the city of God had appeared long before the end of the seventeenth century. The difficulty was in the city of man. The Puritan vision was at once social and theological. The Puritan, while bound for the heavenly city, had to sojourn in the earthly city. It could not be ignored. But the two cities were not bound together in blissful harmony. They were potentially dangerous enemies. In this world, the Puritans had to exercise strong discipline and self-control if they were to maintain within themselves the proper balance between the demands of heaven and the cares of this world. As well as a religious enterprise, Massachusetts was also a political experiment, a test case in the politics of ordering social life. How did the Puritans intend to create and preserve a stable society?

While in England, John Winthrop was elected governor of the Massachusetts Bay Company. At the same time, a number of Assistants were chosen to sit on the General Court of the company. One of their first acts after arriving in Massachusetts was to propose "if it were not the best course that the Freemen should have the power of chuseing Assistants when they are to be chosen, and the Assistants from amongst themselves to chuse a Governor and Deputy Governor, who with the Assistants should have the power of makeing lawes and chuseing officers to execute the same."[16] The proposal was "fully assented unto by the general vote of the people, and ereccion of hands."[17] The General Court of the company had been changed into a legislative assembly. The term "freeman" was "transformed from a designation for the members of a commercial company, exercising legislative and judicial control over that company and its property into a designation for the citizens of a state, with the rights to vote and hold office."[18] A freeman was now defined as a church member. This probably included almost all the adult males in the colony. The Bay Company had become a commonwealth.

Why had Winthrop and the Assistants given up the exclusive powers granted to them by the charter? Certainly it was not based on any desire to represent the private self-interests of groups or individuals. Quite the contrary. The structure of Massachusetts' government was based on a religious model, the idea of the covenant.[19] Covenant theology had developed in response to the problem posed by God's seemingly arbitrary power. God was free to save and damn as He wished. One could never be absolutely sure of salvation. How was the certainty of one's own salvation com-

---

[16] Morgan, *The Puritan Dilemma*, p. 90.
[17] Ibid.
[18] Ibid., p. 91. Generally, see pp. 84–100.
[19] Ibid., pp. 92–94.

patible with God's freedom? The answer was provided by covenant theology. God had freely chosen to commit Himself to a particular plan of salvation. God had chosen to be reasonable. Part of that plan was that sanctified behavior was evidence of justification or potential justification. God was bound to act according to his contract. As John Preston, the architect of covenant theology stated,

> when faith hath once gotten a promise, be sure that thou keeps thy hold, pleade hard with the Lord, and tell him it is part of his Couvenant, and it is impossible that he should deny thee . . . when thou art on sure ground, take no denyall, though the Lord may defer long, yet he will doe it, he cannot chuse; for it is part of his Couvenant. [20]

Besides the contract that linked God and His chosen people, the elect were involved in another contract with other saints both in the church and in the state. The commonwealth of Massachusetts was based on such a covenant. All were committed to a common plan. Everyone was expected to fulfill his part of the contract. Winthrop and the Assistants had freely chosen to surrender arbitrary power. They entered into a predictable and reasonable scheme of government. As Winthrop said, "It is the nature and essence of every society to be knit together by some covenant, either expressed or implied."[21] The Puritan vision of an ordered society was symmetrical. The image of the contract predominated at many levels. The covenant was a symbol of order, of defined relationships. The notion of a covenant was derived by Puritan theologians from common social usage; it carried the simple connotation of a "bargain, a contract, a mutual agreement, a document binding upon both signatories, drawn up in the presence of witnesses and sealed by a notary public."[22] Indeed, covenant theology reflects the tendency to read categories of social organization into spiritual relationships. The flow can also be in the opposite direction. Having read the idea of contract into theology, the Puritans proceeded to translate the theological category back into their own concepts of church and state.

The Puritan commonwealth was created by a covenant. It was assumed that men were bound together for common ends. To make sure that men fulfilled their obligations toward one another, that they did not succumb to the lure of personal gain and pleasure, it was the task of the community to make men accountable for their behavior. John Winthrop clearly spelled out these issues before the assembly in 1637. He concluded that a commonwealth involved the following principles:

---

[20] Perry Miller, *Errand into the Wilderness* (New York, 1956), p. 72.

[21] Morgan, *The Puritan Dilemma*, p. 93.

[22] Miller, *Errand into the Wilderness*, p. 60.

1. No common weale can be founded but by free consent.
2. The persons so incorporating have a public and relative interest each in other, and in the place of their cohabitation and goods, and laws, and in all the means of their welfare. . . .
3. The nature of such an incorporation tyes every member thereof to seeke out and entertaine all means that may conduce to the welfare of the bodye, and to keepe off whatsoever doth appeare to tend to their damage.
4. The welfare of the whole is not to be put to apparent hazard for the advantage of any particular members. [23]

To make sure that these principles were upheld was the responsibility of the town. The town was the major instrument of social and religious control. It was the duty of the town to preserve the delicate balance between the city of God and the city of Man. If the town faltered, so did the entire Puritan program.

The Town

The town was the center of religious life. The inhabitants of a town and the members of a congregation were initially almost identical. The town was both a religious and civil community. The entire weight of Puritan theology and social theory favored the concentration of the population in towns. To live apart from the community was to reject God's grace and to resist the righteous concern of one's neighbor. Isolation was damnation. The solitary individual or family would "degenerate to heathenish ignorance and barbarisme."[24] The town was also a focus of political organization, not only because towns were autonomous centers of local power but because they were the units represented in the assembly. Initially, the magistrates (Assistants) were elected at large by all the freemen of the colony at a session of the General Court (assembly). But the towns, adamant as they were in the defense of congregational independence, were disposed to support a system of locally based representation. Congregationalism abhorred the arbitrary power of religious hierarchy. The town, so closely identified with the congregation, was bent on protecting itself from the arbitrary tendencies of a political hierarchy. The result was that the towns insisted on sending their own locally elected representatives (deputies) to a permanent assembly.[25] The deputies had the authority to select both governor and magistrates. A majority of both deputies and magistrates was required to enact legislation or to approve new taxes. The

---

[23] Miller and Johnson, *The Puritans*, p. 200.
[24] Richard L. Bushmen, *From Puritan to Yankee* (Cambridge, Mass., 1967), p. 57.
[25] Morgan, *The Puritan Dilemma*, pp. 109–114.

covenant that knit together the godly commonwealth was a covenant of towns.

Each town was a commonwealth in microcosm. Its members were bound together by overlapping covenants. The town bore the major burden for preserving intact the Puritan vision of the good society. To this end the town enlisted the support of the entire community. Sin was communal in nature.[26] It corrupted the whole body and called down God's wrath upon the community. Upholding standards of godly behavior was, consequently, an activity that concerned the welfare of everyone. The whole group had promised obedience to God. It was the whole group, therefore, that would suffer the consequences of the unpunished sins of individual members. While the community could not see into the heart of every member, it could at least maintain external compliance with behavioral standards. By so doing, the good community could not only protect itself from God's wrath but would be blessed with temporal prosperity for fulfilling its part of the covenant.[27] Morever, by creating an atmosphere marked by sanctified behavior, the town helped to nurture the receptiveness of the individual soul to God's grace. This emphasis on external conformity could easily lead to an oppressive climate of mutual surveillance and suspicion. The concern of Puritan men and women for their neighbors was always in danger of shading into hypocrisy. It is difficult to describe typical Puritans. Were they loving neighbors or the morbid custodians of each other's behavior? There is evidence for both portraits. The reason for this is the nature of the town itself. Early New England towns were independent, relatively isolated social units. The peculiar kind of social atmosphere that existed in any town was likely to be generated by factors largely internal and specific. Some towns were undoubtedly imbued with a spirit of love and generosity. Others certainly bred a collective paranoia.

Nonetheless, towns shared certain principles. They emphasized collective goals and the responsibilities common to all inhabitants. The New England town, to a surprising degree, approximated the social and religious vision it was intended to resemble. It was a homogeneous social unit, a harmonious blend of church and civil society. The community actively restrained behavior inimical to the welfare of the whole. By eliminating alternatives to godliness, the saints in their towns preserved that delicate balance between the things of God and the affairs of this world. They upheld their part of the covenant. But as the Puritans themselves would admit, this balance required constant watchfulness. There came a day

---

[26] As reflected in Nathaniel Hawthorne's *The Scarlet Letter.*
[27] Morgan, *The Puritan Family,* pp. 9–11.

when the towns were less vigilant. The godly commonwealth faltered. The ordered, stable environment of early Massachusetts gave way progressively to social disorder and dissension. Satan had found his way to New England.

The Merchant

The tension between the two cities, between God and Mammon, did not exist solely on the level of society. It was a deep personal conflict as well. The potential evil within each person, the consequence of original sin, could be controlled only by the application of a continuous self-discipline. The preoccupation with method, order, and regulation, which characterized the Puritan approach to the world, carried over into the notion of vocation. The Puritan was expected to follow his calling, to apply himself to his work with diligence and discipline. A man faithful in his calling, living a well-ordered life, would—like the good society—prosper. Worldly success was to some extent a sign of God's favor.[28] Yet the very act of success, of fulfilling one's vocation, led men away from God and into the city of man. New England had to trade to survive. But trade tended to erect barriers between men, and caused "declension" in the Bible commonwealth. Farmers and merchants were often at odds.[29] What appeared to be a just price or a reasonable profit from the perspective of the merchant who bore the risk often seemed excessive from the view of the agriculturally based community.

The early Massachusetts economy was sustained by the Great Puritan Migration. From 1629 to 1642, some 20,000 Englishmen migrated to New England, the majority to Massachusetts.[30] The newcomers brought materials to the young colony. At the same time, the large number of new colonists provided an important market for the growing agricultural output of Massachusetts. Prices were not left to the law of supply and demand. They were controlled, initially by the assembly and later by the towns. The tendency toward runaway prices in a situation of scarcity was held in check. The English Civil War (1642–1648) brought a period of great migration to an end. Massachusetts found itself short of currency and such manufactured items as window glass, chimney backs, pots, kettles, gunpowder, saws, and axes, but with a surplus of agricultural products.[31] Under these circumstances, trade was essential. The earliest trading pattern

---

[28] Perry Miller, *Nature's Nation* (Cambridge, Mass., 1967), p. 27.
[29] Ibid., p. 28.
[30] Carl Bridenbaugh, *Vexed and Troubled Englishmen* (New York, 1968), p. 472.
[31] Morgan, *The Puritan Dilemma*, pp. 66–67.

was a simple exchange of New England fish for manufactured goods supplied by London merchants.[32] Gradually, a prosperous merchant community developed in the ports of New England, especially Boston. The rise of the New England merchant marked a transformation of the economy that affected every phase of New England life. The relatively self-sufficient agricultural community of the early seventeenth century found itself involved in a complex network of international trade. New England supplied the slave colonies of the West Indies with food and lumber. Credit built up in the West Indies trade was used to support the importation of English goods. The town could not control the complex exchanges that occurred thousands of miles beyond its borders. Prices and profits were set not by the standards of the community but by the erratic fluctuations of an impersonal market. In an economy short of currency, intricate webs of credit and debt developed, binding together local traders and farmers. The small shopkeeper was often attached to a larger network of merchants in Boston. Such ties operated beyond the boundaries of godly control. The growth of relationships that were predominantly economic in character was, from the perspective of the harmonious community, a perversion of personal bonds. When neighbors defined each other as primarily "debtors" and "creditors" rather than as "brothers in Christ," surely the balance between the two cities was disrupted.

Puritan divines rose up against the growing worldliness of the community. They preached harsh, fiery sermons called, appropriately, "jeremiads" against covetousness and dissension. The Puritan synod of 1679 explicitly condemned frauds and deceits invented by shrewd people in their business affairs. "What a shame it is," thought Cotton Mather, "that ever that odious sin of Usury should be pleaded for, or practiced in New England."[33] In his election-day sermon to the Massachusetts assembly (1663), John Higginson reminded the deputies and magistrates that "the Lord stirred up the founders to come to this land not for worldly wealth or a better livelihood for the outward man." New England had been established "as a Plantation of Religion not a Plantation of Trades. Let merchants and such as are increasing cent per cent remember this. If any among us make religion as twelve and the world as thirteen, let such an one know he hath neither the spirit of a true New England man, nor yet of a sincere Christian."[34]

---

[32] Bernard Bailyn, *The New England Merchants in the Seventeenth Century* (New York, 1964), pp. 75–82.

[33] Miller, *Nature's Nation*, p. 31.

[34] Ibid., p. 33.

The culprit in all of this was the merchant. He was seen by the Puritan establishment as the agent of avarice. He had brought the apple into the Puritan paradise. "Suppose a poor man," lamented the minister Chauncy in 1655, "wants a pair of shoes, or other clothes to cover his nakedness, that hath no silver: truely he must be fain almost to sell himself, to get some mean commodities."[35] Who was responsible for this state of affairs? The synod of 1679 indicted the Yankee trader. The hostility of the countryside was the result of experience. Rural districts made their purchases with commodities, or "country pay." Merchants, however, sold their wares for higher prices figured in country pay than the goods were worth in sterling, yet collected their debts at the sterling rate. The class antagonism and regional hostility deplored in the jeremiads "were not figments of an over heated imagination. They were bitter realities, becoming more bitter with the years, and they were tearing the holy and united common commonwealth apart."[36]

The life style of the merchant reflected his participation in a less provincial, more open structure of attachments. His commercial contacts bound him to relatives and factors in London and the West Indies. The merchant stood facing the Atlantic and a world market. The yeoman farmer, encased within his town, faced the frontier and the isolation of a continent. The mutual alienation of merchant and farmer, generated by social and economic polarity, was evident by the 1670s. The merchant, involved as he was in a heterogeneous network that could include London Anglicans and French Catholics in the Caribbean, was more willing to tolerate diversity. He was less attracted to the strict orthodoxy of the Puritan establishment and its narrow adherence to the rather limited categories of "saved" and "damned." The establishment, for its part, was horrified to discover that merchants "would willingly have had the Commonwealth tolerate diverse kinds of sinful opinions . . . that their purses might be filled with coyne."[37]

The seventeenth century beheld a growing disenchantment between the new wealth of a rising merchant class centered in Boston, and the old order upheld by the towns. Merchants were elected to represent Boston in the assembly. But they were unable to command sufficient influence to provide for the selection of one of their numbers as a magistrate. The inland towns remained the bastion of the old order. The merchants felt they were the most important economic group in the colony. Yet they were

---

[35] Ibid., p. 31.
[36] Ibid., pp. 46–47.
[37] Ibid., p. 47.

denied a degree of political leadership and social prestige commensurate with their economic power. Dissatisfaction mounted. The royal offensive against the commonwealth (1675–1688) found the merchant community deeply divided in its loyalties. Only belatedly did the merchants of Boston come to view the abuse of royal power as potentially more threatening to their interests than the overweaning godliness of the commonwealth.

In addition to the interests of merchants and their network of trade and credit, another problem was threatening the homogeneity of New England and its towns—the declining incidence of sainthood. The Halfway Covenant was a response to this vexing issue. Essentially, it helped preserve some sense of religious unity. Those who "believed" even though they had not undergone the experience of "conversion" were accepted into a definite religious structure. If the town was to continue to function as a mechanism of social control, then it was imperative to extend that control to successive generations. The requirements for church membership were made less stringent so that the boundaries of church discipline could be extended to include most of the town.[38] The church had chosen to compromise its purity for the sake of sustaining the religious solidarity of the town. But it was a losing proposition. It became progressively more difficult to integrate a community, divided socially and economically, into the same religious structure. The town was envisioned as a single organic unit. As its control fragmented in one sphere, the consequences would become visible in another. The town stood together or fell as a bundle of interlocking social relationships. This can be seen in the case of land.

Land

Originally, land was owned communally.[39] This was especially true in Connecticut. Newcomers and the children of older settlers received grants of land from the common fields. Plots were located close to the town. This reinforced a concentrated pattern of settlement. People could easily walk to their land from the town square. The town directly regulated the most important resource in an agricultural community. It controlled the land. This pattern buttressed the authority of the town. But as population grew and land use intensified, the town was forced to cut the same pie into ever smaller pieces. One solution was to distribute lands farther away from the town. While this preserved the town's control over land, it upset the close-knit communal settlement pattern. To reduce the time needed to

---

[38] Bushmen, *From Puritan to Yankee*, p. 148.

[39] This section is based on the analysis of Bushmen, especially Chaps. 3, 4, and 5.

walk to their fields, inhabitants moved to the periphery of the town. The original town soon found itself surrounded by several satellite villages. Disputes between the town and its periphery soon developed over taxation, the establishment of new parishes, and the construction of roads and meeting houses. Some inhabitants whose land was located at a considerable distance from the town abandoned the town altogether. They became "outlivers." The long-term solution, however, was to break up the corporate land structure and adopt a system of individual ownership. This process was accelerated by the Crown's attack on corporate grants. By 1690, newly settled towns accepted the private ownership of undivided lands as a legal necessity. The corporate control of the town over land had ended.

The consequence was a marked weakening of the town as a unified structure. Previously a community resource, land now became a commodity in the cash nexus. A powerful economic weapon that could be turned against those who defied the community was laid aside. The division between original inhabitants and newcomers became more pronounced. The original town proprietors controlled most of the valuable land near the center of town. Newcomers were left to fend for themselves on the periphery. The decline of the town as a corporate landowner also reduced its role in the settlement of the frontier. Land speculation increased. Landowners encouraged settlement to help increase land values. Expansion became the prerogative of private enterprise, diminishing the control over growth exerted by the corporate town. As Increase Mather lamented,

> Land! Land! hath been the idol of many in New England. Whereas the first planters were satisfied with an acre a person and twenty for a family how have men since coveted after the earth, that many hundreds, nay thousands of Acres, have been engrossed by one man, and they that profess themselves Christians, have forsaken Churches and Ordinances . . . and all for land. [40]

The place of land in the scheme of town life was transformed. Initially, it was the bastion of communal solidarity. Everyone shared common resources. Now the ownership of land became a cause of envy, a stumbling block in the path of the community. The emphasis on mediation and shared responsibility, the sense of trust that had bound together the leadership of the town and the general polity, gave way. By the 1670s, the communal spirit had slackened. By the 1690s, it had disappeared.[41] Tumultuous

---

[40] Miller, *Nature's Nation*, p. 39.

[41] Kenneth A. Lockridge and Alan Kreider, "The Evolution of Massachusetts Town Government," in *Colonial America*, ed. Stanley N. Katz (Boston, 1971), p. 221. The article was originally published in *William and Mary Quarterly* 23 (1966): 549–574.

town meetings, disputed elections, "bickering, petitioning and ill will" became characteristic of the New England town.[42] It seemed as if the "city upon a hill" had turned into the tower of Babel. The Puritan vision of a harmonious, organic social order serving the common welfare was clouded by the conflicting interests of a changing economic order. The growing economic diversity of New England led to increased social tension and political conflict. The Godly commonwealth gave way to progress.

New England Puritanism, as a social philosophy, was based on medieval models of order and harmony. The Puritan experiment foresaw an enduring, relatively stable social order. The Puritan did not rush out to embrace the gods of change. But it was precisely for this reason that the image of Puritan New England, built in the eye of a hurricane, is so appropriate. For the gods of change whirled inexorably around its borders. All New England was soon enchanted by commerce and land, by the promise of wealth, social mobility, and success. Agriculture and trade flourished. The more the Puritans devoted themselves to their callings, the more they prospered. The contradiction was that the more the labor of the Puritan was rewarded, the greater became the dispersion of society and the more serious its class divisions. From the vantage point of the Puritan clergy, New England was in a state of crisis.

> The more the people worked in the right spirit, the more they transformed the society into something they never intended; the more diligently they labored on the frontier, in the field, in the countinghouse, or on the banks of Newfoundland, the more surely they produced what according to the standards of the founders was a decay of religion and a corruption of morals. [43]

THE DIVERSITY OF ENGLISH COLONIZATION

Until the Navigation Acts (1660–1696) began to establish a framework for English colonial policy, royal government had a minimal impact on the formation of colonial society. The Crown did not provide a framework for institutional development. Besieged at home by internal dissension and then civil war, the Crown was not in a position to impose its will in America. The kind of men and women who participated in colonization, and the models of social organization they brought with them, determined the shape of colonial society. The policies of the Crown during these initial years had less an impact. The fact that Puritan New England was the

---

[42] Lockridge and Kreider, "Massachusetts Town Government," p. 222.
[43] Miller, *Nature's Nation*, p. 48.

project of a religious community is extremely important. The Puritans brought to America their own methods of regulating social life. This was less true of Virginia, where settlement was not controlled by any unit as cohesive as the New England town. In Virginia, the agent of colonization was the company. But the company proved incapable of controlling economic self-interest on behalf of the community. In Puritan New England, however, a concerted effort was made to regulate economic activity in a system that was radically traditional. Greater contrast in this respect existed between New England and its trading partners—the English settlements of the Caribbean.

The West Indies were settled in the spirit of the buccaneer. The men who came to Barbados and Jamaica did not come to save their souls or to raise a family. They came to exploit any available resource. In many cases, initial settlement was the by-product of raiding expeditions against Spanish towns. The spirit of the "rip off" pervaded the growth of West Indian society. The indentured servant who found his way to the tobacco plantations of Barbados in the 1630s and 1640s encountered the harshest labor system in English America.[44] During the 1650s, Barbados turned decisively to sugar production and slave labor. Slavery in the West Indies was the most oppressive in the Americas. In contrast, New England employed considerably fewer white servants than either Virginia or the West Indies. Indentured servitude was more closely supervised by the community. Moreover, slavery never became a major institution in New England, but not because the Puritan was more tolerant than other Englishmen. Slavery was out of harmony with the entire thrust of Puritan society—a society that stressed religious and social homogeneity and a disciplined application to the demands of one's calling. It was not slavery that made the West Indies different from Puritan New England. The two societies were different from the beginning.[45]

English America was a number of diverse enterprises. It included the traditions of religious radicalism, the buccaneer, and the commercial company. Puritan Massachusetts established a unified, homogeneous social order. But a rapid and far-reaching transformation in the economy undermined the established order. Virginia, opened to competing interests in the seventeenth century, formed an economic and social order dominated by the ethos of a stable planter class. In the West Indies, the most rigid pattern of social stratification evolved. The small tobacco planter was

[44] Abbot E. Smith, *Colonists In Bondage* (Chapel Hill, 1947), p. 29.
[45] Richard S. Dunn, *Sugar and Slaves* (Chapel Hill, 1972), pp. 337–341. See the remarks of David Bertelson, *The Lazy South* (New York, 1967), p. 104.

totally eliminated by the great sugar plantation. The West Indies became a major producer of sugar. It mercilessly devoured the lives of black slaves. In the 1660s and 1670s, the English Crown faced the task of integrating these unique local ventures into a common political and economic framework.

VII

The Framework of Empire: The Seventeenth Century

THE ENGLISH CIVIL WAR AND THE RESTORATION

The seventeenth century witnessed a decisive constitutional struggle between Parliament and the Crown. This confrontation took place during a period of growing polarization. Puritan dissenters and a new class of merchants threatened the established religious and social hierarchy. These divisions were evident in the House of Commons, where merchants, tradesmen, and Puritans gained a strong foothold.

The repression of Puritans reached its height under Charles I (1625–1649). The foreign policy of the Crown, favoring as it did, peace with England's commercial rivals, was opposed by merchants. The House of Commons stubbornly defended the "liberties" of Parliament, and an equally resolute monarch seemed bent on expanding royal authority.[1] At issue was the control of the state. Parliament and the Crown were at odds over questions that subsequently divided colonial assemblies and their

---

[1] Christopher Hill, *The Century of Revolution: 1603–1714* (New York, 1961), pp. 44–46.

royal governors. They fought over the levying of new taxes, the control of expenditures, the judiciary, the regulation of military forces, and the accountability of ministers. The struggle became so bitter that Charles I dismissed Parliament for 11 years. It was not until 1640, under great duress, that Charles reconvened Parliament.

The new Parliament immediately impeached ministers of the king, passed an act to prevent the king from dissolving Parliament without its consent, and nullified all nonparliamentary taxes established during the 11 years of personal royal rule. Parliament intended to control the state. The split between Parliament and the king derived from a more general alienation of court and country. The cleavages could not be breached. The result was a civil war (1642–1648) that ended in regicide. The support for Parliament (Roundheads) came from the economically advanced areas of the south and east of England, while the strongholds of traditional agriculture in the north and west backed the king (Cavaliers).[2]

The civil war was not a class conflict. It did tend to pull together the commercially oriented sectors of the society that benefited from foreign trade, the extension of commercial agriculture, and the enclosure laws. But this commercial sector included a combination of the nobility, gentry, tradesmen, and yeomanry. The civil war was geographically based and reflected the religious and economic patterns of different regions rather than the class divisions within regions.[3]

The triumph of the Roundheads in the civil war strengthened the position of commercial interests in the state. Under the new Commonwealth government, England fought a series of commercial wars with the Dutch, passed the first Navigation Act, and upheld the enclosure of common land, thus preserving the gains of commercial agriculture.[4] In Spain, merchants never wielded such influence. Still, merchants and commercial landowners did not feel secure under the Commonwealth. Radical "levelers" began to attack the privileges of the wealthy. The levelers were suppressed, but divisions within the ruling class, deepened by the civil war, left them vulnerable to attacks from below. Under these circumstances, the new commercial order preferred an accommodation with the old regime. The king was restored to the English throne to maintain social stability, property, and discipline, virtues now esteemed by the beneficiaries of the civil war.

The Restoration was a kind of insurance to protect the commercial and

---

[2] Ibid., pp. 121–122.
[3] Barrington Moore, The Social Origins of Democracy and Dictatorship (Boston, 1966), pp. 14–18.
[4] Hill, Century of Revolution, pp. 145–154, 155–159.

propertied classes against the kind of enthusiasm that led to leveling.[5] They made sure their gains remained. All legal decisions made during the Interregnum were confirmed by the king, subject to appeal. Enclosures were upheld, as well as changes in land tenure. The sale of nearly all Crown land made the monarchy financially dependent upon Parliament Perhaps the most enduring legacy was the enhanced position of Parliament. It was now an integral part of the English constitution, no longer dependent on the pleasure of the king. The Triennial Act demanded Parliaments every three years. Parliament retained the right to initiate all money bills and to regulate the spending of funds. In addition, Parliament wrested control of the judiciary from the Crown. The king no longer appointed judges to preside over special executive courts independent of Parliament. The influence of the king's Privy Council was reduced, and the growth of ministerial responsibility continued.

Parliament was the seat of a new social order that no longer pretended to be organic. It represented interests that could not decisively defeat one another. The long-run trend in England was toward the organization of conflicting interests into relatively stable parties that competed for power in Parliament. The representatives of the new economic order (Whigs) and the supporters of a more traditional order of royal power and religious hierarchy (Tories) continued to struggle for political supremacy. But that struggle would be confined for the most part to the boundaries set by established political institutions.[6] The lesson of the civil war was that violent confrontations between the interests that constituted a fairly broad ruling class invited challenges from below. Political power alternated between Whig and Tory, establishing by the eighteenth century what has been called "political stability." The interests represented by levelers, diggers, independents, and fifth-monarchy men, suppressed during the Interregnum, would not seriously challenge the Whig–Tory dominance until the nineteenth century.

It was under these general circumstances that the restored Stuart monarchy under Charles II (1660–1685) reassumed substantial executive power. The king and the Tory party ran the government and distributed patronage. Parliament had strengthened its position during the Interregnum, but a skillful king with adept ministers and support in the Commons could seize the initiative. It was the task of the Whigs to control their opponents as best they could. Charles II was able to make considerable

[5] Ibid., pp. 141–144.
[6] John H. Plumb, *The Origins of Political Stability: England 1675–1725* (Boston, 1967), pp. 159–189.

progress in restoring the vigor of the Crown's executive power, for those who opposed Stuart absolutism were reluctant to rekindle the passions of civil war.

Events in England had their impact on colonial affairs. Three decades of domestic discord (1630–1660) had not been conducive to the formation of a unified royal policy in America. In 1660, with the exception of Virginia and Barbados, there was little royal government in America at all. As regards royal authority, the tie between England and her colonies was provided by charters and not by the presence of bureaucratic officials appointed by the Crown. Only Virginia and Barbados were royal colonies. But even there, the governors appointed by the Crown were left to struggle with local assemblies without much support from the mother country. Royal government faced the stubborn diversity of English America. Not having been a direct partner to the process of colonization and settlement, a royal government with imperial ambitions had to contend with strong centers of local power, organized in assemblies, and resentful of any extension of external political authority. This was the situation faced by the government of Charles II when he and his ministers undertook the restructuring of the political relationships between the Crown and its colonies. Although progressing by fits and starts, Charles initiated a political and economic offensive in America that continued for several decades. The waxing and waning of royal initiative in the colonies was a persistent feature of colonial political life. The American Revolution was the ultimate colonial response to the aggressive extension of British authority in America, but the situation faced by the continental colonies after 1760 was not, in a general sense, without precedence. It was part of a recurrent pattern of imperial centralization and colonial resistance that was established under Charles II a century before.

THE COMMERCIAL FRAMEWORK OF EMPIRE

The first initiative in colonial policy during the Restoration era came not from the ministers and councils of Charles II but from Parliament. The Navigation Acts of 1660, 1663, and 1673 established a definite policy. The act of 1660 provided that all trade with English colonies had to be carried on English ships, with English masters, manned by a predominantly English crew. Trade was not closed to colonial merchants, since all vessels owned and manned by inhabitants of England, Wales, Ireland, and the plantations were placed on equal footing. A vessel from Boston manned by colonial seamen was placed in the same category as a vessel from London with an English master and crew. The point of the act was to exclude England's commercial rivals, especially the Dutch and French, from either carrying foreign products to the colonies or carrying colonial products to Europe.[7] Direct trade between the American plantations and Ireland was restricted after 1663, while Scotland was admitted as a full partner in colonial trade by the terms of the Act of Union (1707).

Had the restraints placed on trade by the Navigation Act of 1660 stopped here, colonial and English merchants would have been free to carry such goods as sugar and tobacco to European markets and to load, in turn, foreign manufactured goods for direct transport and sale in the plantations. But the act of 1660 went on to prohibit the bulk of this trade. It enumerated certain essential commodities like dyewoods used in the woolen industry and important colonial products such as sugar, tobacco, cotton, indigo, and ginger. Based on the philosophy that the colonies were the natural source of specific raw materials that could not be produced in sufficient quantity at home, and that such goods should be monopolized by the mother country, the act stipulated that all enumerated commodities must be shipped to English ports.[8] England was to be the staple for basic colonial products. Enumerated goods destined for European markets had to be reexported from England. The Navigation Act of 1663 extended England's monopoly from the control of basic colonial exports to the regulation of colonial imports. It provided that all commodities of the growth, production, and manufacture of Europe, destined for the plantations, must first be carried to England. England was to be the entrepôt for the bulk of colonial exports, and for all colonial imports of European origin. These acts formed the essential framework of English commercial policy down to the eve of the American Revolution. Spanish commercial organization, in comparison, was not primarily intended to control or stimulate colonial export agriculture. The *flota* system was designed to protect silver shipments to Spain.

The commercial policy designed by Parliament was vigorously and successfully imposed, first in England and then in the colonies, by the executive power of the Crown. For Parliament and the Crown largely agreed on economic policy in the colonies, where commercial dominance and state power were considered to be mutually reinforcing.

The Navigation Acts accompanied a series of commercial wars between

---

[7] Charles M. Andrews, *The Colonial Period of American History*, 4 vols. (New Haven, 1934–1938), vol. 4, *England's Commercial and Colonial Policy*, pp. 61–63.

[8] Ibid., p. 85. Generally, see pp. 85–107.

England and her principal rival, the Netherlands. The Dutch Wars—1652–1654, 1664–1667, 1672–1674—were generally inconclusive, although the English probably captured more Dutch ships.[9] The Far Eastern spice trade remained in the hands of the Dutch. However, the Dutch bid to cut permanently into the colonial carrying trade with English plantations was thwarted. In 1664, England seized the Dutch colony of New Amsterdam, thereby depriving the Netherlands of a major commercial base in the heart of English North America. The Navigation Acts were not paper tigers. England was in a position to enforce her commercial policies.

The acts were not as difficult to implement as might be supposed. It was not a matter of reorganizing the basic nature of colonial trade. The majority of manufactured goods imported into the colonies already came from England.[10] The bulk of Virginia tobacco was carried to England on English ships before 1660. The essential features of New England's commerce were not in violation of the acts, and important exceptions were permitted that favored her maritime activities. New England was allowed to import salt for its fisheries directly from Europe.[11] Most of the salt came from England's commercial ally, Portugal. Wine from Madeira and the Azores—Portuguese possessions—could also be directly imported.[12] Fish, hides, grain, and lumber—commodities possessed by England in sufficient quantity—were not enumerated. These products were the staples of the Northern colonies. New England merchants were free to carry fish and timber to the markets of Southern Europe.[13] The plantations were free to trade with each other even in enumerated commodities. The most important intercolonial trade was between the Northern continental colonies and the English West Indies. Fish, lumber, wheat, bread, flour, and other provisions were exchanged for sugar, molasses, and rum. In addition, colonial merchants could trade with foreign plantations, provided they did not supply them with enumerated commodities nor return with European manufactured goods. The eighteenth-century trade between the Northern colonies and the French West Indies was legal, although it was viewed by English authorities, especially during periods of war, as a disloyal act that

[9] Ralph Davis, *The Rise of the British Shipping Industry in the Seventeenth Century* (New York, 1964), p. 127.

[10] Bernard Bailyn, *The New England Merchants in the Seventeenth Century* (New York, 1964), p. 127.

[11] Andrews, *England's Commercial and Colonial Policy*, p. 109.

[12] Ibid., p. 111.

[13] Curtis P. Nettels, "England's Trade with New England and New York, 1685–1720" *Publications of the Colonial Society of Massachusetts* 28 (1930–1933): 331. See also Andrews, *England's Commercial and Colonial Policy*, p. 88.

benefited the enemy. Colonists also discovered that they could legally carry the trade of foreign plantations to Europe and in time carried considerable quantities of French sugar to Holland.[14]

The Navigation Acts did not ruin colonial trade. They did not destroy the most lucrative and established trading patterns that existed in 1660. They did, however, place critical constraints on the future course of colonial trade and they helped eliminate a promising trade with the Dutch. Overall, the colonies had to pay a higher price for their manufactured goods. During the seventeenth century, many commodities could have been obtained from the Dutch for a third less.[15] Dutch traders had made considerable inroads into the Virginia tobacco trade during the period of the civil war. Still, the basic commercial tie was with England. It was the English merchant who supplied Virginia with perhaps its most crucial necessity— a steady stream of indentured servants in return for tobacco. The Dutch trade was supplementary. It helped ease the drop in tobacco prices by reducing the glut on the London market.[16] It was for this reason that Governor Berkeley and the Virginia planters opposed in vain the enumeration of tobacco. They feared that the London market would be oversupplied and prices would plummet. This is precisely what occurred.

Tobacco was dumped on the English market faster than it could be consumed or reexported.[17] While enumeration was not solely responsible for this glut, it prevented the Virginia planter from selling his tobacco directly to the Dutch and thereby easing the problem of oversupply. In the long run, British merchants developed new markets for Virginia tobacco in Holland and France. But this did not alleviate the immediate problems faced by the small planter. During the civil war, tobacco prices had been at least 3 pence per pound but by 1667 the price had dropped to a half-penny.[18] The small planter who could produce about 1200 pounds of tobacco yearly was faced with a constantly shrinking income out of which he still had to pay local taxes and purchase necessities.[19] Low prices could

[14] Andrews, *England's Commercial and Colonial Policy*, p. 82.

[15] Lawrence A. Harper, *The English Navigation Acts* (1939: New York, 1964), p. 243.

[16] Wesley Frank Craven, *The Southern Colonies in the Seventeenth Century* (Baton Rouge, 1949), pp. 239–242.

[17] The Crown discouraged domestic production because the import duty on tobacco provided an important source of revenue. The duty increased during the Restoration from 2 pence on each pound of tobacco in 1667 to 5 pence in 1685. Tobacco prices remained high in England, preventing an expansion of the home market.

[18] Andrews, *England's Commercial and Colonial Policy*, p. 211.

[19] David S. Lovejoy, *The Glorious Revolution in America* (New York, 1972), pp. 33–35.

only be offset by increasing production.[20] The cost of enumeration fell on the small planter, since his productive capacity was limited. The Navigation Acts helped set the stage for Bacon's Rebellion in the 1670s.

ENFORCEMENT OF THE NAVIGATION ACTS

The Navigation Act of 1660 specified that enumerated goods could be carried only to England or an English plantation. The act was enforced by a cumbersome system of bonding. Ships sailing from England to the colonies had to post bond with the customs officials in England. If they were to load enumerated goods, such as tobacco and sugar, in colonial ports, they had to prove that such goods were carried to a legal destination, that is, to England or another plantation. Customs certificates demonstrated that proper bonds had been given. Other certificates showed that the good had been landed legally. The ship's master, returning to England, could then prove his compliance with the law, and his bond was discharged.[21] The system was reasonably well-administered on the English side of the Atlantic; colonial administration proved to be unsatisfactory. Responsibility for enforcement fell upon the governor, or in the case of proprietary colonies, such as Maryland, upon the Lord Proprietor. Customs officials were established only in those colonies where enumerated goods were produced, namely, the Chesapeake colonies and the sugar plantations of the West Indies.[22] The problem was that the act did not control intercolonial trade. Vessels from Boston that loaded tobacco in Virginia could not bring evidence of bonding, since Boston had no customs service.

For the most part, only ships bonded in England were controlled by the act. Having posted bond, it was in their own self-interest to demonstrate compliance with the law. It appears that unbonded vessels were regularly allowed to clear colonial ports carrying enumerated goods.[23] The result was that enumerated commodities still found their way to Europe. The biggest offenders were probably English merchants. They escaped bonding by stating a destination other than the colonies.[24] After leaving England, they changed course and proceeded to the plantations where they loaded enumerated goods. They then carried their cargoes to illegal

---

[20] Curtis P. Nettels, "British Mercantilism and the Economic Development of the Thirteen Colonies," *Journal of Economic History* 12 (Spring, 1952): 110.

[21] Harper, *English Navigation Acts*, pp. 161–162.

[22] Lovejoy, *Glorious Revolution*, p. 14.

[23] Andrews, *England's Commercial and Colonial Policy*, p. 118.

[24] Ibid.

destinations. New England merchants also evaded the law. They picked up tobacco, especially in the Abermarle Sound region of North Carolina, and returned to Boston. There they made up composite cargoes composed of fish, lumber, and tobacco, and set sail for France, Holland, or Spain. The trade in enumerated goods between New England and other areas of the British Isles, specifically, Ireland, Scotland, and the Channel Islands, was also illegal. Reports came to the Plantation Board in England alleging wholesale violations of the acts by New Englanders. These reports were certainly exaggerated. But Parliament, in the midst of a maritime struggle for commercial supremacy with the Dutch, was not about to see the Navigation Acts undone from within.

The Plantation Duty Act of 1673 outlined a new customs system to tighten up enforcement of the Navigation Acts. It addressed the problem of unbonded vessels loading enumerated commodities. Any vessel that could not produce a certificate demonstrating that bond had been posted in England had to deposit a bond in the colonial port of clearance stating that the enumerated goods in question were to be taken either directly to another colonial port or directly to England. In addition, vessels not bonded in England had to pay a duty on the enumerated goods they loaded. This "plantation duty" was a penny per pound on tobacco.[25] It tended to undercut the profitability of the illegal trade in tobacco, since there was a rebate on tobacco reexported from England of all but a half-penny per pound of the original duty. Even if the colonial merchant brought his tobacco to an illegal destination, such as Ireland, he would find himself undersold by reexported tobacco from England.[26] For the most part, colonial merchants confined their activities to intercolonial trade, either with other English colonies or with foreign plantations in the West Indies. English merchants generally monopolized the carrying of enumerated commodities to England. Their superior credit and market operations gave them a considerable advantage over colonial merchants. While the plantation duty did raise a small revenue, its object was certainly regulation and not taxation. In order to receive and retain bonds and to collect the new duty, it was necessary to install a large number of customs officials in the colonies. In royal and proprietary colonies, many of these officials were appointed by the governor. The new customs system was also extended to the Northern colonies.

If the Virginia planter had come to appreciate the meaning of empire in the 1660s, New England merchants developed a similar consciousness

---

[25] Ibid., pp. 119–120.
[26] Ibid., pp. 120–121.

in the 1670s and 1680s. A horde of petty bureaucrats descended upon New England in search of lucrative new positions in the colonial customs service. Characteristic of this new group was Edmund Randolph, a notorious critic of the Godly commonwealth, who secured for himself the position of collector of customs for New England in 1679. During the first 9 months, Randolph attempted some 17 seizures of goods and vessels that he maintained were in violation of the Acts. He brought 10 of these to trial before local courts. He lost all the cases. His actions were not simply the efforts of a disinterested public servant. Randolph stood to gain a percentage of the goods confiscated if the merchants were convicted. Some of the seizures were certainly justified. But Randolph was also guilty of flagrant customs racketeering, for in a period when the colonial bureaucracy was in its infancy, "perquisites, fees, bribes and gifts—not salaries—were the main financial rewards for public service."[27]

Customs officials were convinced that colonial merchants violated the Navigation Acts, and merchants and planters were just as sure that customs officers were guilty of fraudulent practices. The colonial response to the Acts was generally hostile, a situation further complicated by genuine confusion over the exact interpretation of certain provisions. Culpeper's Rebellion in the Albermarle region of North Carolina (1677) spoke for disgruntled planters who feared that collection of the new plantation duty on tobacco would lead the New England merchants, who monopolized their trade, to raise prices for imported goods.[28] A heated dispute developed in Maryland over the applicability of the plantation duty to the tobacco trade with Ireland. Baltimore came close to losing his charter and an unpopular customs officer lost his life. The Lords of Trade in England were beseiged by petitions from the colonies requesting specific exemptions. They were almost always denied. In New England, there was a general spirit of noncooperation.

While New England merchants were becoming aware of the price of membership in the empire, they did not feel that the liabilities outweighed the benefits.[29] Denied the political dominance in New England that they felt was warranted by their economic position, they were generally supportive of stronger imperial ties. Massachusetts was still controlled by towns loyal to the vision of a Puritan commonwealth, a vision that relegated the lapsed or dissenting merchant to an inferior role in political decisions. Many merchants saw the advent of royal officials as providing

---

[27] Bailyn, *New England Merchants*, pp. 163–165.

[28] Lovejoy, *Glorious Revolution*, p. 12; Bailyn, *New England Merchants*, p. 151.

[29] Bailyn, *New England Merchants*, p. 159.

allies in their quest for greater political power.[30] Still, the sympathies of the merchant community were divided. Colonial trade and agriculture were being forced into a preconceived pattern of exchange, a pattern whose parameters were not set by the representatives of colonial interests. Fundamental decisions about trade and production, decisions that could mean ruin or prosperity for important economic interests in the colonies, were to be made in London, far removed from the direct control of merchants and planters.

True, the Navigation Acts were not ruinous. But what was to prevent the imposition of restrictions genuinely deleterious to trade? The thrust of imperial reorganization was such that the priorities of individual colonies stood to be reordered in terms of the overall priorities of English diplomatic and commercial policy. The economic position of the colonies was precarious. Readjustments in the commercial framework established by the Navigation Acts occurred frequently enough to drive this point home every generation. The colonist in both North America and the West Indies displayed considerable opposition to the gradual tightening of the imperial commercial system during the Restoration. The English response was not compromise but, rather, greater insistence that the colonies adjust to the dictates of imperial policy. They did. The vast majority of colonial commerce and agricultural production was carried on in concert with the Navigation Acts. But the tension caused by the imposition of the Acts during the Restoration fed into the political confrontations that occurred in several colonies in the aftermath of the Glorious Revolution (1688–1689).

Commercial policy was the heart of England's empire in America. Even immigration was based on mercantile theory. The Crown was willing to admit dissenters and foreigners because a growing population contributed to colonial production and increased the demand for English products.[31] Growing sea power and commercial strength put her in a position to protect the integrity of an international trading system. She was intent upon defending this system not only from potential European rivals but also from the disruptive impact of competing colonial interests. Economic orthodoxy as outlined in the Navigation Acts was elevated to the position of an official state ideology—to be obeyed, not questioned.[32] Heresy, in terms of colonial policy, was an economic and not a religious affair. The dominant role assigned to commercial organization in English America stands

---

[30] Ibid., p. 160.
[31] Nettels, "British Mercantilism," pp. 107–108.
[32] Lovejoy, *Glorious Revolution*, p. 20, and generally, pp. 1–20.

in vivid contrast to the concerns of Spanish royal government in the Indies.

COLONIAL ADMINISTRATION

The role of the Crown in Hispanic America was clear. The Hapsburg bureaucracy provided a relatively stable political context that was able to contain and balance the economic interests of miners, merchants, landowners, and royal officials. Administrative reorganization in seventeenth-century English America, coupled with the establishment of the navigation system, helped to create a situation of economic and political instability. Had the revolution occurred in the midst of such a rapidly shifting social environment, it would have generated a violent internal struggle for political power. In the eighteenth century, as the colonial economies adjusted to the navigation system, a more stable political culture began to emerge, while in Spanish America, the Bourbon reform program disrupted established economic and political patterns.

In English America, the restored Stuart monarchy, using the executive power of the Crown, initiated a strong attack against the political diversity and relative autonomy of the colonial governments. The goal was to establish a more uniform and centralized system of royal administration. Political institutions designed and controlled by the executive power of the king, rather than local institutions subject to the traditions of particular colonies, were to form the new focus for colonial political life. But when the Crown finally acted (1675), it faced the opposition of assemblies, towns and county courts, local institutions that had gained the legitimacy of tradition. By contrast, in Spanish America, the Crown had acted immediately to uphold its authority.

For in only a few instances had the English Crown exercised direct authority in its plantations. Virginia became a royal colony in 1624 after the company's charter was terminated. But if that act had indicated the beginning of a royal initiative in the colonial sphere, the initiative was short-lived. Barbados and Jamaica were added to the list of royal colonies, but not as the result of any overall design of royal government. Both were placed under direct Crown administration by acts of Parliament—Barbados in 1652 and Jamaica in 1661.

In the 1670s, the Crown began a concerted effort to bolster its authority in America. In those colonies where the Crown already exercised direct authority through its governors, it sought to curtail the powers of local institutions, especially the assemblies, and to increase its own jurisdiction over internal affairs. The governor of Jamaica was instructed to extend Poyning's Law to the colony in 1678. Under its terms, the assembly would have been limited to a passive role in legislative matters. The assembly was allowed to consider only those laws drafted by the king and based on the suggestions of the royal governor and his council. The approval of such a measure would have constituted a virtual revolution in procedure, since it was the custom of assemblies to initiate laws and levy taxes. The adamant resistance of Jamaicans and the shaky legal foundations for the demand persuaded the Crown to drop the issue.[33] In Virginia, the powers of the assembly also came under attack.

Bacon's Rebellion (1676)

Politically, Virginia was dominated by a class of wealthy planters who controlled county government and whose lines of authority extended to the assembly and the governor's council. Sir William Berkeley governed Virginia in alliance with a favored group of planters. He used his powers of patronage to appoint his supporters to important county posts. The immediate cause of rebellion stemmed from Berkeley's ineffective Indian policy. Frontier settlements were being menaced by the strongest Indian attack in several decades. Berkeley's response was viewed as inadequate. Nathaniel Bacon led a frontier war against the Indians that the governor maintained was unauthorized. What began as a frontier conflict rapidly became an attack on the privileged oligarchy that dominated the colony.[34] The rebellion mobilized two distinct groups. It was led by substantial planters who were opposed to the privileges and policies of the Berkeley clique. Their dissatisfaction was based to a considerable degree on their exclusion from privilege. Ordinary settlers whose economic base was being undermined by the fall in tobacco prices were also active. Their discontent was directed not only at Berkeley but at the rising social influence of the very planters who challenged Berkeley's "Green Spring" faction.[35] The rebellion, although the most destructive insurrection before the Revolution, was short-lived. Bacon died from exhaustion and exposure after driving Berkeley from Jamestown, and the rebellion collapsed. None of the factions involved in the uprising developed a permanent identity as an oppo-

[33] Leonard Labaree, *Royal Government in America* (New York, 1930), pp. 219–222. In addition, see Lovejoy, *Glorious Revolution*, pp. 22–23.

[34] Charles M. Andrews, Ed., *Narratives of the Insurrections 1675–1690* (New York, 1915), pp. 15–141. See also Craven, *Southern Colonies*, pp. 360–393.

[35] Bailyn, *New England Merchants*, pp. 103–106.

sition group with specific goals. When news of the events reached England, a force of 1100 men was quickly dispatched to Virginia. This decisive royal response was evidence of the new role the Crown intended to play in shaping the course of colonial affairs.

Berkeley had governed Virginia by tying together royal government and the interests of an elite group of planters. The Crown proceeded to undo this alliance by driving the planters into opposition. Berkeley had worked through the assembly. After the rebellion, the new royal initiative attempted to break the control of the assembly over local affairs. Symbolic of the change this policy engendered was the role played by Robert Beverly. He had been a member of Berkeley's Green Spring faction. He now became a symbol of the assembly's "independence and resistance to the Crown's attack upon their authority."[36]

The Crown considered "that the rebellion of Virginia was occasioned by the Excessive power of the Assembly."[37] In some respects, the Crown's interpretation was no doubt correct. The assembly represented the interests of particular planters. They used the assembly to secure their own dominance over internal colonial affairs and this had provoked the opposition of other groups. But by attacking the rights and privileges of the assembly rather than a specific group, the Crown was in fact challenging the political instrument of the entire planter class, a class whose position was consolidated rather than undermined by Bacon's Rebellion. The small planter, mobilized during the insurrection, was faced with a system of county government dominated by the family ties of wealthy planters. Indeed, he began his exodus from the Tidewater region.

In the aftermath of the rebellion, many planters who previously identified their interests with the cause of royal government had reason to question such an identity. Legally, the position of the assembly was quite vulnerable. It met not by right but by the pleasure of the king. Its legitimacy was based on instructions given by the Crown to the governor. It was not protected by any sacrosanct constitutional guarantee. On the eve of the rebellion, the assembly had drafted a charter it hoped the Crown would approve. The draft granted the assembly a virtual monopoly of local power and authority. The assembly claimed the right to approve all taxes and impositions. The role of the Crown was to be passive. It could review laws passed by the assembly. The assembly considered that it was merely seeking direct confirmation of what had already come to be established procedure. They sought assurances that "the rights of Englishmen"

---

[36] Lovejoy, *Glorious Revolution*, p. 62.
[37] Ibid., p. 50.

would be guaranteed.[38] Of course, in this instance, the rights of Englishmen actually meant the right of an elite group of planters to control Virginia. The king had no intention of approving such a charter. Provisions of this nature placed obstacles in the path of royal government. When a new charter was issued by the Crown, it failed to confirm any of the guarantees sought by the assembly. The status of the assembly remained uncertain. But so did the position of the planter class whose interests were represented by that body. As the Crown continued to attack the assembly, questioning and overturning established procedures and laws, the planters used all the political skills of the House of Burgesses (assembly) to defend themselves from the arbitrary power of the Stuart monarchy.[39] The legacy of the Restoration in Virginia was to pit colonial self-interest against Crown policy, centering the conflict in a specific institution—the assembly. The Stuarts transformed the assembly from a potential ally to an opponent. The intensity of the conflict ceased only when the momentum of the royal offensive was undercut by the overthrow of the Stuarts in 1688.

In royal colonies where the Crown exercised direct authority, it challenged the legislative powers of the assembly and determined that such bodies could convene only at the pleasure of the king. The boundary between local privileges and the royal prerogative was extended in favor of the Crown. In most colonies, however, the nature of the political tie to the Crown was based on a charter. Typically, charters granted extensive rights to the groups, corporations, or individuals who held them. Lord Baltimore's charter in Maryland specifically empowered him "to Ordain, Make and Enact Laws of what Kind soever . . . of and with the Advice, Assent, and Approbation of the Free-Men of the same Province."[40] Chartered colonies, in particular the Commonwealth of Massachusetts, tended to use their chartered rights to circumvent the demands of royal policy. In 1665, the Massachusetts General Court (assembly) refused to accept the credentials of a royal commission dispatched to investigate conditions in the colony, arguing that the commission's authority was "inconsistent with the maintenance of the laws and authority here so long enjoyed and orderly established under the warrant of His Majesties Royal Charter."[41] Colonial charters were clearly an impediment to the extension of executive control. The Crown proceeded to strike against chartered colonies through

---

[38] Ibid., p. 38.

[39] Ibid., pp. 69, 53–69.

[40] Jack P. Greene, Ed., *Great Britain and the American Colonies 1606–1763* (Columbia, 1970), p. 23.

[41] Bailyn, *New England Merchants*, p. 120.

the Lords of Trade, a permanent committee of the king's Privy Council established to oversee colonial affairs. The Lords opposed the establishment of additional chartered colonies and attempted to convert those already in existence to the royal type.

William Penn, a personal friend of the king, was granted the proprietorship of Pennsylvania in 1681 in spite of the opposition of the Lords of Trade. But his charter contained more stringent royal controls than had been characteristic of other chartered grants. In 1684, the Lords initiated a general attack on the chartered colonies in the courts, which led to the revocation of the Massachusetts charter. The Baltimore grant in Maryland was especially hard-pressed during this period. Charles II died in 1685. His successor, James II, continued to extend the prerogatives of royal government in America. A policy of political consolidation was undertaken whose basic contours bore a striking resemblance to Spanish viceregal government. The experiment began with the establishment of the Dominion of New England under the governorship of Sir Edmund Andros in 1686. The heart of the Dominion was Massachusetts, but Rhode Island and Connecticut, pressured into surrendering their charters, were also placed under its jurisdiction. Subsequently, New York and New Jersey were added to the Dominion, administered by the deputy governor, Francis Nicholson.

The Dominion struck at the institutional foundations of Puritan dominance in Massachusetts. The General Court (assembly) was suppressed. Legislative power, including the right to levy taxes, was placed in the hands of the governor and his council. Overall judicial responsibility was also placed under their jurisdiction. The councilors received their commissions from the Lords of Trade. The new royal government also brought religious toleration for Anglicans and disestablished the Puritan church. It was no longer to be supported by public revenues. Massachusetts did not display much overt resistance to such monumental changes. The leadership of the colony was deeply divided. The Puritan oligarchy had used the authority of the charter to restrict the participation of religious dissenters in colonial affairs. Many of these dissenters were Anglican merchants or "moderates" whose enthusiasm for a colonial government run by religious zealots was not keen. Important segments of the merchant community were alienated from the Puritan leadership when the Crown began its attack on the charter. So Dominion government enjoyed the initial support of many merchants and moderates who believed their influence would be heightened under Governor Andros. By the 1680s "merchants welcomed any help they could get gaining an amount of political power proportionate to their economic and social influence."[42] By aligning themselves with the new royal administration, they hoped to strengthen their political position and ameliorate some of the disturbing effects of the Navigation Acts. The Puritan community, for its part, profoundly disoriented by the events leading to the establishment and demise of the Dominion, looked within itself to discover the cause of God's disfavor. In Salem, the community uncovered rampant witchcraft.

If merchants felt politically impotent under the aegis of the Godly commonwealth, their influence was even less forceful in the Dominion. The charter had favored the interests of the Puritan community. But it had, at least, protected the merchants against the aggressive and often fraudulent enforcement of the Navigation Acts. Now royal government, it appeared, threatened everyone's interest and afforded protection to no one. The towns resisted the imposition of new taxes levied without their consent. The Dominion government reacted quickly to quell such opposition. It restricted the authority of town government, limiting the frequency of town meetings to a single annual assemblage. The inhabitants were "forbidden to convene at any other time under any pretense whatsoever."[43] The last citadel of New England Puritanism, the town, was under siege. The position of merchants was also in jeopardy. Governor Andros insisted on an interpretation of the Navigation Acts that prohibited aspects of trade, such as the exchange with the French West Indies, that were actually legal. Overall, the Acts were more rigidly enforced than ever before. New England commerce experienced serious contraction.[44] The interests of merchants and Puritans joined in a coalition against the Andros administration. Overt confrontation, however, was triggered by events in England.

The Glorious Revolution

It was not just the king's subjects on the American side of the Atlantic who felt the brunt of executive power. In England, there was also a renewed assertion of royal authority. The charters of cities and boroughs were attacked as the Crown sought to control local patronage. Moreover, the Stuarts followed a policy of peace with France during a period when mercantile interest began to see French power as a direct threat to English

---

[42] Ibid., p. 160.

[43] Viola F. Barnes, *The Dominion of New England* (New Haven, 1923), pp. 96, 85–96.

[44] Ibid., pp. 135–173.

commercial strength. When James II suspended the Test Act (an act that required all officeholders, including the king, to be members of the Church of England), he alienated the staunch Anglican sympathies of the Tories, until then, strong supporters of the royal prerogative. A temporary alliance between prominent Whigs and Tories resulted. William, King of Holland, was invited to take up the English throne. James II fled to France in 1688. The Glorious Revolution reasserted the rights of Parliament against the extension of executive power. It made explicit what had been merely implicit during the Restoration. The king could not rule without the support of Parliament. The Crown never again assaulted the liberties of Parliament. The Bill of Rights restricted the dispensing power of the king. No law could be suspended without the approval of Parliament. The ability of the Crown to finance a policy independent of Parliament was regulated by the judicious control of royal revenues. The king was granted an annual salary. Even customs revenue was granted for a specific number of years. Parliamentary supervision of the executive increased. Annual budgets drawn up by the treasury were submitted to Parliament. It set up its own committees for examining public accounts and exercised the right to criticize royal appointments.[45] The rights of Parliament, or more specifically, the rights of the propertied classes in England to protect themselves from arbitrary executive power, had been upheld. A temporary alliance of Whigs and Tories was achieved on behalf of their mutual interests. Certainly, the Glorious Revolution was not arranged to protect the interests of colonial subjects; it had been an internal affair, a quiet coup d'état rather than a revolution. But it provoked a profound and complex reaction in America.

The reorganization of colonial political institutions had been carried out by the executive agencies of the Crown. It was the Lords of Trade and not Parliament that attacked chartered colonies and established the Dominion. Parliament itself was being challenged by the extension of royal prerogatives in England. Surely both actions were part of a larger whole. The rights of Englishmen were everywhere besieged. Colonists antagonistic to royal government in America tended to identify themselves with the Whig opposition to royal power. The Glorious Revolution had destroyed the legitimacy of Stuart absolutism at home; certainly the Revolution also abrogated the thrust of royal policy in America as well. At least so it appeared to important groups in the colonies.

As news of events trickled into Boston, Andros, without instructions from England, hesitated to act. Since the Dominion was clearly identified with the overthrown monarchy, its legitimacy was thrown into question. The failure of Andros to declare his loyalty immediately for the new king

[45] Hill, *Century of Revolution,* pp. 277–280.

was taken as a demonstration of continued support for James II. Rumors of a conspiracy to deliver Massachusetts to James II with the support of the French and Indians in Canada made the silence of the governor appear more ominous still. Another fear was that Andros might indeed declare for the new king and that there would be no relief from arbitrary government.[46] On April 18, 1689, the inhabitants of Boston, directed by a "group of gentlemen" composed of merchants, former magistrates, ministers, and some members of the governor's council, toppled the Dominion.[47] The interests of Puritans and merchants had combined against the Crown. In May, a new assembly was elected. The Commonwealth was reestablished under the interim leadership of the former governor, Bradstreet. Meanwhile, the colony's agent in London, Increase Mather, entered into negotiations for a new charter from the king.

The events of April were not a bid for independence. The colonists wished only to return to concepts of empire more consistent with their interests and more in conformity with the rights of Englishmen. As Increase Mather argued in his pamphlet, *A Vindication of New England,* "No Englishmen in their Wits will ever Venture their Lives and Estates to Enlarge the King's Dominions abroad, and Enrich the whole English Nation, if their Reward after all must be to be deprived of their English Liberties."[48] Furthermore, colonial interests had a fairly concrete interpretation of what such liberties entailed. For example, when the New York assembly drafted a *Charter of Liberties and Privileges* (1683) that it hoped the proprietor would accept, the charter provided that all legislative power, including the power to levy taxes, be placed in its own hands. The charter also called for triennial meetings of the assembly. The privileges claimed by the New York assembly were not unique. Colonial leaders were well aware of constitutional developments in England. They attempted to defend their own interests from the executive power of the Crown by claiming for their assemblies privileges similar to those enjoyed by Parliament.[49] When Parliament struck against the king, supposedly it also struck a blow for English liberties in the colonies. In the aftermath of the insurrections that disrupted the course of royal government in America, colonists justified their actions by stressing the symmetry of events on both sides of the Atlantic. The *Declaration of the Gentlemen, Merchants and the Inhabitants of Boston,* drawn up on the day of the revolt against Andros, argued that their action was in compliance with "the Patterns which

---

[46] Lovejoy, *Glorious Revolution,* p. 242.
[47] Ibid., pp. 240–242.
[48] Ibid., p. 292.
[49] Ibid., pp. 114–121.

the Nobility, Gentry and Commonality (in England) have set before us."[50] It is clear from the language of the declaration that the leaders of Massachusetts viewed their actions within the context of an international "Popish Plot" wherein the "great Scarlet Whore" aided by the "absolute and Arbitrary" authority of the king had sought "no less than the Extinction of the Protestant Religion" and "English Liberties." Parliament, the Protestant King William and the gentlemen, merchants, and inhabitants of Boston had all acted in unison to thwart such an "infamous Design."[51] Such contentions were partially self-serving. They were also erroneous.

The Whig–Tory coalition that united temporarily to topple James II had not done so to reorder colonial policy. If colonial leaders assumed that the split between the king and Parliament also reflected a fundamental division regarding the thrust of colonial affairs, they were soon set straight. There were not, in fact, two separate colonial policies representing anything so simplistic as "Arbitrary Authority" and "English Liberties." Commercial interests were well-represented on the Lords of Trade. Its membership included a prestigious group of merchants, diplomats, economists, and expansionists. The English Board of Customs, responsible for administering the Navigation Acts, consistently furnished the Lords with information and had considerable influence on that body.[52] Enforcement of the Navigation Acts passed by Parliament and the extension of royal control in the colonies were mutually reinforcing policies. Commercial interests in England may have opposed the growth of executive power at home. But in the colonies, royal power was not inconsistent with commercial policy. The Navigation Acts subordinated the colonial economy to the requirements of a commercial empire whose center was England. Politically, the men who designed commercial policy were not about to propose constitutional equality between colonial assemblies and Parliament. Colonial interests, on the other hand, judging from the arguments they produced to justify the rebellions of 1689, saw the empire as an empire of equals based on equal privileges for those who dominated the affairs of particular colonies. There was potential for bitter conflict over constitutional issues, over the rights of powerful interest groups within each colony and their relationship to imperial interests represented by Parliament. The political "resettlement" in the wake of the Glorious Revolution largely avoided overt conflict; but the essential issues remained unresolved.

---

[50] Andrews, *Narratives of the Insurrections,* p. 181.

[51] Ibid., pp. 175–178.

[52] Winfred T. Root, "The Lords of Trade and Plantations 1675–1696," *American Historical Review* **23** (1917): 25–31.

The Lords of Trade were not purged by the new king. They continued to direct colonial policy. William, however, was not opposed to assemblies on principle, as tended to be true of the Stuarts. Assemblies were not, in fact, necessarily inimical to imperial interests as long as they remained sufficiently subordinate to the power of royal governors and their councils. The momentum of the Lords had been undercut both by the Glorious Revolution at home and by the scope of colonial reaction in America. Maryland, New York, and Massachusetts all had their insurrections. Moreover, as England plunged into war with France (1689–1697), the Lords were pressed by other duties in addition to the implementation of colonial policy. Attempts to consolidate the continental colonies were abandoned. But the Lords continued to oppose the existence of private chartered colonies (proprietary) or the granting of chartered privileges to royal colonies. For the most part, the attitude of the Lords was upheld by the king. The proprietary status of Maryland was terminated. New York and Maryland were confirmed as royal colonies. Like Virginia, they enjoyed assemblies but by virtue of the king's instructions. They met not by right but at the pleasure of the king.

Only Massachusetts received the privilege of an assembly guaranteed by royal charter. In no small measure, this was due to the skillful negotiation of the colony's agent, Increase Mather. The Massachusetts assembly was the only lower house in the colonies granted the power to select the members of the governor's council. Still, the charter was a disappointment to the Puritan faction. The virtual independence enjoyed by the old Commonwealth was not restored. The king now appointed the governor, who in turn appointed judges, sheriffs, and justices of the peace. The hand of royal government had certainly been strengthened in comparison with the terms of the old charter. Liberty of conscience was granted to Anglicans, and voting privileges were tied to property—not to church membership. Consequently, the franchise could no longer be manipulated to maintain the same degree of Puritan dominance in the assembly. The Godly commonwealth would have to be shared with dissenters and merchants. A homogeneous polity organized to support the earthly pilgrimage to salvation was irreparably lost.

The diverse reactions in America to the events of the Glorious Revolution underscores the tentative nature of colonial politics. While the insurrections generally deflected the momentum of the royal initiative, they were not produced by similar sets of internal conditions. They were uncoordinated events that reflected the peculiar nature of local politics. Only in Massachusetts was the rebellion the unified response of previously divided interests. In New York, the rebellion of Jacob Leisler created in-

tense hostility between competing groups, which came very close to provoking civil war. When royal government resumed in a very tense atmosphere, Leisler was tried and executed for treason. Behind the insurrections
that disrupted the colonies in the late seventeenth century in Virginia
(1676), North Carolina (1677), New England, New York, and Maryland
(1689) was a profound instability in the nature of colonial leadership. In
each of these colonies, no single group had an unchallenged claim to exercise legitimate authority. Had rebellion provoked a drive for independence
under these conditions, the result might well have been a series of destructive civil wars. The task of constructing a unified political system from
the ruins of empire would have appeared as hopeless in English America
as it subsequently did in Spanish America.

An assembly was not viewed as a political institution to be shared by
adversaries. It was an institution that provided a particular group with
the machinery to dominate internal affairs according to a specific procedure
and to ward off the potential interference of royal officials. This was in
fact how assemblies were used in both Massachusetts and Virginia. The
principle of exclusion was not seen as fundamentally incompatible with
the rights of Englishmen. Catholics, with the exception of Maryland, were
everywhere excluded. The Puritans had attempted to limit the participation of Anglican merchants. The interests of Virginia planters certainly
came to overshadow the small freeholder. In the context of the seventeenth
century, when colonial interests invoked the rights of Englishmen, they
meant that men of wealth and property, socially preeminent, had the
right to determine local affairs in a manner consistent with their interests.
In England, this was accomplished through Parliament. In America, the
assembly was viewed as the bastion of such rights. But in seventeenth-century America, it was not always clear exactly who the socially preeminent
were, since class divisions were less sharply drawn than in England. The
tendency was for factions to develop within that relatively broad layer of
society where men could claim some degree of wealth, property, and status.
It was this condition that reinforced political instability. The trend during
the eighteenth century was toward a more stable political situation. In
some instances, particular groups, such as the Virginia planters, gained a
predominant social position and their interests dominated the assembly.
In others, where particular interests could not defeat one another, there
were more serious divisions. But in both situations, the assembly provided
an institutional setting for political battles. As colonists became more diverse religiously (Dissenters and Puritans in Massachusetts), ethnically
(the Germans and the Scotch–Irish on the frontier), economically (farmers and merchants in New England), and culturally (the East versus the

West), the colonial assemblies came to "represent" these interests. The assembly absorbed conflict by confining it to the boundaries and procedures of a specific political institution.[53]

The agreements between the Crown and its rebellious colonies approved the calling of assemblies. But fundamental problems remained unresolved. The boundaries between the local authority of the assembly and the scope of royal control were not clearly defined. The result was a prolonged struggle between the Crown and colonial assemblies. There was not, as we have seen, a very significant division between Parliament and the Crown over the direction of colonial policy. Yet, the colonists persisted in the belief that such a split existed. This belief was supported by the fact that the Crown structured political relationships, while Parliament confined itself to the direction of commercial policy. This division continued after the Glorious Revolution, lending credence to the belief that a colonial assembly resisting the authority of the Crown could find strong support for such a policy in Parliament.

---

[53] Bernard Bailyn examines colonial politics from this perspective in "Politics and Social Structure in Virginia," in *Seventeenth-Century America*, ed. James Morton Smith, (Chapel Hill, 1959), pp. 90–115. See also Bernard Bailyn, *The Origins of American Politics* (New York, 1968), pp. 99–108.

Map 5 English and French America (1750).

VIII

The Framework of Empire:
The Eighteenth Century

THE STRUCTURE OF TRADE

The Crown's political initiative was weakened by the Glorious Revolution but Parliament retained its keen interest in the enforcement of the Navigation Acts. England was in the throes of a commercial revolution that depended heavily on the control of colonial exports. As late as 1640, the mainstay of English commerce was woolen cloth. It accounted for almost 90% of all English exports. By the turn of the century (1699–1701), woolens constituted only 47% of England's exports.[1] The dynamic element in the English commercial system during the latter half of the seventeenth century was the growth in the reexport trade of colonial products to Europe. This expansion was based on England's monopolization of enumerated colonial products, especially sugar and tobacco. The most spectacular growth was in the tobacco trade. Tobacco imports to London from the Chesapeake

---

[1] Ralph Davis, "English Foreign Trade, 1600–1700," *Economic History Review* 7 (1954):150.

region grew from 7 million pounds in the period 1662–1663 to 22 million pounds in 1699–1701.[2] About ⅔ of these imports were reexported to Europe. London imports of West Indian sugar also increased dramatically, from an average of 148,000 cwt (hundredweight equalling about 100 pounds) in 1663–1669 to 371,000 cwt in 1699–1701, ⅓ of which was reexported.[3] The reexport of these commodities more than trebeled during the four decades 1660–1700.[4] Fundamental changes in the organization of production and distribution made such growth possible. Sugar and tobacco were transformed from luxury products to cheap commodities that could be sold on a mass-market basis. The growth of the English reexport trade in sugar and tobacco was closely tied to the expansion of the slave labor system in the West Indies and Virginia.

The Navigation Acts were designed to protect this expanding trade. Enumeration, control of the carrying trade, and the domination of colonial markets were the pillars of English commercial policy. They provided English merchants with ready access to colonial products and ensured a protected market for English manufacturers. All English and colonial merchants were free to trade within the commercial system.[5] This freedom is in striking contrast to the Spanish system of the same period, which restricted trade to specific ports and granted a monopoly to the merchant guild of Seville and Cadiz. England followed a policy of internal free trade a full century before the Spanish Bourbons adopted *comercio libre*. From the perspective of other European nations, the English commercial system was, of course, a monopoly. Foreign nations had access to colonial markets only indirectly through English intermediaries. While, in theory, all aspects of trade were opened to colonial merchants, in the main, the carrying of enumerated commodities to England, and their reexport to the continent, was dominated by British merchants. So was the movement of English goods to the colonies. Colonial merchants confined the larger part of their trading activities to other English colonies or to the foreign colonies of other European powers. By the end of the seventeenth century, the fundamental importance of colonial trade to English commercial prosperity was indisputable. Of all English exports, 40% were either the reexport

---

[2] Ibid., p. 152.

[3] Ibid.

[4] Ibid., p. 159.

[5] Under the terms of the Act of Union (1707), Scotland joined England and Wales in the Kingdom of Great Britain. Scottish merchants participated in the navigation system on an equal basis. Glasgow merchants became important carriers in the Virginia tobacco trade during the eighteenth century.

of colonial products to Europe or the direct export of English manufactured goods to the colonies.[6]

The English Civil War and the Glorious Revolution had extended the influence of commercial interests on English foreign policy. During the last quarter of the seventeenth century and much of the eighteenth, commercial policy and foreign policy were inseparable. They constituted a single policy, labeled by historians as "mercantilism," that had both economic and strategic aspects. Mercantilism implied four interrelated propositions:

1. that wealth is essential to power;
2. that power is essential to wealth;
3. that wealth and power are each proper ultimate ends of national policy;
4. that there is long run harmony between these ends though there may well be times when military security demands economic sacrifices.[7]

England's commercial system was not designed and defended simply to fill the merchant's pocketbook. Trade was considered to be the wealth of nations. The navigation system was a strategic enterprise established in the national interest to promote and sustain the power of England relative to other state systems. In terms of the international balance of power, commercial ties had profound political implications. Treaties ending international conflicts between 1650 and 1763 were filled with intricate commercial arrangements. Establishing and defending commercial networks was part and parcel of the drama attendant upon the international competition for empire. During the seventeenth century, England successfully shielded her newly formed trading monopoly from Dutch penetration. Direct Dutch trade with the English continental colonies was eliminated. At the same time, England used every means available to penetrate what remained of the Spanish commercial monopoly in Hispanic America. The protection and dismemberment of trading systems was a crucial objective in the three centuries of international conflict that pitted the French, Dutch, English, Spanish, and Portuguese against each other in various combinations. The threat of Dutch and Spanish rivalry to English America had dwindled by the time of the Peace of Utrecht in 1713. The great challenge to English commercial hegemony in the eighteenth century came from France, an adversary the English faced everywhere in the colonial

---

[6] Davis, "English Foreign Trade, 1660–1700," p. 150.

[7] Charles Wilson, "Mercantilism: Some Vicissitudes of an Idea," *Economic History Review* 10 (1957): 181–182.

world—in continental North America, in the West Indies, and in the Far East.

The Glorious Revolution checked the royal attack on colonial charters and assemblies in America. The constitutional relationship between the executive authority of the Crown and the power of the local assembly was not defined by acts of Parliament. Over time, the assembly tended to gain ground at the expense of the executive. Yet, during the same period, from the Glorious Revolution to the end of the French and Indian War (1688–1763), Parliament reacted vigorously to problems posed by certain colonial economic practices. In 1696, it passed a comprehensive bill to ensure a more uniform and systematic application of the entire range of Navigation Acts. Essentially, the Navigation Act of 1696 created machinery for enforcement that was less dependent on colonial participation. The Plantation Duty Act of 1673 had extended bonding and clearance procedures to colonial ports. But responsibility for putting such procedures into effect was left to the governors, courts, and local officials of the several colonies. Under the provisions of the old Act of 1673, the colonial customs service, for all intents and purposes, was organized from the American side of the Atlantic. The organization of the customs service was, consequently, far from uniform. In Virginia, the collectorships went to members of the governor's council who were both influential planters and political leaders of consequence. The customs posts in Maryland went to the favorites of the governor. They were nothing less than racketeers out to make their fortunes.[8]

Stuart policy approached the problem of developing a consistent system of commercial administration by attempting to set up uniform political institutions directly dependent on the Crown. This program of internal reform was cut short by the Glorious Revolution. William III, more cautious than his Stuart predecessors, dealt with the problem of colonial trade by separating commercial organization from political administration.[9] The Navigation Act of 1696 removed responsibility for the establishment of a satisfactory customs service from the jurisdiction of particular colonies and placed it directly under the control of the English Board of Customs Commissioners, a subdivision of the Department of the Treasury. The Navigation Acts were to be administered by a single organization that stretched to both sides of the Atlantic. This was accomplished without any significant alteration in the organization of local political institutions. The Act of 1696 did not provoke a constitutional crisis.

---

[8] Thomas C. Barrow, *Trade and Empire: The British Customs Service in Colonial America 1660–1775* (Cambridge, Eng., 1967), pp. 44–45.

[9] Ibid., p. 38.

Under the terms of the Act of 1696, the colonies were divided into customs districts. There were 34 districts in 1710, staffed by 42 permanent officials appointed by the Board of Customs Commissioners, paid by the English Exchequer, and supervised by a Surveyor General. To as great an extent as was feasible, the control of the customs service was centered in London. Colonial institutions were bypassed. Bonding and registration of ships was centrally regulated. Bonds had to be forwarded to London, where a general register of all vessels was kept. Prosecution under the act could be removed from the jurisdiction of local colonial courts and placed in the hands of special imperial tribunals, the vice-admiralty courts. A reasonably uniform system for the administration of the Navigation Acts was thus established which could circumvent the obstructive tendencies of local institutions.[10] There were still some stumbling blocks that caused friction. The respective jurisdictions of colonial common law courts (they practiced trial by jury and were notoriously reluctant to convict colonial merchants accused of violating the Navigation Acts) and the vice-admiralty courts (cases were heard by judges appointed by the Admiralty in England) were not clearly defined.[11] Still, the Act of 1696 had created a customs system that was administered from London and whose operation did not create serious problems during the period of Whig supremacy (1714–1760).

The Whig ministries were content to maintain the integrity of the navigation system. This was the first and primary concern of colonial policy. As Pitt had said in the 1730s when England was threatened by the Franco–Spanish alliance of 1733 (The Family Compact), "When trade is at stake it is your last Retrenchment; you must defend it or perish."[12] The maintenance of England's commercial policy and the vigorous Parliamentary response to matters involving colonial trade were not inconsistent with a minimal concern for constitutional issues. Problems that concerned the rights and powers of local assemblies remained unresolved. Still, England's colonial policy was proving to be an enormous success both commercially and strategically. Wealth was producing power and that power yielded wealth. Basic reforms in the nature of colonial political institutions did not appear likely to add much to an already successful system.

England's commercial expansion in the latter half of the seventeenth

---

[10] Ibid., pp. 39–59.

[11] Charles M. Andrews, *The Colonial Period of American History*, 4 vols. (New Haven, 1934–1938), vol. 4, *England's Commercial and Colonial Policy*, pp. 258–260. See also Carl Ubbelohde, *The Vice Admiralty Courts and the American Revolution* (Chapel Hill, 1960), pp. 3–22.

[12] John H. Plumb, *England in the Eighteenth Century: 1714–1815* (Cambridge, Eng., 1950), p. 71.

century was closely tied to the reexport of enumerated colonial products. The reexport trade continued to be important during the eighteenth century. But in terms of the pace of expansion, the dynamic component in British trade during the eighteenth century was the phenomenal growth in the export of British manufacturers to colonial markets.[13] British exports to the colonies increased six times over between 1700 and 1770.[14] The growth of this trade was especially important, since it compensated for the drop in England's traditional export—woolens. Moreover, the new export trade stimulated the growth of British industry as never before:

> The process of industrialization in England from the second quarter of the eighteenth century was to an important extent a response to colonial demands for nails, axes, firearms, buckets, coaches, clocks, saddles, handkerchiefs, buttons, cordage and a thousand other things; a variety of goods becoming so wide that the compilers of the Customs record tired of further extending their long schedules of commodities and lumped an increasing proportion of these exports under the heading of "Goods, several sorts." [15]

Britain's trade with the Southern colonies and the West Indies was a simple exchange of enumerated commodities for manufactured goods. The commercial tie between Britain and the Northern colonies was more complex. The fundamental problem was that the Northern colonies produced little that could be exported to Britain in exchange for manufactured goods. The result was a persistent and serious deficit in the balance of payments. During the period between 1698 and 1717, New England imported goods valued at an average of £103,500. Her average annual exports to Britain in the same period amounted to £37,400, leaving an annual deficit of £66,100 or £1,189,800 for the entire 18-year period.[16] During much of the eighteenth century, England was self-sufficient in foodstuffs and hence there was no demand for the agricultural surplus of the Northern and Middle colonies. The central problem of New England's commerce was to find a legal outlet for her products that would provide her with the credit needed to purchase British manufactured goods. To do this, merchants built up a series of commercial exchanges.

First of all, New England merchants exported provisions, lumber, and

---

[13] Ralph Davis, "English Foreign Trade, 1700–1774," *Economic History Review* 15 (1962–1963): 291–292.

[14] Barrow, *Trade and Empire*, p. 144.

[15] Davis, "English Foreign Trade," p. 290.

[16] Curtis P. Nettels, "England's Trade with New England and New York, 1685–1720," *Publications of the Colonial Society of Massachusetts* 28 (1930–1933): 322–350.

rum to Newfoundland in exchange for the settlers' fish. On the island, they maintained stores and resident factors who managed the sale of cargoes and the purchase of fish on commission. For the most part, the New Englanders did not carry the bulk of the fish to its final destination. Instead, they sold it to trading vessels that came to Newfoundland in the summer from England, Ireland, Spain, and Portugal. In return, they received wines, brandy, linens, coin, and bills of exchange. Purchasing Spanish wines in Newfoundland that had not first passed through British customs was, of course, a violation of the Navigation Acts.[17]

A second trading pattern involved the export of New England fish and timber to Southern Europe. Direct trade in nonenumerated commodities with the ports of Southern Europe was not prohibited by the Navigation Acts. Returns were in pieces of eight and bills of exchange drawn on London. Salt for the New England fisheries could also be imported directly from Southern Europe. Since Britain's trade with Southern Europe was increasing during the eighteenth century, Spanish merchants in ports like Bilbao had bills of exchange received from British merchants to pass on to the New Englanders. Despite their denials, New England merchants probably loaded contraband Spanish and Portuguese wines as return cargoes.[18]

The most important trade of the Northern colonies was with the British West Indies and the foreign sugar colonies of France and Holland in the Caribbean. They exported fish, lumber, horses, wheat, bread, flour, pipe staves, candles, hoops, and shingles.[19] Of such diversity were the cargoes dispatched to the West Indies that the vessels resembled floating general stores.[20] Northern merchants returned with bills of exchange, molasses, rum, and sugar. Of these returns, molasses, a by-product of the sugar refining process, took on the greatest significance. New England distilleries depended on a steady supply of cheap molasses to make rum. Molasses was also used extensively in cooking and could easily be made into a home-brewed beer. During the seventeenth century, New England imported the bulk of its molasses from the English colonies of the West Indies. Progressively, however, the English West Indian planters began to set up their own distilleries, exporting rum to Britain and the continental colonies. The cost of molasses began to rise. An alternative supply was found in the French and Dutch sugar islands. The French government prohibited the

---

[17] Ibid., pp. 329–330.
[18] Ibid., pp. 331–333.
[19] Ibid., pp. 333–339.
[20] Richard Pares, *Yankees and Creoles: The Trade between North America and the West Indies before the American Revolution* (London, 1956), pp. 37–38.

importation of rum to protect the French brandy industry. Neither the French nor Dutch sugar colonies developed an extensive rum industry during the colonial period. Consequently, the French sugar island had only one major outlet for molasses, the English continental colonies. New England distilleries had at their disposal a cheap supply of foreign molasses. While New England rum was inferior to the English West Indian product, it had a decided advantage in price; New England rum sold for about half the cost of West Indian rum. The trade between the Northern colonies and the foreign sugar islands was not illegal as long as it did not involve enumerated commodities or European products. But the trade came under heavy attack from West Indian planters whose interests were well-represented in London.[21]

West Indian sugar enjoyed a monopoly of the English market. Nearly 40% of English sugar imports had been reexported in the late seventeenth century. But during the eighteenth century, the reexport trade fell drastically in the face of competition from cheaper French sugar. By the 1730s, only 5% of English sugar imports were reexported to European markets.[22] Expanding sugar production in the British West Indies, combined with a shrinking reexport market, threatened to glut the English market and drive down prices. At the same time, Ireland and the continental colonies were importing large quantities of French sugar. The strategy of the West Indian planters was to expand their protected market. This is essentially what the Molasses Act of 1733 accomplished. The direct trade between France and Ireland, in which Irish foodstuffs were exchanged for French sugar, wine, and brandy, was prohibited. Hereafter, Ireland was chiefly supplied with British West Indian sugar. Ireland also became an important market for West Indian rum. Importations had reached 2 million gallons annually by 1763.[23] The addition of Ireland to the protected home market was further supplemented by the progressive expansion of the Scottish market after the Act of Union in 1707. The overall result was that supply lagged behind demand, keeping colonial sugar prices in the home market well above those prevailing on the continent of Europe.[24]

The Molasses Act was also intended to create a protected market for West Indian rum and sugar in the mainland colonies. A prohibitive duty

---

[21] Gilman S. Ostrander, "The Colonial Molasses Trade," *Agricultural History* 30 (April, 1956): 77–79.

[22] Richard Sheridan, "The Molasses Act and the Market Strategy of the British Sugar Planters," *Journal of Economic History* 17 (1957): 64. Reprinted in *Essays in American Colonial History*, ed. Paul Goodman (New York, 1967).

[23] Ibid., p. 76

[24] Ibid., p. 83.

of 6 pence per gallon was placed on imported foreign molasses. This amounted to a 100% tax, and it could have ruined the New England rum industry. A heavy duty of 5 shillings per hundredweight was also placed on imported foreign sugar. Unable to profitably load return cargoes of molasses and sugar, the Northern trade with the foreign West Indies would have been seriously handicapped. But as it applied to the North American colonies, the Molasses Act was never rigidly enforced. Systematic procedures to circumvent the act were soon developed. Some foreign molasses and sugar was smuggled into the colonies, avoiding colonial customs altogether. But much of it was disguised as British by bribing customs officials in the West Indies to issue certificates for imaginary quantities of English West Indian molasses and sugar.[25] At times, a small quantity of foreign molasses was declared and the duty paid, while the bulk entered duty-free. The Molasses Act became a dead letter in the colonies. Few serious attempts to enforce it occurred during the 31 years of its existence. During the 1750s, for example, Massachusetts legally imported less than half the molasses and rum it exported, not to mention the large amounts it consumed domestically. Over the entire lifetime of the act, duties on only a half million gallons were collected. In 1750, Massachusetts alone was importing about 1 million gallons of molasses annually, the vast majority of it illegally.[26]

The trade between the Northern colonies and the French West Indies posed serious problems to British authorities, especially in wartime—which was 35 years of the period between 1689 and 1763. England's principal colonial rival was France. Sugar from the French West Indies sustained a lucrative French reexport trade to other European nations. The English Northern colonies were the principal source of provisions for the French West Indies. This trade then, from one perspective, helped support the colonial empire of Britain's rival. On the other hand, the profits from the trade enabled colonial merchants to purchase British manufactured goods. If the Molasses Act was to be rigidly enforced, Northern merchants would lack foreign money to underwrite purchases of British goods, creating the fatal danger—that the Northern colonies would be driven to manufacture for themselves and would develop exports in competition with British products.[27] That Parliament was concerned over such a possibility is shown by the laws passed to prevent the growth of colonial manufactures. The Woolens Act (1699) and the Hat Act (1732) prohibited the exportation

---

[25] Pares, *Yankees and Creoles*, p. 57.

[26] Ostrander, "Colonial Molasses Trade," pp. 80–83.

[27] Curtis P. Nettels, "British Mercantilism and the Economic Development of the Thirteen Colonies," *Journal of Economic History* 12 (Spring, 1952): 112.

of such commodities beyond the colony in which they were produced. The Iron Act (1750) was designed to limit the production of finished ironwares in the colonies and to encourage the growth of finished iron products in Britain. The naval stores program (1704) was a constructive attempt to stimulate the production of tar, pitch, turpentine, resin, masts, and yards in the Northern colonies. The hope was that Northern commerce could be restructured to resemble that of other plantations—a direct exchange of raw materials for finished products. But the exportation of naval stores was never sufficient to replace the importance of foreign trade. The Northern colonies did support an important shipbuilding industry. By the time of the Revolution, close to a third of all ships under British registry were colonial-built.[28] Since many of the vessels were constructed for colonial merchants, the industry did not support as large a volume of British purchases as might be expected. Still, shipbuilding probably netted more returns than all other native products carried to Britain.[29] During periods of war, the Northern colonies received returns for provisioning British warships and equipping expeditions. But in the long run, the problem of the Northern colonies persisted. Without the French trade, the Northern colonies could not maintain their volume of British imports. Concern over the possible development of competitive colonial industries usually outweighed strategic considerations. The Whig ministries acquiesced to a situation in which the nonenforcement of the Molasses Act as it pertained to the continental colonies gained the force of official policy.[30] Only during the British blockade of French West Indian ports during the Seven Years War (1757–1763) was the trade, at times, effectively halted.[31]

To an extent, then, the Northern colonies did not fit into the navigation system. A crucial market for Northern products existed outside of Britain and her plantations. To this degree, the Northern colonies showed less economic integration relative to British and colonial markets than was true of other plantations, especially those in the South and the West Indies. The Northern colonies "smuggled" molasses, sugar, and some marginal goods, such as wine and brandy. But they smuggled to earn returns to purchase British goods. Certainly, the colonial customs service, as it developed in the eighteenth century, was in sad need of reform. But it was not the efficient enforcement of the Navigation Acts that was primarily responsible for maintaining the navigation system. By the eigh-

---

28 Andrews, *England's Commercial and Colonial Policy*, pp. 81–82.

29 Nettels, "England's Trade," p. 393.

30 Barrow, *Trade and Empire*, pp. 134–137.

31 Richard Pares, *War and Trade in the West Indies, 1739–1763* (London, 1936), p. 393.

teenth century, "commercial habits, business connections and credit relationships" were developed that "rendered the colonies dependent upon England and minimized the likelihood of any sudden change."[32] In addition, England had the most extensive merchant marine and was readily becoming the manufacturing center of Europe. In the Spanish empire, where British goods did not enjoy a protected market, she successfully competed against the French and the Dutch. If enforcement of the Acts was lax, colonists were restrained from illegal trade by the economic advantages of trade with England. Illegal trade was naturally in those products that Britain could not supply as cheaply or as plentifully as other nations. The list of such commodities is not particularly impressive.[33] In the main, such smuggling as there was centered on primary agricultural products produced neither in England nor in other plantations. In some cases, such as tea, smuggling was encouraged by high import taxes levied in Britain. When tea was reexported to the colonies, the initial import tax was not refunded. It was during the period of excessive taxation of tea in Great Britain (1723–1767) that the chief smuggling of tea in the colonies developed. Dutch tea regularly undersold the overtaxed British product.[34] Nonetheless, illicit trade never accounted for more than a small part of the regular trade.[35]

Compared to the situation in Spanish America, England's control over the markets and produce of the colonial world was remarkable. She attained all the major goals of her commercial policies. She eliminated foreign shipping in the colonies, controlled the flow of enumerated products, and was the major supplier of colonial markets.[36] Commercially, England was the great success story of the eighteenth century. To appreciate the fundamental strength of the economic links between England and her colonies, it is worth recalling the concurrent eighteenth-century situation in Spanish America. The markets of the Spanish colonial world had been usurped by the French, Dutch, and British, who successfully penetrated the Spanish monopoly. Not only did they carry on extensive illicit operations from their island bases in the Caribbean, but they openly participated in the fleet system, establishing centers in Cadiz and Seville.

---

[32] Lawrence A. Harper, *The English Navigation Acts* (1939: New York, 1964), p. 243.

[33] Barrow, *Trade and Empire*, pp. 149–152.

[34] Oliver M. Dickerson, *The Navigation Acts and the American Revolution* (Philadelphia, 1951), pp. 87–91.

[35] Barrow, *Trade and Empire*, pp. 141–151; Harper, *English Navigation Acts*, pp. 253–274; Dickerson, *Navigation Acts*, pp. 63–91.

[36] Harper, *English Navigation Acts*, p. 253.

The silver of New Spain and Peru was flowing into British coffers in Jamaica, providing specie for the continental colonies and supporting British trade in the Far East. A major share of Spanish colonial exports went to the British, French, and Dutch. If the control of trade is used to define an essential aspect of a colonial system, then the Spanish colonial system was a tenuous arrangement. The French colonial system also had notable commercial weaknesses. In spite of persistent efforts, the French colonies in North America—Quebec and Louisiana—were unable to provision the French sugar colonies in the West Indies; they relied instead on the British continental colonies. By the standards of the day, the British system was certainly more in accord with mercantile ideas. The volume of illicit commodities making their way from Europe to the English colonies via the West Indies, compared to the situation in Spanish America, was certainly not very great.

The Navigation Acts provoked serious antagonism when they were initially adopted by Parliament in the seventeenth century, but during the eighteenth century, colonial dissatisfaction was comparatively minor. Opposition to the navigation system as it existed prior to 1763 played a negligible role in precipitating the American Revolution.[37] Whig policy was devoted to the expansion of trade. The first speech delivered by George II (1727–1760) to Parliament echoed the Whig preoccupation with trade. It was drawn up by the prime minister, Robert Walpole.

> We should be extremely wanting to ourselves if we neglected [to extend] our Commerce upon which the richness and grandeur of this nation chiefly depend. It is very obvious that nothing would more conduce to the obtaining so public a good, than to make the exportation of our manufacturers, and the importation of the commodities used in the manufacturing of them as praticable and easy as may be; by this means, the balance of trade may be preserved in our favor.[38]

These were precisely the objectives that the maintenance and defense of England's commercial empire accomplished. This success helped to underwrite the Whig policy of interfering as little as possible with the internal political organization of colonial life. As long as commerce prospered, administrative reorganization appeared to be unnecessary. In the meantime, colonial assemblies extended their control over local affairs.

The expansion of trade—and the colonies were an integral part of this expansion—was essential to the solvency of the state. Indirect taxes on trading operations collected in Britain—customs duties and excise taxes—

---

[37] Dickerson, *Navigation Acts,* pp. 31–57.
[38] Barrow, *Trade and Empire,* p. 131.

provided the state with its major source of revenue. This was a feasible arrangement, since exports and enumerated colonial imports like tobacco all passed through British ports. From 1736 to 1738, taxes on trade brought well over 4 million pounds into the treasury each year, while the land tax, the major form of direct taxation, yielded about a million pounds.[39] The state maintained an adequate financial base by organizing trade. Fiscal policy, until the Seven Years War placed new burdens on the treasury, did not seem to require a major overhaul of colonial administration.

COLONIAL ADMINISTRATION

The seventeenth century in England was a period of intense constitutional conflict. During the Restoration, Tories supported a strong monarchy and the established Anglican Church, while the Whigs tended to support toleration for dissenters and favored constitutional limitations on royal power.[40] The Stuarts chose their ministers from among the Tories, but the House of Commons remained the stronghold of the Whigs. The consequence was the persistence of serious constitutional problems throughout the period (1660–1688). The Glorious Revolution was a constitutional triumph for the Whigs. Progressively, the Tory party, tainted by Stuart absolutism, declined, and by the 1720s, no longer formed "a viable base for political action."[41]

The eighteenth century, especially during the reign of the first Hanoverians, George I (1714–1727) and George II (1727–1760), was the period of Whig supremacy. The constitutional problems of the seventeenth century had been resolved. The executive power of the Crown, exercised through its ministries, could no longer be sustained without a majority in the House of Commons. The king, no matter what the emergency, was powerless to raise a regiment, levy a tax, or suspend a law without the consent of Parliament. While the king still appointed judges, they held office "on good behavior" and could not be removed "at the pleasure of the King." The hostility between the executive and the House of Commons was largely ameliorated. The king chose his ministers from

---

[39] Gabriel Ardant, "Financial Policy and Economic Infrastructures of Modern States and Nations," in *The Formation of National States in Western Europe*, ed. Charles Tilly (Princeton, in press).

[40] Stanley Katz, *Newcastle's New York: Anglo–American Politics 1732–1753* (Cambridge, Mass., 1968), p. 4.

[41] Ibid.

the Whig leadership, some of whom, like William Pitt, had been leaders in the House of Commons. Political conflict during the eighteenth century ceased to be constitutional. Its object was no longer to challenge the essential nature of the balance between Parliament and the executive. Rather, political activity "was conducted within the amorphous groups of Whigs and pitted Whig against Whig."[42] The character of politics was intensely factional. To maintain their political support in Parliament, ministers managed an extensive patronage system on both sides of the Atlantic.

If a ministry could not be sustained without support in Parliament, it could not function in the absence of royal approval. Ministers were the king's men. There was no "prime" minister in the sense of a specific office. But, typically, a particular minister came to enjoy the special confidence of the king and became the most influential member of the executive. Such an individual was, in practice, a prime minister. The custom was for the king to appoint his most trusted minister to the position of Lord High Treasurer. This was true of Robert Walpole for two decades (1722–1742). When an influential minister found that his policies had lost royal favor, he tendered his resignation. During the seventeenth century, the major advisory body to the sovereign was his Privy Council. It consisted of those who held household offices or were responsible for the departments of state. It was an unwieldy body of about 60 members of varying political views, and was unsuited for rigorous discussion and the formation of policy.[43] Gradually, over the course of the eighteenth century, the Privy Council was superseded by a new institutional development, the Cabinet, or Cabinet Council. It was composed of the great officers of state, such as the Lord of the Treasury, the secretaries of state, and the First Lord of the Admiralty.

Constitutionally, colonial administration was the responsibility of the Crown, since the colonies were settled under the authority of royal grants. Issues pertaining to colonial administration rarely received the attention of Parliament. The Whig ministries (1714–1760), by and large, preferred to isolate colonial policy from political controversy by dealing with colonial administration in terms of the authority inherent in the royal prerogative. Until the conclusion of the second great colonial war of the eighteenth century, the Seven Years War (1757–1763), "Parliament did not pass a single act dealing primarily with local colonial administration."[44] The

---

[42] Ibid., p. 5.

[43] David Ogg, *England in the Reigns of James II and William III* (Oxford, 1955), pp. 333–335.

[44] Leonard Labaree, *Royal Government in America* (New York, 1930), p. 4.

colonies provided the Whig ministries with a significant source of political patronage beyond the control of Parliament. The maintenance of this patronage system and the preservation of executive jurisdiction over colonial administration were generally considered to be more important than involving Parliament in measures to bolster the authority of prerogative power in America. On the few occasions when Crown officials tried to bolster their instructions to colonial governors by Parliamentary act, either the executive itself, divided over the advisability of such a precedent, did not vigorously pursue the issue, or the Commons proved unwilling to grant the executive such a blanket increase in its authority.[45]

The question "Who was responsible for colonial administration?" is easily raised but not so readily resolved. In England itself, responsibility for administration in terms of general policy guidelines was shifting from the cumbersome machinery of the Privy Council to a small council or cabinet of the most important ministers. Under the Stuarts, the Privy Council was involved in framing administrative policy. The Lords of Trade, as constituted in 1675, was the most important body for the consideration of colonial policy.[46] It was, relative to the Privy Council, a committee of the whole. But a select group of influential royal councilors Council was involved in framing administrative policy. The Lords of Trade, with the support of the king, spearheaded the reorganization of colonial administration that ended with the Glorious Revolution. That initiative had attempted to abolish colonial assemblies or at least to reduce their significance in the control of internal administration. Under King William (1688–1702) the assembly was permitted to continue as a basic element in colonial political life, but at the king's pleasure rather than by virtue of rights guaranteed in royal charters.

William brought to the English throne an aggressive foreign policy directed against France. This policy was supported by major commercial interests that viewed France as the principal threat to England's colonial empire. In the ensuing Anglo–French conflict (1689–1697), England's trade losses were serious. The blame was placed by the House of Commons on the inefficiency of the Lords of Trade, who were responsible for colonial defense and the organization of the convoy service. The system of placing all administrative responsibility in the hands of the entire Privy Council instead of separate, select committees was attacked as creating a situation in which "everybody's business is nobody's." In a direct chal-

---

[45] Ibid., pp. 33–34. See also Jack P. Greene, Ed., *Great Britain and the American Colonies 1606–1763* (Columbia, 1970), p. xxxiii.

[46] Winfred T. Root, "The Lords of Trade and Plantations, 1675–1696," *American Historical Review* **23** (1917): 20–41.

lenge to the traditional authority of the Crown, the House of Commons proposed to remedy this state of affairs by establishing its own council of trade complete with administrative responsibilities in the colonies. William countered by establishing in 1696 a special committee of experts (the Board of Trade) to deal with colonial policy that met most of the objections of the House. During the eighteenth century, the Board of Trade was the most important executive agency of the Crown, charged with overall responsibility for colonial administration.[47]

The Board of Trade

The Board of Trade was commissioned by the king as primarily an agency for overseeing and improving the course of trade between England and her plantations as well as between England and other foreign powers. This intent is clear from the language of its commission. It stated, in part:

> Whereas We are extremely desirous that the Trade of Our Kingdom of England, upon which the strength and riches thereof do in a great measure depend, should by all proper means be prompted and advanced; and whereas we are pursuaded that nothing will more effectively contribute thereto than the appointment of knowing and fit persons to inspect and examine into the general Trade of Our said Kingdom and the severall parts thereof. . . We do by these presents authorize and impower you Our said Commissioners . . . to enquire, examine into and take an Account of the state and condition of the general Trade of England, and also of the severall particular Trades in all Forreign parts, and how the same respectively are advanced or decayed, and the causes or occasions thereof.[48]

Colonial administration, as outlined in the commission was a secondary consideration—a corrolary of commercial policy. In Spanish America, the priorities were quite different. A bureaucracy, specifically designed to control colonial administration, sustained royal authority.

The attention of the Board was directed not to constitutional issues, but, rather, to problems of a mercantile variety. The Board was asked to examine the potential for the production of naval stores, to see how the colonies might be more effectively settled, and to seek the most effectual means to encourage the "Fishery of this Kingdom." Generally, it was instructed to find new staples or sources of raw material while expanding

---

[47] Ibid., p. 39.
[48] Greene, *Great Britain and the American Colonies*, p. 128.

colonial markets for British manufactured goods. Regarding direct colonial administration, the Board had several duties. It was to draw up instructions for royal governors and was responsible for their supervision; the governor was expected to correspond with the Board. The Board was expected to be a source of information on colonial problems that could be passed on to other executive agencies. It could submit nominations for governor, deputy governor, and the provincial council to the king's Privy Council. All laws passed by local assemblies were to be reviewed by the Board, and its recommendations forwarded to the Privy Council. The Board was also expected to oversee colonial finances, as it was enjoined "to require an Account of all Monies given for Publick uses by the Assemblies in Our Plantations, and how the same are or have been expended or laid out." [49] Complaints from the colonies concerning "oppressions" and "maladministrations" were also to be directed to the Board.

While the Board was burdened with extensive obligations in the supervision of colonial administration, its ability to determine or enforce policy was remarkably limited. By comparison, the Council of the Indies exercised comprehensive and decisive authority in Hispanic America. But as an advisory body to the Privy Council, the Board of Trade had no right to act on its own. Its authority rested on the influence of its individual members—in particular, the President of the Board—with the king's chief ministers or with Parliament. This became increasingly the case as the eighteenth century wore on. During this period, the significance of the Privy Council as a policy-making body declined considerably. The Board theoretically was responsible to the Privy Council, which had a separate committee to consider Board recommendations, but the real power no longer resided in the Privy Council. The Board had to find support for its administrative policies either in Parliament or in the king's Cabinet Council; without such support, the Board of Trade was virtually powerless. Tied as it was to the Privy Council, it was constitutionally outflanked by the growth of ministerial government. The Secretary of the Treasury (Prime Minister) and the Secretary of State for the Southern Department not only came to exercise an informal veto over the policy recommendations of the Board but they appropriated for themselves, or for their departments, functions that originally fell in the province of the Board's commission.

The Board lost its ability to fill positions in the colonial bureaucracy. The First Lord of the Treasury and the Secretary of State virtually monopolized appointments during the period of Whig supremacy (1714–1760).

---

[49] Ibid., p. 130.

The Board tended to become an adjunct to the office of the Secretary of State for the Southern Department; and copies of any document sent by the Board to the Privy Council had to be sent to the office of the Secretary of State as well. Although, initially, the Secretary of State was concerned with colonial affairs only as they concerned defense and diplomacy, the concerns of internal administration gravitated to his office. This dominance of the Secretary of State over the Board continued during the period that the Duke of Newcastle held the office of Secretary (1724–1746). Newcastle took over practically all correspondence with colonial governors. He virtually ignored the Board on questions of colonial administration and frequently failed to inform its members of orders and instructions issued by his office. The Board of Trade was reduced from a policy-making organization to a bureau of information for other government agencies.[50] It still exercised important aspects of routine administration, considering petitions and scrutinizing colonial legislation. But between the formal lines of authority was the growing influence of the Lord High Treasurer and the Secretary of State, who could intervene at any stage in the established process of administration or circumvent the process altogether. The problem of the Board of Trade was that it never acquired ministerial status; as the cabinet system evolved, the influence of the Board over administrative policy continued to decline.

The Board persisted in its attempts to protect the integrity of royal authority. But if it found the assembly to be a stubborn adversary, it also discovered that its own diminished status in the scheme of British government was a major stumbling block to the achievement of its objectives. The Board endeavored to hold colonial governors to the faithful execution of their instructions, while exercising but slight control over either their appointment or removal. It proposed reforms to bolster the floundering fortunes of royal authority only to find that ministerial support for such policies was not forthcoming. Colonial administration was not a clearly defined central administration. Not only were responsibilities spread over ministries, boards, and councils but the distribution of administrative functions was subject to periodic revision. Such revisions were often the result of slow, incremental changes. They did not represent a desire to reconstitute colonial administration in accordance with specific policy objectives. Colonial administration was divided, with different agencies and officials frequently at loggerheads. That such a situation was allowed to continue reflects the low priority assigned to colonial administration

---

[50] Oliver M. Dickerson, *American Colonial Government 1696–1765* (1912: New York, 1962), pp. 108–115.

during the Whig period and the weight assigned to commercial problems, a bias clearly evident in the commission of the Board itself.

Commercial policy always interested Parliament, and the Board of Trade found strong support there for its recommendations about trade, especially in the House of Commons.[51] The Board exerted the most influence on commercial policy; it was less successful as an administrator. It was frequently requested by Parliament to prepare reports on such questions as the production of rice, naval stores, and other staples, the state of colonial commerce, and violations of the trade laws, and was often directed to draft bills pertaining to trade.[52] British merchants exercised great influence over the Board in matters touching their interests. The Board, for its part, proved "ever responsive to conditions of trade and the opinions of merchants."[53] To the extent that Board proposals enjoyed the support of mercantile interests, they were likely to find advocates in the House of Commons and the backing of a ministry unwilling to alienate powerful British interest groups. When it came to commercial policies, whether initiated by the Board or independently introduced into Parliament by concerned parties, action was quickly taken. The willingness of Parliament to consider legislation over a wide range of economic issues, from general trade to currency regulation, and the success of the Board in marshalling support for many aspects of its own mercantile program, stand in stark contrast to the Board's inability to enlist support to strengthen royal authority in America.

The Board's difficulties, especially during the Whig ministries, also stemmed from the political orientation of the chief minister, Robert Walpole (1721–1742), and Newcastle (1724–1746), the Secretary of State. In terms of British administration, Walpole's policy was "to avoid issues involving fundamentals and all debates over basic principles, to restrict the active role of government and act only when it was expedient or necessary to do so."[54] Newcastle shared the same basic assumption. These principles naturally colored their approach to colonial affairs. Rather than tamper with colonial administration, they preferred to maintain the *status quo* of patronage and trade. They were unwilling to provoke a constitutional crisis in the colonies by enforcing the unpopular policies of the Board of Trade. Any bill geared to reform colonial administration—the acknowledged province of the executive—was not likely to get very far in Parliament without the strong support of the king's ministers.

---

[51] Ibid., pp. 127–131.
[52] Ibid., pp. 128–129.
[53] Labaree, *Royal Government in America*, p. 60, pp. 60–62.
[54] Greene, *Great Britain and the American Colonies*, p. xxxi.

Both the ministry and powerful interest groups in Parliament viewed the "colonial" problem as first and foremost a commercial problem. Trade was "a national preoccupation." Contemporaries would have agreed with the concise formula of Daniel Defoe (1728):

> Trade is the Wealth of the World; Trade makes the Difference as to Rich and Poor, between one Nation and another; Trade nourishes Industry, Industry begets Trade; Trade dispenses the natural Wealth of the World and Trade raises new Species of Wealth, which Nature knew nothing of.[55]

Since trade and industry flourished during the eighteenth century, it is not difficult to understand why contemporaries did not appreciate the Board's view that the situation in the colonies warranted Parliamentary intervention. As it attempted to grapple with serious constitutional problems, the Board operated under a series of handicaps that reduced its effectiveness, thereby facilitating the assembly's rise to power.

Closely supervised, bureaucratic organization in Spanish America was more extensive and professional. But Spain set out to control society more completely, concerned as she was to gain access to the wealth of the Indies, especially precious metals. England wished to control trade, and this did not require a large bureaucracy in the colonies.

The Royal Governor and His Council

By 1730, most of the continental colonies had become royal provinces. The proprietors of the Carolinas and the Jerseys had sold their rights to the Crown. Although returned to the nominal authority of the Baltimore family in 1716, Maryland was, for most intents and purposes, a royal province. Pennsylvania remained a proprietary colony; the Penn family still appointed the governor, but the rights of the assembly were clearly defined in a Charter of Liberties. Connecticut and Rhode Island continued to be self-governing colonies under the charters granted during the seventeenth century. The struggles between the prerogatives of royal authority and the rights of colonial assemblies, the most important internal development in eighteenth-century America, centered in the royal colonies.

The structure of government in royal provinces was based on the will of the king as it was expressed in the commission and instructions given to royal governors. The commission was a standardized document that granted to the governor all the necessary powers to establish and maintain a provincial government; it was the legal basis for all political authority.

---

[55] Plumb, *England in the Eighteenth Century*, p. 20.

The governor's commission was drawn up by the Board of Trade and approved by the Privy Council, a warrant was issued under the king's name, and the commission was sent through the royal seals. The powers granted to the governor in his commission were of such a general nature that they provided little specific guidance in respect to the execution of his office.

The governor's instructions defined actual policy.[56] They covered a variety of topics. Some were uniform and applied to all royal provinces, such as those that defined the powers of the governor over his council and the assembly; other instructions pertained to specific problems in various provinces. Although they followed a standardized pattern, the instructions were sometimes revised, and care was taken to make sure that each new draft reflected any changes in the policies of the home government. When drafting the instructions, the Board was assisted by other governmental agencies that had a special interest in colonial administration. The Commissioners of the Customs usually reviewed the instructions that related to trade, and suggested appropriate changes. Other interested parties could also suggest revisions. British merchants were especially active in this regard. They concerned themselves with any instructions that affected their interests. They were successful, for example, in persuading the Board to include instructions prohibiting the governor from approving colonial laws that placed duties on British imports, even though the governors themselves often supported such measures.[57] Although the colonies maintained agents in London to represent their views before the Board, they appear to have had but slight effect on the drafting. When the instructions had been prepared, they were reviewed by the Privy Council. The final draft received the signature of the king.

These documents—the commission and instructions—defined the role of the governor as it pertained to crucial matters like the framing of legislation, provincial finance, and the administration of justice. The governor, with the consent of his council, had authority to summon the assembly. Although normally he consulted the council before dissolving or proroguing an assembly, the governor could act on his own. He had an absolute veto over all colonial legislation. Control of provincial finance was the joint responsibility of both governor and council; money could be paid out only under their warrant. Acting with his council, the governor could create courts and appoint judges. The governor and council constituted the highest colonial court of appeals in civil cases.

---

[56] Labaree, *Royal Government in America*, pp. 31–36. See also Leonard Labaree, *Royal Instructions to British Colonial Governors, 1670–1776*, 2 vols., (New York, 1967), vol. 1, pp. vii–ix.

[57] Labaree, *Royal Government in America*, p. 60; generally, pp. 60–63.

The council usually had 12 members. Their names were listed in the governor's instructions. In most cases, a majority were held over from the previous administration. They were not his hand-picked men, but it was possible for the governor to exercise some control over the council's composition, especially if he had well-placed connections in London. The governor kept a list of nominations before the Board, and sometimes a well-connected governor could secure the appointment of his favorite candidate. It was not uncommon for the Board to appoint councilors other than the candidates nominated by the governor—a practice that could seriously undermine the governor's influence with those seeking appointments. Councilors were almost exclusively colonists of considerable prominence in their respective provinces. Once appointed, a councilor normally served for life, unless suspended by the governor or the Board.

The council was the governor's advisory board, the upper house of the assembly, and the highest court of appeals. Only in its legislative capacity did the council exercise authority independent of the governor. The council was entitled to an equal voice in all legislation. This independence was at times compromised, since the governor often presumed not only to attend legislative sessions of the council but to act as a presiding officer and even to cast a vote. This situation caused considerable controversy in New York. It was finally resolved by the British Attorney-General who prohibited the practice.[58] But, generally, constitutional conflicts between the governor and his council were rare. Personal interests, rather than fundamental issues of authority, were at the root of most quarrels. For the most part, the governor and his council functioned together reasonably well.[59]

The governor's instructions did not envision an equal balance between the authority of the assembly and that of the governor and council. The intent was to relegate the assembly to a subordinate role, concentrating authority in the office of the governor and in the council. But to accomplish this, royal government had to extend its control over powerful local interests that demanded political power commensurate with their wealth and social prestige. What was to be the role of planters, merchants, and professionals in colonial government? In England, the constitutional conflicts that stemmed from the growth of new economic and commercial groups had been resolved. The royal executive could not function without the support of powerful groups represented by Parliament. In America, the quest for power gravitated to the elected assembly. It became the focal point for local and popular interests attempting to turn colonial govern-

---

[58] Ibid., pp. 159–162.
[59] Ibid., p. 163.

ment to their own advantage. Since the governor's instructions placed important limitations on the role of the assembly, the political influence of that body could only be extended at the cost of executive power. This is in fact what occurred. Assemblies acquired great constitutional significance in the structure of royal government, not by right but by usage and custom. They established precedents and doggedly maintained them in the face of royal instructions to the contrary. The assembly attracted the politically ambitious because it provided a major avenue for extending personal power and a means to protect group interests.

There was a competing avenue of political advancement. Individuals could court the favor of the governor and perhaps receive an influential position in the colonial bureaucracy. This was, to some extent, the career pattern of the royal councilor. In Virginia, the governor was authorized to designate naval officers, sheriffs, judges, county magistrates, the receiver-general, and clerks of various sorts. The list varied from province to province. The point is that a burgeoning administrative bureaucracy might have provided a counterweight to the assembly. If colonial interests could have been tied into an extensive patronage system managed by the governor, then the elite might have been more effectively controlled, as was the case in Spanish America. Under such circumstances, a significant group of imperial bureaucrats dependent upon their jobs might have allied themselves with the governor against the assembly. While this pattern did emerge on a minor scale, it never predominated.

The appointive power of the governor was, in practice, sharply curtailed. The Navigation Act of 1696 placed the American customs service under the authority of the Customs Commissioners in London. The Board of Trade, the Secretary of State for the Southern Department, and the Prime Minister (Secretary of the Treasury) all made appointments to the colonial bureaucracy. To complicate matters still further, control over specific offices shifted at times from one department to another, reflecting internal bureaucratic struggles. Colonial administration was, at its worst, a spoils system. Lucrative positions often went to men who resided in England and held their offices as sinecures. They collected the salary but farmed out the work to deputies who received a small fee for their labors. Absenteeism was "constant, flagrant and unchecked."[60] The most important appointments to provincial administration were usually made by officials in London. Colonial patronage was an adjunct to the complex patronage system manipulated by the Whig ministries.

Filling positions in colonial administration did not provide the governor

---

[60] Ibid., p. 104, 102–104.

with a very significant political base. The governor soon discovered that an official appointed directly from Great Britain was extremely difficult to control. He was, as often as not, a thorn in his side rather than a dependable subordinate. Unless a governor had powerful connections in Britain, the strategy of adroitly utilizing the patronage system to secure the support and loyalty of the colony's elite was not likely to succeed. Even when the governor could make appointments, they were often limited in nature. The governor of Massachusetts, for example, had little authority over town government. Although the governor of Virginia supposedly could appoint sheriffs and magistrates, in practice he was restricted to lists drawn up by county officials.[61] County government in Virginia was the prerogative of leading planter families. The major career path for the politically ambitious planter, merchant, or lawyer extended from towns and counties to the assembly.

In several colonies, the assembly grew in response to westward expansion, further complicating the task of the governor, who had to cope with an expanding number of delegates. In Massachusetts, every town with at least 40 voters was obliged to send a representative to the assembly. While, in a few instances, specific colonial assemblies were not responsive to the demands of western settlers, notably in North and South Carolina, the general trend was toward a fairly equitable apportionment. Western interests, integrated into the political life of the assembly, did not provide ready allies for the embattled executive.[62]

In Spanish America, political power was an extension of bureaucratic authority. From the viceroy to the town *regidor*, authority was the consequence of a position in a bureaucratic hierarchy. In this respect, English America was fundamentally different. While the governor sat at the top of a colonial bureaucracy that could command considerable influence, local government continued to develop beyond the purview of imperial control. The assembly, rather than royal administrators, controlled political organization.

The Assembly

During the eighteenth century, assemblies succeeded in acquiring powers that, according to the instructions of the Board of Trade, belonged to the governor and his council. To be sure, the colonial bureaucracy continued

---

[61] Wesley Frank Craven, *The Southern Colonies in the Seventeenth Century* (Baton Rouge, 1949), pp. 293–294.

[62] Bernard Bailyn, *The Origins of American Politics* (New York, 1968), pp. 32–33.

to grow, and this development placed added patronage in the hands of the governor. But whatever advantage the governor might have gained thereby was more than offset by the success of the assembly in strengthening its hold over vital aspects of provincial administration. Of fundamental importance was the assembly's control over revenue. The royal executive did not have the power to levy taxes under its own authority, a principle upheld by the Attorney-General of Great Britain. The Board's position, however, was that the assembly was obliged to make general revenue grants (perpetual taxes) to pay for civil administration. The Board insisted that all funds raised by the assembly should be controlled by the governor and council. In almost all the royal colonies during the eighteenth century, assemblies refused to make revenue grants under these conditions. In the conflicts that resulted, colonial administration often came to a standstill.

The struggle in New York was particularly acrimonious. Governor Hunter refused to approve any revenue bill that did not conform to the Board's directives. The assembly demanded that all money raised by its enactments be placed in the hands of a treasurer that it approved. In the ensuing deadlock, no appropriations were made for 5 years (1710–1715). Hunter reported that the "officers of the government are starving, the forts on the frontier are in ruins, the French and Indians threaten us everyday, no public money nor credit for five pounds in the public account."[63] In this case, a compromise was reached. But the persistence of succeeding assemblies continued. By 1748, the New York assembly had secured almost complete control over financial administration. Some of the methods used to obtain such mastery, characteristic not only of the New York assembly but other assemblies as well, were as follows: Assemblies insisted that all funds be administered by a treasurer of their choosing; they passed detailed and specific appropriations, usually of short duration; and they refused to allow the council to amend money bills registered in the lower house.[64] They made "appropriations for salaries to officials by name and not by office—an effective limitation on the governor's power of appointment and removal." They "attached these salary bills as riders to bills for the payment of the forces on the frontier—which latter measures the governor could not afford to veto."[65] In addition, money bills might contain the provision that appropriations could be made without the governor's warrant. The control over provincial finance was not confined to New York. The same powers came to be exercised by virtually every provincial

---

[63] Labaree, *Royal Government in America*, p. 285.
[64] Ibid., pp. 431–432.
[65] Ibid., p. 287.

assembly, and the tactics employed were of a similar nature in all the colonies. For their part, governors gave in to the demands of the assembly rather than see a province brought to the brink of financial ruin. During periods of war with France—1702–1713, 1744–1748, 1756–1763—when the home government placed a premium on a harmonious spirit of cooperation, governors were loath to provoke damaging conflicts with their assemblies. Using its dominance over financial administration, the assembly came to direct a considerable patronage system of its own. When money was granted for special purposes, such as the payment of troops, funds were placed in the hands of commissioners named in the bill. The assembly was able to nominate and appoint officials to "collect, hold and apply funds arising from provincial revenues."[66] In addition, the lower house was able to control the income from many offices that were filled by the governor. They fixed all fees by statute, denying the power of the governor and council to establish them by executive order. Another curb was thus placed on the significance of the governor's patronage.

During the course of the eighteenth century, the lower house was able to acquire other important privileges. The role of the assembly in establishing colonial courts became customary, although the governor maintained the right to appoint judges. The lower house secured control over its own internal proceedings similar to that exercised by Parliament. They nominated their own speaker; enjoyed freedom of speech and debate; representatives were free from arrest during legislative sessions; and they set their own house rules. But the crux of the assembly's dominant position in the structure of royal government was the power of the purse. Royal government was, to a large extent, financially dependent on the grants of local assemblies. To permit the home government access to colonial revenues beyond the control of the assembly, was to strike at the heart of the assembly's power. The lower house was well aware of that fundamental truth. This was precisely the threat posed by Parliamentary taxation after 1763. Royal government would, for the first time, enjoy financial autonomy. The instructions could be enforced.

The ascendance of the assembly during the Whig period (1714–1760) was, in certain respects, based on the declining influence of the Board of Trade. The Board experienced great difficulty in mobilizing ministerial support behind its rigid insistence that the terms of the governor's instructions be strictly enforced. But weakness at home was not the only determinant in the Board's failure. The Board faced an uphill struggle in the

---

[66] Jack P. Greene, *The Quest for Power, The Lower House of Assembly in the Southern Royal Colonies, 1689–1776* (Chapel Hill, 1963), p. 223.

colonies; the spirit of the Board's program ran counter to the direction of colonial institutional growth. In the seventeenth century, the principle of control by dominant colonial groups over administration was firmly established. The royal government did not aggressively attempt to stake out its claim to control important aspects of institutional life until the last quarter of the seventeenth century. It could only gain ground at the expense of groups and institutions already in America. Royal power was, from the beginning, pitted against local power. The dynamics of this situation, expressed in the insurrections that followed on the heels of the Glorious Revolution, continued into the eighteenth century. The recurrent pattern to build a strong basis of political support. The cycle could also have been neutralized if the royal government had succeeded in coopting vital colonial interests into an imperial bureaucracy—the Spanish pattern. But for reasons already discussed, this never occurred on a scale sufficiently large to build a strong basis of political support. The cycle could also have been broken by force. This was the strategy that provoked the American Revolution.

The discrepancy between the governor's instructions and the powers that assemblies came to exercise helped to fuel a persistent pattern of conflict between local assemblies and royal government. The Board denied the assembly fundamental rights enjoyed by Parliament. The constitutional powers that Parliament secured in the Civil War and the Glorious Revolution were not passed on to colonial assemblies. But the liberties of Parliament did provide an ideological foundation for the assembly's resistance to royal authority. Had the assembly simply accepted the role assigned to it by the governor's instructions, it would have exercised very little control over the money it provided to pay for administration; and it would have lost control over aspects of its own internal organization, such as nominating the speaker and setting house rules.

Even though assemblies were able to abrogate important aspects of royal instructions, the colonial executive continued to exercise powers in America that were not characteristic of royal government in Britain. For example, the governor and council had the power to establish constituencies and apportion representation. Judges in some provinces continued to be appointed at the pleasure of the king rather than during good behavior. Although the assemblies had made important gains during the eighteenth century that had the force of custom in America, the Board of Trade refused to grant official cognizance to such deviations from the governor's instructions. Whenever a new governor arrived, determined to enforce the longstanding policies of the Board, the assembly was likely to find itself fighting the same battles over again. The Board could have revised the governor's instructions to reflect the enhanced constitutional role of the assembly. This was never done. The consequence was a persistent tension in colonial political life.

Assemblies held their powers by custom and usage but not by right. When the Board attained a new significance under the direction of the Earl of Halifax (1748–1761), it quickly initiated a new offensive on the issue of permanent revenues. But the intervention of the Seven Years War compelled the Board to abandon its aggressive stance.[67] The tenuous position of the assembly reinforced the distrust of colonial leaders. The boundaries between royal authority and local power remained unclear; or, perhaps more accurately, whenever an assembly thought the issue was resolved, it discovered that the Board did not concur. The Board was prone to follow a rigid and doctrinaire position. It maintained that instructions had constitutional weight and should be enforced, a policy that threatened the precedents set by the several assemblies. The Whig ministries were generally accommodating and moderate. But what if the ministry should be radically reorganized? Would the policies of the Board become the program of a new government? This is, in fact, the direction of events after 1760.

The financial policy of the Crown was that each province should bear the cost of its own administration. Hopefully, this would take the form of long-term grants or perpetual taxes. In the seventeenth century, the Crown had achieved some success in this regard. A perpetual tax of 2 shillings per hogshead on tobacco had been passed by the Virginia assembly in the aftermath of Bacon's Rebellion. A similar tax had been granted to the proprietor of Maryland. The Crown obtained a share of this tax when Maryland became a royal colony. But during the eighteenth century, of all the assemblies, only the Jamaican lower house (1728) approved a permanent revenue act. The funds yielded by these revenues, while they covered the cost of the governor's salary, did not prove sufficient to cover the cost of civil administration. In all the royal colonies, therefore, the Crown faced the problem of establishing an independent financial base to support administration. In Spanish America, the royal tax on silver production paid for imperial administration.

The assemblies steadfastly resisted the precedent of approving expenditures they could not control. Facing a determined opposition, the Crown could have turned to alternative sources of financial support, thus circumventing the lower house altogether. The Crown enjoyed some private

---

[67] Dickerson, *American Colonial Government*, pp. 40–53, 191–193.

revenues in a number of colonies. The right to collect land rents (quit rents) was acquired by the king when certain proprietary colonies became royal provinces. The quit rents in the Carolinas were used to defray all or part of the cost of the governor's salary; the quit rents from Virginia probably amounted to £6000 or £7000 annually. But the funds were not applied toward the colonies. They were used instead to finance patronage positions in Britain.[68] The most substantial source of private Crown revenue came from Barbados and the Leeward Islands, where the king had relinquished his claims to quit rents in exchange for a perpetual duty (4.5%) on the major exports of the islands, notably sugar. The surplus from these duties, after defraying the cost of island administration, went to pay part of the salary of the governor of South Carolina.

The private revenues of the Crown, even if they were more systematically applied to colonial administration, would still have been insufficient to cover the cost of the civil bureaucracy. There were still other alternatives. The ministry could have sought a specific appropriation from Parliament for purposes of colonial administration; or direct taxes might have been imposed on the colonies by Parliament. Both steps were fraught with political dangers. The first would surely bring in its wake wholesale Parliamentary intervention in colonial administration. The second was likely to unleash unprecedented colonial opposition. Either course was certainly out of character in the Whig world of Walpole and Newcastle. Whereas the Board continued to be appalled at the progressive deterioration of royal authority, the Whig ministries do not appear to have been overly concerned. If they did not favor direct taxation, it was not primarily because they shrank from the consequences. Colonial taxation appeared to be not only unwise but unnecessary and positively harmful. Newcastle, for example, while committed to the defense of the colonies, opposed "novel or harsh measures of colonial government likely to dampen or forfeit colonial good will and thus injure British trade with the colonies."[69] It was trade and not constitutional issues that preoccupied the Whig ministries. The fine points of administration were of secondary importance.

Confronting the determined opposition of assemblies to providing permanent revenues, the Whig ministries were willing to concede the point and accept periodic or even yearly grants. They did, in fact, get half a loaf for their efforts. Many royal colonies did prove to be self-supporting,

---

[68] Dora Mae Clark, *The Rise of the British Treasury* (New Haven, 1960), p. 103.
[69] Bernhard Knollenberg, *Origin of the American Revolution 1759–1766* (New York, 1961), p. 22.

especially during the years of Anglo–French peace (1713–1744). The assemblies did pay the salaries of royal officials, albeit on their own terms. And an important objective of Whig policy was thereby achieved. Self-contained sources of patronage that did not require a very heavy investment of Crown revenues were made available to the king's ministers. The cost of patronage in America was, to a considerable extent, paid out of the colonial treasury. But in this exchange, a crucial precedent was set over the course of half a century. No revenues would be raised in the colonies without the consent of local assemblies.

The policy that the colonial system should pay the cost of its own administration without either direct taxes or Parliamentary appropriations was shattered by the great colonial wars. Britain fought two major wars with her most determined colonial rival, France. King George's War, called the "War of Austrian Succession" in Europe (1744–1748), was generally inconclusive in America. The Seven Years War, known in America as the "French and Indian War" (1756–1763), brought Anglo–French conflict to its height. The cost of colonial defense in both the West Indies ment. While assemblies made considerable grants for colonial defense, and the North American continent was paid out of funds voted by Parlia- such expenditures were frequently reimbursed by Parliament.[70] Before the period of the great wars, Parliament occasionally granted funds for projects that concerned colonial administration. The Carolinas were purchased from their proprietors with Parliamentary funds. In addition, the treasury began to request regular grants for the civil administration of Nova Scotia and Georgia. But the conduct of war, especially the Seven Years War, necessitated unprecedented Parliamentary expenditures in the colonies. The treasury was making regular shipments of from £50,000 to £150,000 in specie to support the war effort in the colonies. It was to be expected that such large expenditures would lead to increased Parliamentary scrutiny of colonial affairs. As war debts mounted, Parliament and the new king George III (1760–1820) began to examine the financial structure of the empire. They were faced with administering and defending an empire greatly expanded by the acquisition of Quebec at the Peace of Paris in 1763. At the same time, they endeavored to reduce Britain's enormous debt. Their solution was to raise revenue in America by act of Parliament. The view of empire changed dramatically. They began to count profits directly, in terms of cash returns to the treasury, rather than indirectly, in terms of the general increase in trade. As the ministry attempted to reorganize financial policy, it discovered that accepted practices could not

---

[70] Clark, *Rise of the British Treasury*, pp. 84–85.

be changed without challenging what the assemblies considered their most basic rights. The executive faced assemblies that emerged from the Seven Years War with an enhanced view of their position in the scheme of royal government. The assemblies resisted the new ministry with determination and revolution.

IX

The Reorganization of Empire
1760-1776

THE NEW EMPIRE

The French and Indian War (1756–1763) ended in British victory. France lost the greater part of her colonial empire in North America at the Peace of Paris (1763). She ceded Quebec and most of her forts in the interior of the continent, such as Detroit, Michilimackinac, Vincennes, Chartres, and Mobile. British claims to all the territory east of the Mississippi River, with the exception of New Orleans and its environs, were acknowledged by France. It was a costly victory. The North American war was but one front in a larger conflict that raged on the European continent and on the high seas. The British debt had increased to £140,000,000.[1] Peace found Britain with a greatly enlarged continental empire that threatened to place additional burdens on the already debt-ridden treasury. British regiments numbering some 8000 officers and men had to be main-

---

[1] John C. Miller, *Origins of the American Revolution* (Boston, 1943), p. 82.

tained in Quebec and in the frontier fortifications vacated by the French.[2] The civil administration of Quebec required direct financial support, as did the administration and defense of Georgia and Nova Scotia.

George III (1760–1820) assumed the British throne in the context of expanded imperial obligations and a huge war debt. He appointed a new ministry. Newcastle, who had exerted great influence on colonial policy for almost 40 years, relinquished his post as First Lord of the Treasury in 1762. He was a consistent opponent of "any alteration that may be proposed, of the present constitution, or received usage and practice, with regard to . . . our settlements in America."[3] In spite of strong pressure during the war, Newcastle steadfastly resisted proposals to levy taxes in the colonies. But the new ministry faced an altered colonial situation. If the empire was not to be a charge on the British treasury, then permanent revenues raised in the colonies and applied toward administration were a necessity. While many colonies paid for their own administration and supported the war effort, the assembly of Massachusetts was not disposed to tax itself to sustain the civil administration of Nova Scotia or to maintain troops in East Florida. The addition of new territories that could not possibly be self-supporting in the immediate future presented, from the perspective of the new ministry, a problem that had to be resolved in terms of the empire as a whole and not in terms of specific quotas, grants, or requisitions made by individual assemblies.[4] The new ministry advocated direct Parliamentary taxation in the colonies. These revenues would be applied toward the overall cost of imperial administration. Financial policy was now directed to a single imperial unit rather than to separate individual colonies.

In the winter of 1765, the Grenville ministry proposed a modest colonial revenue bill to the House of Commons. The Stamp Act required that licenses, newspapers, legal documents, and clearance papers used by merchants must all be printed on specially stamped paper. Agents appointed by the British government were commissioned to sell the paper in the colonies. Stamp duties had already proved their worth as revenue measures in Britain. The Stamp Act was virtually self-enforcing. Unstamped documents were simply void.[5] It was in the interests of individual

[2] Bernhard Knollenberg, Origin of the American Revolution 1759–1766 (New York, 1961), p. 87.

[3] Ibid., pp. 22–23.

[4] Miller, Origins of the American Revolution, p. 10. See also Lawrence Henry Gipson, The Coming of the Revolution (New York, 1954), pp. 73–75; and Jack P. Greene, Ed., The Reinterpretation of the American Revolution 1763–1789 (New York, 1968), pp. 32–33.

[5] Miller, Origins of the American Revolution, pp. 110–111.

citizens to make sure their documents and legal papers were properly stamped. The Stamp Act was a modest beginning in colonial taxation. It was estimated that the cost of maintaining the British army in North America came to about £350,000 annually. The Stamp Act was expected to raise only about £60,000 a year, but it was immensely popular in Parliament.[6] It passed without so much as a division in the House. The weight of direct Parliamentary taxation in Britain fell on landowners. By the end of the Seven Years War, land was taxed at the rate of 4 shillings in the pound. Landed interests in Parliament were strong, and favorably responded to the proposals of the Grenville ministry. They hoped such measures might relieve their own tax burdens.[7]

As the Stamp Act demonstrated, Parliament and the executive were determined to play a new role in colonial affairs. During the period of the great Whig ministries (1722–1760), colonial policy was set by executive agencies. The old division of labor placed the regulation of trade in the hands of Parliament and left administrative and financial policy to the Crown. This division became less pronounced under the exigencies of the new empire. Colonial assemblies now confronted not only the particular administrative challenges posed by royal officials in their specific provinces but a general threat to their local powers provoked and authorized by Parliament itself. If this constitutional shift in the formation and organization of colonial policy was viewed as an event of minor importance to the executive and Parliament, it was seen as a particularly ominous precedent in America. The Stamp Act passed through the channels of British government quietly and smoothly, but provoked an unprecedented constitutional crisis in America, a crisis unforeseen by either Parliament or the king's ministers. It is important to understand why this should be the case. Apologists of imperial policy have stressed the moderate sums that Parliament intended to raise by the various revenue measures approved after 1763. But such measures became caught in the peculiar net of colonial political beliefs and practices, and they could not be dislodged. Both Spain and England initiated reforms after the Seven Years War which led to resistance and rebellion. But in English America, a well-organized opposition reacted immediately.

THE CONTEXT OF THE STAMP CRISIS

Royal governors could not construct a political base in the colonies sufficiently powerful to control the assembly. By 1763, colonial assemblies had placed important restraints on the executive. The establishment and

---

[6] Ibid., p. 113.
[7] Ibid., pp. 87–88.

maintenance of these restrictions were directly related to the assembly's control over taxation and expenditures. Still, colonial political life was unsettled. In America, the executive retained powers that it could no longer legally exercise in England. The uncertain nature of the assembly's power was due to the fact that its established "customs" had no legal foundation. During the Whig period, assemblies had considerable leeway to maneuver politically, since the hard line of the Board of Trade was not usually backed by the ministry. Parliament, for its part, rarely intervened to bolster royal authority. In the years immediately following the Peace of Paris (1763), this situation changed. The lines of colonial policy hardened behind the united front of the king's ministers and Parliament. The assembly faced what it considered a determined attempt to subvert its liberties. The uncertain boundary between the rights of the assembly and the authority of the Crown was now more clearly defined. Parliament, it appeared, was intervening to uphold powers that colonial leaders identified with Stuart absolutism. In responding to the new imperial offensive, colonial elites struggled not so much to assert new rights as to maintain old rights secured during the last half century.

The Stamp Act was not an isolated incident. It occurred as one of a series of measures that caused deep concern throughout the American colonies. The Board of Trade forbade its governors to approve any colonial legislation that did not include a suspension clause. Under the terms of this instruction, any act of a provincial assembly that amended or repealed an existing act had to be passed with a clause that suspended its operation until the new law was approved by the Privy Council. The application of this instruction alarmed colonial leaders in Virginia (1759), Massachusetts (1761), and South Carolina (1761). They viewed this action as an unwarranted intrusion of royal authority in the legislative process. The Privy Council had generally been relegated to a passive role. It could only invalidate acts passed by the assembly. The practice universally accepted in the colonies was that a law passed by the assembly and approved by the governor and his council went into effect immediately and was valid until specifically suspended by the Privy Council. The implication of the suspension clause was that all colonial laws were invalid until specifically approved by the Privy Council.[9]

There were other measures that provoked hostility in the period immediately preceding the Stamp Act. In New York and New Jersey (1761), the Board of Trade demanded that judges be appointed by the governor

---

[8] Bernard Bailyn, *The Origins of American Politics* (New York, 1968), pp. 106–161.
[9] Knollenberg, *Origin of the American Revolution*, pp. 57–72.

at the king's pleasure rather than during good behavior, as was the practice in both those colonies and in Britain. When Governor Hardy of New Jersey violated his instructions and continued to appoint judges in the customary fashion, he was immediately dismissed.[10] The executive evidently intended to press for what it considered to be full royal authority over judicial appointments.

In 1761, Judge Thomas Hutchinson of the Superior Court of Massachusetts upheld the right of the courts to issue general writs of assistance. The writs empowered customs officers, accompanied by local constables, to search—and if necessary break into—homes and stores for smuggled goods without presenting any grounds for such a search. The merchants vigorously opposed the decision. The assembly passed a bill forbidding courts to issue general writs, but the governor refused to approve the measure.[11] The incidents outlined above, whether they concerned the suspension clause, judicial tenure, or writs of assistance, were local in nature. Their impact was largely confined to the provinces in which they occurred. In responding to these challenges, assemblies usually faced the traditional adversary—the governor and his instructions.

Prior to the passage of the Stamp Act, the most significant and disturbing indication of the dramatic change in colonial policy came from Parliament in the guise of a Navigation Act. The Sugar Act (1764) marked a decided shift in the attitudes of both the king's ministers and Parliament about the role of trade in the empire. The old navigation system was designed to regulate trade. The core of the program was enumeration, control of the carrying trade, and the domination of colonial markets. As it existed before 1763, the organization of commerce had not occasioned significant colonial opposition in the eighteenth century. The plantation duty (1673), designed to restrict the flow of enumerated commodities to legal channels, and the molasses duty (1733), intended to protect the sugar plantations of the West Indies, were the major customs duties collected in America. Serious attempts to collect the molasses duty did not materialize until after 1763. Regulation was the major function of the trade duties. The annual cost of the customs establishment, for example, ran between £7000 and £8000, while the duties collected averaged around £1500 per year.[12]

The Sugar Act introduced as a major element in the new navigation system the principle of raising revenue by taxing trade. The provision that caused the greatest concern was the extension of the Molasses Act of 1733.

---

[10] Ibid., pp. 72–75.
[11] Ibid., pp. 67–70.
[12] David Hawke, *The Colonial Experience* (New York, 1966), p. 342.

While the duty on molasses imported from the foreign West Indies was reduced from 6 to 3 pence per gallon, it was clear that the Grenville ministry intended to enforce its collection. A squadron of British warships was dispatched to American waters to aid the customs service. The tax on foreign molasses was still considered to be prohibitively high. It was seen as a direct threat to the trade of the Northern and Middle colonies. The merchants of these colonies carried provisions to the French West Indies and returned with cargoes of molasses to meet the demand of the domestic rum industry. A crucial trading cycle was in danger of being disrupted. To meet these objections, the duty was lowered still further to a penny per gallon in 1766. But the lowered duty now applied to all imported molasses, British as well as foreign. The Sugar Act was clearly a revenue measure.

The Sugar Act placed new impositions on other items as well. Wines imported directly from the Azores of Medeira, Spanish and Portuguese wines imported from Britain, foreign coffee and indigo, and British-grown coffee and pimento were all taxed. The Sugar Act raised substantial revenues in the continental colonies, and it aggravated a postwar depression in trade with the West Indies.[13] This depression resulted both from the British policy of heavily taxing foreign molasses and from a new restrictive French policy as well. The French sugar islands of Martinque and Guadaloupe, important markets for Northern agricultural products and a chief source of foreign molasses, were closed to foreign trade.[14] Although the embargo was subsequently lifted, the temporary consequence was to glut the British West Indies with Northern produce. The price of agricultural products plummeted, while the cost of molasses was pushed upward by the contraction in supply. The passage of the Stamp Act coincided with a slump in the Northern trade, a slump attributed to the high duty on molasses.

At the same time the Sugar Act was passed (1764), Grenville announced his plan to raise additional revenues by means of a stamp tax. He proposed to wait a year before laying such a bill before Parliament. News of the acts, one passed, the other proposed, reached the colonies at the same time. Virtually every assembly that met in 1764 protested against the new measures. The New York assembly declared that, by long-established custom, the rights and privileges of colonists included their exemption from taxes not granted by themselves. This custom was "a right . . . inseparable from the very Idea of Property, for who can call that

---

[13] Miller, *Origins of the American Revolution*, pp. 101–102.

[14] Dorothy Burne Goebel, "The 'New England Trade' and the French West Indies, 1763–1774: A Study in Trade Policies," *William and Mary Quarterly* 20 (1963): 347–352.

his own which can be taken away at the Pleasure of another?"[15] Opposition to the proposed stamp legislation as a violation of basic rights, privileges, or liberties was a common theme expressed in the documents composed by the assemblies. The Sugar Act was not attacked as frequently on constitutional grounds because it was seen as part of an old dispute between Northern merchants and West Indian planters. Nonetheless, it is evident that assemblies viewed taxation by Parliament as a basic change in the constitutional relationship between the colonies and Great Britain.

THE STAMP ACT CRISIS

Evidently, whatever news the ministry received about the widespread colonial opposition to stamp duties did not cause much concern. The Stamp Act was passed by Parliament in February, 1765, and was to take effect in November of that year. In August, the colonies broke forth in a torrent of protest. There were riots in Boston, New York, and Philadelphia. Everywhere, commissioners who had been appointed to distribute stamped paper were forced to resign. They were snubbed by their friends, intimidated by unruly mobs, and burned in effigy. In Boston, a mob pillaged the home of the stamp distributor, Andrew Oliver, and demolished his shop. Similar episodes occurred in other provinces, where crowds not only attacked the home of stamp distributors but destroyed the property of customs collectors and other royal officials. In Newport, Rhode Island, the homes of two prominent lawyers who defended the Stamp Act were plundered. The Collecter of Customs in Newport fled to the safety of a British man-of-war in the harbor. The Boston mobs vandalized the homes of the Comptroller of the Customs, the Register of the Vice-Admiralty Court, and the Lieutenant Governor, Thomas Hutchinson.

The provincial assemblies were also active. In May, the Virginia Assembly passed a series of resolutions—The Virginia Resolves—pertaining to the subject of taxation. The fifth resolution, approved by the narrowest of margins, was subsequently overturned. But it did not contain any principles not already implied in the four resolutions retained by the Burgesses. It was objectionable mostly for its forthright language. It stated:

> Resolved Therefore that the General Assembly of this colony has the only and sole exclusive Right and Power to lay Taxes and Impositions upon the Inhabitants of this Colony and that every Attempt to vest such Power in any other Person or Persons whatsoever other than the General Assembly aforesaid has a manifest Tendency to destroy British as well as American Freedom.[16]

---

[15] Knollenberg, *Origin of the American Revolution*, pp. 189–190.

[16] Edmund S. and Helen M. Morgan, *The Stamp Act Crisis* (Chapel Hill, 1953), p. 92; generally, pp. 88–113.

There were two additional resolutions, more forceful in their implications, that were not accepted by the Virginia House of Burgesses. But newspaper accounts printed all the resolutions, and as they circulated through other colonies, the Virginia Assembly appeared more outspoken than was actually the case. Following Virginia's example, Rhode Island, New York, Pennsylvania, South Carolina, Connecticut, Massachusetts, Maryland, and New Jersey approved resolutions defining their rights. In many instances, they acted on the model resolutions supposedly passed in Virginia, incorporating aspects of the apocryphal fifth, sixth, and seventh resolutions. In all cases, the assemblies forcefully expressed their conviction that Parliament's right to tax the colonies was constitutionally limited. They did so in terms more explicit than the limited and sometimes vague objections made the year before.[17] Massachusetts asked each colonial assembly to send representatives to a special meeting "to consult together on the present circumstances."[18]

The Stamp Act Congress convened in New York on October 7, 1765. Nine colonies were represented. New Hampshire declined to attend but later approved the proceedings. Virginia, North Carolina, and Georgia were prevented from attending because their respective governors refused to convene the assembly so that delegates might be selected. In New Jersey and Delaware, the same situation occurred, but a rump group of assemblymen held informal elections and sent delegates. The Congress adopted a series of rights and grievances. The most important declarations concerned the constitutional basis for taxation. They stated, in part,

> That his Majesty's Liege Subjects in these Colonies, are entitled to all the inherent Rights and Liberties of his Natural born Subjects, within the Kingdom of Great Britain.
> That the only Representatives of the People of these Colonies, are Persons chosen therein by themselves, and that no taxes ever have been, or can be Constitutionally imposed on them, but by their respective legislature.
> That all supplies to the Crown, being free Gifts of the people, it is unreasonable and inconsistent with the Principles and Spirit of the British Constitution, for the People of Great Britain to grant his Majesty the Property of the Colonists.[19]

The Stamp Act Declarations also objected to provisions in the Sugar Act, especially the revenue aspects of the measure, and requested its repeal. The uncertain division between the rights of assemblies and the limits of execu-

---

[17] Ibid., p. 99.
[18] Gipson, *Coming of the Revolution*, p. 89.
[19] Morgan and Morgan, *Stamp Act Crisis*, pp. 106–107.

tive power were clarified by the Congress. The assemblies intended to protect their privileges by continuing to exercise control over revenue.

But the crisis had not yet passed. Consignments of stamps began to arrive in the colonies. Since all the commissioners had resigned, there was no one legally qualified to distribute them. The stamps were placed in forts, were held aboard ships in the harbor protected by man-of-wars, or were placed in the custody of municipal councils. Under the provisions of the Stamp Act, a court could not be held, a ship could not clear port, and a newspaper could not be printed without the use of stamps. The act was defied. Newspapers appeared, ports were opened, and a number of courts began to do business—all without the use of stamps.[20] Colonial leaders had successfully undermined the act. In the highly charged political atmosphere of 1765–1766, attempts to implement the Stamp Act by force of arms would undoubtedly have provoked armed resistance. But this was not the response of the British government. British trade was disrupted by the disturbance in the colonies. Colonial merchants and planters refused to pay their debts while the Stamp Act was in effect, thereby bringing considerable pressure to bear on mercantile interests to push for repeal in Parliament.

Before news of the crisis precipitated by the Stamp Act reached England, the Greenville ministry was dismissed by the king. The Rockingham ministry, although it lasted only a year, was more responsive to British merchants. The Stamp Act was repealed and the crisis passed.[21] But to ensure its repeal, the ministry was obliged to pass the Declaratory Act. It asserted the legislative authority of Parliament "in all cases whatsoever." Its passage was considered a formality in the colonies. The reference to "legislative" authority was construed as a distinction between "legislation" and "taxation." Parliament intended no such distinction. It considered the Declaratory Act to be an affirmation of its authority to tax the colonies.[22] A year later, a new ministry placed before Parliament both a revenue measure and a plan to reorganize the enforcement of the navigation system (Townshed Act, 1767). The conflict was renewed.

COLONIAL SUPPORT FOR RESISTANCE

Behind the opposition to the policies of the new British empire, there were certainly strong motives of self-interest. Merchants rapidly mobilized

---

[20] Gipson, *Coming of the Revolution*, p. 104.
[21] Miller, *Origins of the American Revolution*, pp. 155–160.
[22] Morgan and Morgan, *Stamp Act Crisis*, pp. 282–296.

in response to the Sugar and Stamp Acts. Both of these acts placed heavy duties on trade. The duties levied by the Sugar Act fell heaviest on the trade of the great colonial ports: Boston, Philadelphia, New York, and Charleston.[23] The main burden of the Stamp Act also fell on trade and shipping. Under the act, ships "had to have stamps for every clearance; for every cocket or bill of lading; for every agreement concerning compensation for transfering goods from one place to another; and for each of four bonds concerning enumerated goods, iron and lumber."[24] These stamps would have cost about £2 for each clearance. Merchants in the commercial provinces were "instigators of the first discontent in the colonies." [25]

The alienation of the merchant community was a crucial development. Merchants played a more extensive role in their communities than the strict definition of "merchant" implies.

> They were not only wholesale and in many cases retail dealers, but the principal importers, exporters, shipowners, bankers, insurers, wharfingers and warehousemen in the chief port cities, with influence comparable to that of the combined mercantile, banking, shipping, import and export, and marine insurance interests in these cities today. Furthermore, the merchants and their lawyers were constantly in touch with each other across colonial lines.[26]

Merchants certainly responded to what they considered to be the ruin of their trade; they were deeply involved in the events of the Stamp Act crisis.[27] Nonetheless, the discontent of the merchant community was but one aspect of a much larger constitutional issue that concerned the rights of the assembly and its position as a bastion of powerful colonial groups.

The issue was the reorganization of the empire and the threat this posed to dominant provincial groups. Colonial leaders were quite aware that the Crown's patronage and influence produced majorities in Parliament. They were also conscious of how their own assemblies countered the extension of such executive "influence" in America. The attempt to levy taxes by act of Parliament was repugnant, not only because it would drain colonial finances but because it would destroy the most important check on the misuse of executive power that the assembly could wield—its control of

---

[23] Oliver M. Dickerson, *The Navigation Acts and the American Revolution* (Philadelphia, 1951), pp. 185–187.

[24] Ibid., p. 191.

[25] Arthur M. Schlesinger, Sr., *The Colonial Merchants and the American Revolution 1763–1776* (1917: New York, 1957), p. 591.

[26] Knollenberg, *Origin of the American Revolution*, p. 140.

[27] Schlesinger, *Colonial Merchants*, pp. 66–68.

the purse. This control was considered to be a right essential to the pre-servation of liberty and property, a right won by Englishmen in the his-toric clash between Parliament and the Crown. A royal government that could ignore the taxing power of the assembly could exert the full range of executive power, precisely the situation assemblies wished to avoid. What Parliament viewed as an intelligent program to place an expanded empire on a firm financial footing was viewed in the colonies as a consti-tutional revolution precipitated by the most treacherous of motives—the destruction of liberty and property. That the Crown could enlist Parlia-ment's support in such a perverse scheme only demonstrated the extent to which patronage and "influence" had perverted the British constitution. Skillfully applying the fruits of colonial taxation where it could create the most influence, the executive would soon be able to regulate the entire range of colonial administration—the governor, the judiciary, the court, and the town. Colonial taxes would feed and enlarge the executive patronage system, and its grasp would spread to the assembly. Liberty would be ex-tinguished. Or so it appeared on the American side of the Atlantic.[28] The Stamp Act precipitated violent and almost universal resistance in conti-nental North America because it was seen as a vital aspect of a much larger imperial program designed to upset the constitutional balance be-tween the assemblies and the executive.

The scope and intensity of the measures taken to reorganize the empire reinforced this perception. By 1765, the colonists had witnessed the fall of the Pitt ministry (1756–1761), a ministry that was considered to be favorable to colonial interests. They had experienced a new and disturbing initiative in judicial tenure and legislative procedure. The Grenville minis-try demanded stricter enforcement of the whole range of Navigation Acts. Customs officers who held posts in the colonies but farmed them out while continuing to live in Great Britain were ordered to their posts. The navy was used in peacetime as an arm of the customs service. A standing army of British regulars was maintained on the continent to guard the frontier. Not a few colonial leaders saw the army as a direct intimidation to ensure compliance with unpopular measures. The Sugar Act had modified the terms of the old navigation system. Revenue as well as regulation became an important tenet of the navigation program. In addition, both the Sugar and the Stamp Act affected the court system. They expanded the jurisdic-tion of executive or Vice-Admiralty Courts.

In Britain, any violation of a revenue measure was tried by a jury in the Exchequer Courts, but in America, those who failed to comply with the

---

[28] Bailyn, *Origins of American Politics*, pp. 3–28.

acts could be prosecuted by customs officials before the Crown-appointed provincial Vice-Admiralty Judge. The case could even be brought to the Vice-Admiralty Court in Halifax, Nova Scotia. At the discretion of the prosecutor, violations could also be tried in colonial courts. The new judicial machinery was not extensively used by royal officials. But colonists, especially merchants, were concerned about potential use and possible abuse. It appeared that the Vice-Admiralty Courts were being expanded specifically and consciously to bypass the provincial common law courts. The Crown, establishing greater financial power in America, was bolstering this by superimposing its own judicial system wherein cases were tried by Crown judges rather than by juries.[29] The Stamp Act crisis was a response to a series of measures that constituted, from the perspective of local assemblies, a concerted effort to curb their powers, thus threatening basic rights and liberties.[30] While the immediate crisis subsided after the repeal of the Stamp Act (1766), the Townshend Acts (1767) reinforced the belief that Parliament and the executive were determined to undermine American liberties.

The repeal of the Stamp Act did not return colonial administration to the *status quo* that had existed prior to 1760. The Sugar Act remained in effect, raising a revenue of about £50,000 between 1766 and 1767.[31] The provisions regarding Vice-Admiralty jurisdiction also remained on the books. The declaration of the Stamp Act Congress had pointedly objected to the revenue aspects of the Sugar Act while affirming that "Trial by Jury is the inherent and invaluable Right of every British Subject in these Colonies."[32] The Townshend Acts were objectionable on both these counts. They placed new duties on colonial imports and created four additional Vice-Admiralty Courts. The new tax measure was attached to a comprehensive reorganization of the customs service. A separate Board of Customs Commissioners was established in America. The new board began to enforce provisions of the Sugar Act that had been largely ignored. Ships traveling more than two leagues (miles) from the coastline had to carry cockets containing a complete list of their cargoes and stating the contents of all packages and their destination. The cockets were to be issued by the customs service for a fee. Any goods not covered by cockets were to be confiscated.[33] The old navigation system placed few restrictions on intercolo-

---

[29] Carl Ubbelohde, *The Vice Admiralty Courts and the American Revolution* (Chapel Hill, 1960), pp. 58–80.

[30] Knollenberg, *Origin of the American Revolution*, pp. 13–14.

[31] George L. Beer, *British Colonial Policy 1754–1765* (1907: Gloucester, 1958), p. 283n.

[32] Morgan and Morgan, *Stamp Act Crisis*, p. 106.

[33] Dickerson, *Navigation Acts*, p. 179.

nial trade in nonenumerated commodities. Now the bulk of intercolonial trade, and even coastal trade within the same colony, could be subject to expensive bureaucratic monitoring, since the best shipping channels often departed more than 7 miles from the coast. Enforcement of these burdensome regulations was selective. Harassment was especially disruptive in New England and South Carolina.[34]

The most ominous aspect of the Townshend Acts was that the taxes collected were to be directly spent to maintain and expand the customs service. Receipts over the cost of collection could also be applied toward the general support of civil administration in the colonies. If there was any policy in the eighteenth century that virtually every colonial assembly had resisted with all the political skill it could command, it was the notion that the assembly should grant taxes to the governor for spending at his discretion. The Crown, with the approbation of Parliament, now intended to create a general fund that could be expended by the ministry for political purposes. In the context of colonial culture, there was nothing more political than an unrestrained executive bureaucracy. The Townshend Acts proposed to expand the customs bureaucracy, to create additional Vice-Admiralty Courts, and to pay the salaries of other royal officials by taxing trade. The patronage system was to be enlarged and its control placed more firmly in the hands of the executive. The colonies, it seemed, were being asked to pay for their own oppression. They refused.

The actions and reactions of the continental colonies and the British Parliament finally provoked armed conflict in April, 1775. Underlying the events that occurred between the conclusion of the Seven Years War and the battles of Lexington and Concord was a fundamental dilemma. The Crown considered financial and administrative reorganization to be essential ingredients in the reconstruction of the empire. It was a program of centralization designed to draw resources from the colonies so that they could be placed at the disposal of the empire as a whole. The new tax revenues could be used to support an imperial program designed by the executive and removed from the adverse influence of provincial assemblies. This reorganization, however, was bound to generate a basic structural shift in the constitutional balance between the assembly and the executive. The empire could be restructured only at the expense of the assembly. Colonial ideology related concretely to the defense of a particular institution. The "Rights of Englishmen," "Liberty" and "Property," were coterminous with the privileges of assemblies. The Revolution preserved a political instrument. It preserved the assembly.

During the eighteenth century, planters, merchants, tradesmen, and

---

[34] Ibid., p. 210.

western farmers had identified with local rather than imperial institutions. The patronage power of the Crown was weak. It could not turn to an entrenched class of officeholders for support. The new empire challenged the assembly. By so doing, it threatened the broad spectrum of colonial interests tied to assemblies. Indeed, the assembly was a key instrument in organizing the resistance to imperial policies. It issued declarations and petitions instrumental in forming colonial opinion. The Committees of Correspondence were organized by assemblies. The Stamp Act Congress and the Continental Congress could claim a legitimate political status because they were the creations of the several assemblies. The Revolution had a center. The center held together remarkably well. There were, certainly, pockets of support for the Crown. But Toryism, for the most part, was not a class movement. No specific colonial interest group can be identified as Tory.[35] The western counties of North and South Carolina did tend to support the Crown. But western farmers and frontiersmen in general were staunch supporters of the Revolution. Tory support on the southern frontier (North and South Carolina and Georgia) was the exception. In these colonies, the eastern seaboard planters, entrenched in the assembly, refused to expand the legislature to represent western constituencies.

Armed struggle between hostile colonial groups did not play a major role in the American Revolution. The assembly organized the forces of independence and held together the structure of local power. In Spanish America, the problem was both independence and the internal balance of power between antagonistic groups. Independence was simultaneously civil war. The Crown recruited loyalists in Peru to crush rebellion in Chile. In North America, the British Crown found less organized support in its rebellious colonies. The Revolution was a constitutional conflict, the final episode in the battle over the rights of the assembly. The strength of the assembly consisted in the fact that it provided the foundation for colonial ideology while it orchestrated the organization of local government. No provincial institution played such a role in Spanish America.

---

[35] Greene, *Reinterpretation of the American Revolution*, p. 46.

Conclusion

THE BEGINNINGS

The epic of Spain in America commenced before the Reformation. Against the cultural and linguistic diversity of pre-Hispanic America, Spain advanced a single language and a single faith.[1] The Spanish state moved decisively in the immediate post-Conquest period to impose a uniform administrative system on the conquests of individual *conquistadores*. The thrust of Spain in America, as in Europe, was toward the construction of a universal order. In America, as in Iberia, unity was the creation of the political determination of the Spanish state. The comprehensive institutions that Spain cast upon the Americas—the church, the state bureaucracy, and the Inquisition—provide a measure of the strength of state participation in the formation of Hispanic culture. The Crown carefully orchestrated the institutional development of colonial society, confidently applying royal practices in Spain to conditions in America. Authority was

---

[1] Octavio Paz, *The Labyrinth of Solitude* (New York, 1961), pp. 89–116.

expressed in institutions constructed and organized by the state bureaucracy. Institutionally, political life reflected the will of the state and not the volition of local interests.

English America was formed during a struggle between Parliament and the king. As a result, the Crown's ability to intervene in the process of society-building was limited at a crucial moment. The conflict in the mother country provided a model of resistance for colonial leaders to follow. In the Spanish Indies, colonization occurred at precisely the moment when the power of the Castilian Cortes was declining. The conquest was undertaken on behalf of the King of Castile. It was in Castile that the Crown had been most successful in minimizing the institutional basis of opposition to royal authority.[2]

Hispanic society was not simply the product of a royal bureaucracy. It also represented the aspirations of conquerors. Yet, even the impact of the *conquistador* tended to reinforce the uniformity of Spanish colonial institutions. The *conquistador*, resting on the labor of a preexisting, easily controlled agricultural society, skillfully reproduced the aristocratic social patterns he had known in Spain. Desirous as he was to enter that world of status and wealth defined by the Crown, the *conquistador* built his new society on the comprehensive institutions provided by the Spanish state. What cultural diversity there was came out of pre-Hispanic America. While merchants, craftsmen, and professionals were also well-represented among the early settlers, they took their places in a cultural system defined by the aristocratic ethos of military adventurers and by the religious and political surveillance of the royal bureaucracy.

The most immediate problems posed by the conquest of a vast, diverse continent were unification and control, and colonial administration was organized for those ends. The Indian population was subdued and subordinated by the new ruling class of *encomenderos*. But the *encomendero* class itself was the target of a royal program that reduced its political significance by installing a class of state officeholders. The rapid extension of royal government to the territory encompassed by the conquest depended on the existence of wealth that could be readily taxed. Precious metals provided the financial base to establish a bureaucratic order. The Crown would have played a more modest role in America if it had paid for imperial organization directly.

Spain alone, of all the nations that came to the Americas, conquered an extensive agricultural society. Spain alone had immediate access to valu-

---

[2] Woodrow W. Borah, "Representative Institutions in the Spanish Empire in the Sixteenth Century: The New World," *The Americas* 12 (January, 1956): 223–233.

able resources—silver and gold—that she could readily use to support royal government. The pace and scale of Spanish colonization was unparalleled anywhere in America. In two decades, her empire expanded from a few Caribbean islands to a huge continental expanse. In the rest of the Americas, colonization was a slow, painful process. Companies, proprietors, and colonists tried with little success to locate valuable resources. The English starved in Virginia; the French went hungry in Quebec. Eventually commercial agriculture and furs, rather than Indian labor and precious metals, formed the basis for other early colonial systems.

Spanish America was the creation of the Renaissance and pre-Reformation Europe. More than a century was to lapse before the English successfully established a permanent settlement in America. English America was the product of both a different culture and a different age. English settlement was the project of commercial companies. Colonization occurred as commerce became a more significant aspect in the English economy and the European system. The control of international trade, rather than political dominance over territory in Europe, provided the new key to the wealth of nations. The Spanish Hapsburgs, using Castile as their base, attempted to maintain a dynastic empire in Europe during the sixteenth century. They identified the power and wealth of the state with territorial dominance, as exemplified by their tendency to export political and religious institutions of control to their possessions in both Europe and America. The preponderant position of Spain in Europe was short-lived. As the seventeenth century was to demonstrate, it was not the state controlling the most territory, but the state carrying the most trade, that gained preeminence. The Dutch and the English emerged from the international conflict of the late sixteenth century as Spain's greatest rivals. It was in this atmosphere of the heightened importance of commercial enterprise that England came to America. England in America was more self-consciously a commercial venture. Spain in America was more explicitly an activity of political and religious domination.

England in America was the achievement of a multiplicity of gods, political arrangements, and economic activities. Institutional development reflected the predisposition of those who participated in colonization and the impact of immediate conditions more than it represented the political will of the English Crown. In its numerous enclaves, the English colonies incorporated a religious and economic diversity that was the offshoot of the English Reformation and a growing economic complexity. This is not to suggest that there was no diversity in Spanish America. The important point is that different groups in English America—planters in Virginia, merchants and Puritans in Massachusetts—came to control the political, social, and religious life of entire provinces. Wealthy miners and merchants may have dominated specific *cabildos* in Spanish American towns. But the overarching political and religious structure, while at times open to their influence, was not of their own creation. The English Puritans originated the congregational system in Massachusetts. The colonial assemblies were initially the extension of popular and familiar procedures practiced by commercial companies. The assembly was not an institution of royal control as was the Spanish *audiencia*. With its diverse political and religious institutions, English America enshrined the usages, customs, and prejudices of particular groups of colonists. The local character of institutions in English America stands in sharp contrast to Hispanic state institutions. This does not mean that the Spanish empire was socially and politically homogeneous; there were differences of consequence both within and between New Spain and Peru. Still, the *audiencia* and the *cabildo* appeared everywhere in Spanish America. By contrast, there was no county court in Massachusetts, and the town meeting did not develop as a significant political institution in Virginia. In English America, local institutions gave expression to the peculiar economic and social conditions of each colony. In Spanish America, the diverse conditions of an entire continent had to find expression in the same set of standardized institutions.

ROYAL GOVERNMENT

The Spanish state dispatched bishops and judges to America. The English sent customs officials. The Spanish state organized an administrative system that stretched from the viceregal capital to the provincial *cabildo*. Power in Hispanic America was bureaucratically based. Men of influence, even if that influence was of purely local significance, typically had a foothold in the bureaucratic structure. Wealth, status, and power were bound to the instruments that tied Spain to America. The bureaucratic weakness of the English Crown presents a striking contrast to the pervasive instruments of royal power that flourished in Spanish America. The influence exerted by the English Crown on provincial society was more limited. The "selectmen" of a New England town, for example, were simply not the creations of royal government. Appointments to county offices in Virginia were regulated by local interests. In English America, lines of authority and influence extended from local political units to the assembly. Although part of the scheme of royal government, the assembly was not governed by the partisans of the Crown. Wealth and status predominantly derived from an individual's position in locally based communities rather than from a bureaucratic office. Royal government in English America was less an overarching structure of power and influence than in Hispanic America.

Colonial administration in the *audiencias* of Spanish America carried out a royal program that was both normative and utilitarian. As a political and religious structure based on kingship and salvation, the Hapsburg bureaucracy was the bastion of a universal moral order that systematically arranged political and religious life. At the same time, the bureaucracy was also a financial organization charged with the task of filtering revenues to the treasury in Madrid. It was an economic watchdog continuously urged by the Council of the Indies to curtail economic practices prejudicial to Spanish commerce. The Hapsburg bureaucracy was most successful in providing for colonial life a normative context that legitimized the religious and political authority of the Spanish state. The importance attached to the maintenance of the normative order reflected the determined adherence of the Spanish Crown to its pre-Reformation origins. As a commercial enterprise established to maintain the Indies as a market for Spanish products and as a source of raw materials to be reexported or utilized by Spanish industry, the achievements of the imperial system are less impressive. The interdependence between the Spanish economy and the economic activities of her colonial possessions deteriorated during the seventeenth century.

Spain failed to crush the Dutch revolt, and the Armada (1588) was unable to clear the North Atlantic sea lanes for Spanish shipping. These setbacks weakened her position as an international entrepôt for the Indies trade. Spain's eroding economic status was reinforced by the decline of the Castilian textile industry in the late sixteenth century. By the seventeenth century, Spain could not meet the demand for manufactured goods nor could she provide a direct market for important colonial exports, such as dyewoods, indigo, and cochineal (red dye), that were used in textile industries. Increasingly, the *flota* system became a complex marketing operation for non-Spanish commodities. The *flota* system continued to operate until the Bourbon program of *comercio libre* was introduced in the eighteenth century, but it was no longer a monopoly system. While it still remained an important channel for the importation of European goods and an outlet for colonial products, the *flota* system had to compete with the contraband operations of the British, French, and Dutch based in the Caribbean islands they controlled. Spain simply could not control the colonial economy from a position of economic, commercial, and military weakness. During the seventeenth century, the economic links that bound America to dependence on Spain were cast aside. The crisis in the Indies trade occurred "not because the American economies were collapsing but because they were developing and disengaging themselves from their primitive dependence on the mother country."[3]

The decline in the Indies trade contributed to economic depression in Spain, but the economies of the New World showed vigorous signs of self-sufficiency. Domestic production of wine, olive oil, and wheat expanded, further depressing the demand for Spanish agricultural products. Internal investments in sugar refineries, cacao, textile production, and leather goods—geared to the demands of domestic markets—increased. The *obrajes* of Quito provided basic textiles for a vast market that extended throughout the Viceroyalty of Peru. In New Spain, the *obrajes* used the cochineal of Oaxaca and the indigo of Guatemala in the production of woolens, silks, cotton mantles, and linen.[4] Silver remittances to Spain dropped not only because of increased competition from colonial agriculture and industry but because colonial merchants purchased contraband merchandise from the English, Dutch, and French. Peruvian merchants invested in the contraband goods brought to the Pacific coast on the Manila—Acapulco fleets. As international rivalry mounted, a greater share of the Crown's silver receipts were spent locally on defense and less were returned to Spain. All these factors underscored Spanish economic weakness in a global economy centered on the commercial dominance of England and Holland. By 1650, the Indies had ceased to be the private economic preserve of the Spanish Crown. It was a shared empire. The silver mines of New Spain and Peru lubricated the commercial transactions of an international trading system that involved Spain's historic European enemies.

Although the monopoly system collapsed, bureaucratic organization was vigorously maintained. This was possible because silver provided an adequate financial base for the bureaucracy. Royal government depended on the existence of wealth that could be readily taxed. Had the wealth of the Indies not defrayed the cost of imperial administration and external defense, the entire edifice might have collapsed under the weight of economic depression in Spain. While Spain continued to profit from the financial system run by its bureaucracy, as time went on, the bureaucracy remitted a decreasing share of American wealth to Madrid. This decline in treasury returns occurred during a time of continued economic growth and substantial silver production in the Americas.

---

[3] John Lynch, *Spain Under the Hapsburgs*, 2 vols. (Oxford, 1964–1969), vol. 2, *Spain and America 1578–1700*, p. 193.

[4] Brian R. Hamnett, *Politics and Trade in South Mexico, 1750–1821* (Cambridge, Eng., 1971), p. 3.

The heart of the problem was commercial. Since Spain could not supply American markets with sufficient manufactured goods to meet growing demands, and since she did not provide an adequate outlet for colonial exports, her role in determining the structure of the colonial economy was less forceful than that played by Great Britain in the economic organization of English America. The *flota* system, while it adequately protected silver shipments, proved an inflexible commercial instrument. The erratic fleet sailings were a deterrent to the growth of colonial exports. One of the consequences of this situation was to stimulate economic activities in the colonies oriented toward domestic markets. As the importance of Spain's economic links to America decayed, the capacity of those links to generate contributions to the royal treasury also declined. Desperately attempting to develop new sources of revenue, the Crown adopted expedients, such as the sale of bureaucratic offices, that weakened its control over the bureaucracy and, in the long run, reduced its revenues. Unwilling to finance the collection of important taxes, such at the sales tax (*alcabala*) and Indian tribute, by maintaining a class of well-paid officials, the Crown farmed out tax collection to individuals and corporations. The bureaucracy was sold to local interests. The ability of the Crown to monitor the performance of public officials at the local level, such as the *corregidor* and his assistants (*tenientes*), had so deteriorated that when the Crown finally reformed local administration in the eighteenth century, it eliminated the *corregimientos* entirely, substituting a new system of intendancies.

While the direct ties between the Spanish and American economies languished during the seventeenth century, the close relationship between the bureaucracy and local economic structures continued. Bureaucratic officials were often investors in economic activities expressly forbidden by the Laws of the Indies. Treasury officials in Zacatecas (New Spain) advanced credit to miners, thereby providing capital for the industry. *Corregidores*, often financed by merchants, issued cash, basic equipment, and commodities to the Indian population. In return, the Indians redeemed their debts in the products of the region. These goods were then turned over to merchants who sold them at considerable profit. In Oaxaca, the production of cochineal, a dye essential to the textile industry, was supported by a complex network of interests involving *corregidores*, Indian communities, the *obrajes*, the merchant guild (*consulado*) of Mexico City, and the *audiencia*.[5] In the Kingdom of Quito, *Oidores* invested in the *obrajes* that supplied textiles to much of the Viceroyalty of Peru. Compromised by its economic entanglements, the Hapsburg bureaucracy played

---

[5] Ibid., pp. 5–8.

a self-interested role in the implementation of royal cedulas pertaining to important economic practices. Notable in this regard were the vain attempts of the Council of the Indies to regulate the use of Indian labor. The bureaucracy and local interests combined to moderate or reverse the plans of the Crown.

While the collapse of the Indies trade marked the economic disengagement of the Hispanic world, it did not precipitate an estrangement between colonial society and royal government. The bureaucracy continued omnipresent in the Spanish Indies. It preserved a normative order while it influenced the organization of economic life. It provided a structure for both the pursuit of salvation and self-interest. Influenced by wealthy Creoles and Peninsular Spaniards, the bureaucracy was not just the tool of the Crown. Creoles purchased seats on the local cabildo; they became corregidores, held treasury offices, and eventually even dominated the Viceregal Audiencias of Lima and Mexico City. When wealthy creoles coopted the bureaucracy to the detriment of the royal exchequer and the Laws of the Indies, one consequence was to tie their class to the maintenance of royal government.[6] The Hapsburg bureaucracy positioned itself between the demands of a weak state and strong local pressures. The bureaucracy provided a way of balancing in different ways, at different places and at different times, the financial interests of the Crown, the religious mission of the church, and the economic interests of miners and merchants, Creoles and Peninsular Spaniards. Underlying what appeared to be a uniform symmetrical structure of offices arranged hierarchically from the august viceroyalty to the municipal council (cabildo), was in fact a decentralized series of relatively autonomous units that could circumvent the apparently superior jurisdiction of other bureaucratic bodies and officials. The local cabildo, the audiencia, the viceroy, and the bishop could all be arrayed against one another in a complex bureaucratic struggle that might, at root, pertain to the financial operations of the corregidor. The Hapsburg system of competing jurisdictions reinforced the local character of compromises between officials and influential groups. When there was conflict, it almost always centered in the bureaucracy. But the government of Charles III (1759–1788) embarked upon a program of bureaucratic and commercial reform that aggressively asserted the authority of the Crown, and challenged the old Hapsburg system.

---

[6] Gabriel Ardant, "Financial Policy and Economic Infrastructures of Modern States and Nations," in The Formation of National States in Western Europe, ed. Charles Tilly, (Princeton, in press).

In the late sixteenth century when the Hakluyts urged the Queen and their fellow Englishmen to undertake a program of colonization in America, they submitted a design to increase and control trade. When successful colonies were finally established in the early seventeenth century, they were organized under the auspices of joint stock companies. Colonial English America was a commercial enterprise. The framework of empire was provided by Navigation Acts passed by Parliament. Compared to the character of Spanish America, institutions of royal control did not exercise as decisive an influence on the development of colonial society. These two phenomena, the primacy of commercial organization and the weakness of the royal government, were closely related. The English Civil War enhanced the constitutional position of Parliament and retarded the growth of an independent royal executive. The attempt of the restored Stuart monarchy to expand institutions of royal control in both England and America was thwarted by the Glorious Revolution in England and by a series of insurrections in America that led the new monarchy to restore colonial assemblies and to abandon the Stuart program of Dominion government. The development of English America occurred during English commercial expansion when mercantile interests could decisively influence domestic and foreign policy.

The defeat of royal power in England decreased the significance of Crown institutions. There was no royal official in England equivalent to the Spanish *corregidor* or the French intendant. Compared to the central importance of the royal bureaucracy in both France and Spain, royal government in England was fundamentally curtailed by the political events of the seventeenth century. The Crown alone could not set up in America the kind of royal government already repudiated at home. After the Glorious Revolution, the expansion of royal power would have required the active participation of Parliament. Given the commercial orientation of English foreign policy, we should ask, as did Walpole: What additional advantage was to be gained by the aggressive extension of royal government in the colonies?

European states in the eighteenth century extended central administration to extract greater resources from local units. Had England constructed a more comprehensive bureaucratic organization in colonial America, the primary rationale would certainly have been extractive—to monitor the collection of new taxes. But until the period of the Seven Years War (1756–1763), such a policy appeared, from the perspective of mercantile interests, to be both undesirable and unnecessary. Great Britain's growing trade provided the foundation for her fiscal capacity. The great bulk of her revenues came from the taxation of commercial activities.[7] Already established as an entrepôt for colonial products, especially sugar and tobacco, she was able to tax these imports when they entered Britain rather than having to rely on the more expensive and complex procedure of setting up a bureaucratic apparatus to tax colonial production at its source. The strength of Britain's military and commercial position within the global European economy made it possible for her to maintain at home a single financial operation that could tax colonial imports and foreign reexports channeled through her seaports. This system proved adequate until the Seven Years War. Direct taxation in the colonies was viewed as commercially unsound, since it would reduce the ability of the colonies to purchase British manufactured goods. Walpole's ministry (1722–1742) completed the abolition of all duties on the export of British manufactures.[8] In America, royal government developed in juxtaposition to a diminished royal authority in England and a commercial program that did not appear to require an extensive bureaucracy. England's economic strength was based on her role as the entrepôt for colonial products and the supplier of manufactured goods, a position reinforced by the superiority of her industrial capacity. England defined the colonial problem as primarily a commercial problem.

The Spanish state faced a different problem in the post-Conquest period. The production of precious metals was the most valuable economic activity in the Indies. To tap this wealth effectively, the Crown sent its bureaucracy directly to the source of production to control the movement of raw ore to the refinery and from there to the royal mint, where the Crown's share was deducted. The silver mines of New Spain and Peru solved the problem of supporting royal administration. A Cortes was never convened in the New World because the Crown did not levy direct taxes.[9] Financially, the Spanish system was extractive and it required, in accordance with the practices of the period, an extensive bureaucracy to oversee its operation. The bureaucracy was charged with the collection of internal taxes on sales and production. Consistent with the experience of other state systems, the Crown found it extremely difficult to efficiently tax an economy characterized by small scattered enterprises and dispersed economic transactions. The Crown was most successful in taxing silver production since mining, refining, and minting were relatively concentrated activities.

---

[7] For a discussion on this point, see Ardant, "Financial Policy."

[8] William Kennedy, *English Taxation, 1640–1799* (1913: London, 1964), pp. 96–99.

[9] Borah, "Representative Institutions," pp. 252–253.

In English America, royal government was not generally a tax-gathering agency. The customs service collected the plantation duty, and the customs was the most extensive bureaucratic organization in America. But it was not established to provide a revenue for the British exchequer. In fact, the maintenance of the customs service in America was at the expense of the British treasury. The function of the customs was to regulate trade rather than to collect taxes. As a regulatory agency, the American customs was by no means a model of effectiveness. Officials appointed to the customs regularly leased their duties to subordinates in the colonies while they remained in England collecting their salaries. Customs officers were easy marks for a well-placed bribe. The success of the navigation system can certainly not be attributed to the high standards of British bureaucrats in America. It was England's commercial strength, superior credit operations, and cheap, competitive manufactured goods of high quality that provided the real cement of the empire. Were this not so, the Navigation Acts would have been as difficult to enforce as many aspects of the Laws of the Indies.

The economy of Hispanic America may have disengaged itself from dependency on Spain. Still, the impact of the Spanish bureaucracy on the organization of economic life remained strong. In English America, royal officials did not play so direct a role in the economy. There was no royal monopoly on mercury; no large royal treasury; no sales tax; and no merchant *aviadores* capitalizing the economic activities of royal officials. Instead there were enumerated commodities to be transported to England and reexported to additional European markets. There were demands for English manufactured goods to be filled. The Spanish empire was based on silver. The British empire was based on tobacco, sugar, fish, and rum. The British economy, and the navigation system that supported it, exerted a tremendous influence on colonial production and consumption. The opening of additional tobacco markets by British merchants stimulated production in the Chesapeake region and fostered the growth of plantation agriculture and the slave labor system. The activities of New England merchants were geared to offset the persistent balance of payments deficit they incurred with Great Britain. The navigation system maintained, and was intended to maintain, the economic dependence of English America on Britain. Mercantile interests in Britain were determined to avoid the "fatal danger" —that the Northern colonies would begin to manufacture for themselves. In fact, it may well be that the domestic economies of New Spain and important areas of Peru were more self-sufficient and industrially productive between 1650 and 1750 than either the Southern or Northern colonies. The present pattern of economic underdevelopment and dependency, characteristic of Spanish America, is not inherent in the colonial situation of the seventeenth and eighteenth centuries. It is a phenomenon that should be explained rather than assumed.

The continued vitality of the navigation system—British trade continued to prosper—and the opposition of the Whig ministries (1714–1760) to colonial taxation made an aggressive extension of royal power appear unnecessary. Royal government was allowed to deteriorate. It was not, of course, the policy of the Whig ministries to reduce the significance of royal authority in America. It was the provincial assemblies that systematically attacked royal power and established common precedents that undermined the governor's constitutional position. The lever used to dislodge the power of the governor was the control exercised by the assembly over the granting and disbursement of revenues. The power of the royal executive to levy taxes unilaterally was eliminated in the political upheavals of the seventeenth century. The cost of administration in America was usually defrayed by the appropriations of individual assemblies. While assemblies appropriated funds to cover these costs, they did so on their own terms. Although the Board of Trade insisted that they had to establish permanent revenues to support royal administration, the assemblies refused to make such grants. Using the control of the purse, they continued to gain ground throughout the eighteenth century. By the end of the Seven Years War, the assembly dominated political life in the colonies. The restricted patronage power of the governor made it extremely difficult for him to create a political base in the assembly. The limited scope of the royal bureaucracy prevented it from developing into a structure that could absorb significant colonial interests. The institution that expressed and channeled the political aspirations of influential colonial groups was the assembly.

Both in English and Spanish America colonists turned royal government to their own ends. In Spanish America, wealthy colonists infiltrated bureaucratic structures. They prevented the enforcement of royal cedulas inimical to their interests by waging covert and complicated bureaucratic struggles. In English America, opposition to the Crown was directly expressed in local assemblies. Conflict had a sharpness that was absent in the byzantine politics of Hispanic America. In Spanish America, royal government encompassed both the city of god and the city of man. The bureaucracy distributed political power, financed economic activities, and saved souls. Royal government in English America did not control salvation. The New England Puritan saved his soul without the assistance of intervening royal institutions. An internal, moral universe was constructed in Massachusetts before the Crown rescinded the colony's charter. In Virginia, laymen controlled the Anglican vestry. The social organization of Virginia gave free rein to the interests of planters. The Crown did not impose a system of religious or social priorities. Both god and the economy underwent a profound change in seventeenth-century England and this social turbulence was exported to America. Royal government was not a moral, unified enterprise on the scale of Spanish America. It was, much more self-consciously, an enterprise to be evaluated in the customs house.

The colonies of English America did not inherit a common religious framework. They were divided religiously, ethnically, and economically. But they did inherit a common political institution—the assembly. The assembly was the locus of internal conflicts and a center of opposition to the Crown. It levied taxes; appointed officials of local significance; supported religious establishments; issued paper currency; protected merchants and planters; and controlled its own system of patronage. It was the assembly that upheld "liberty," safeguarded the "rights of Englishmen," and protected "property;" it furnished a common ideology. In English America, the assembly sustained the moral universe.

THE REORGANIZATION OF EMPIRE, AND INDEPENDENCE

In the period following the Seven Years War, both England and Spain undertook substantial reforms that provoked strong resistance, and ultimately revolt, in their colonies. The object of the Bourbon reform program was to reconstruct colonial administration. Bourbon policy was influenced by the doctrine of Enlightened Despotism. The Bourbons saw Spanish backwardness as the consequence of a poorly organized state in which an inefficient local bureaucracy squandered financial resources before they could be remitted to Madrid. If the state could directly control local government with its own cadre of loyal officials staunchly safeguarding the interests of the Crown, then a more powerful and efficient state system could be constructed. Acting from a position of strength, the state could reform society. Tradition was no longer to be a sufficient justification for the existence of institutions. Practices were judged in terms of their usefulness to the state, and an administrative structure was judged particularly useful if it took resources from local units and applied them toward the more general welfare of the state. This basic philosophy of reform, already applied in Spain, was applied to America after 1763. But Bourbon reform in Spain was cautious and tentative compared to the vigorous program pursued in America. At home, the monarchy was more reluctant to alienate its traditional bases of support—the church and the aristocracy. In America, less prudence was displayed. Since the colonial bureaucracy played such an important role in colonial life, a basic shift in its goals and organization was bound to have serious consequences.

The critical importance of the Bourbon reforms consists in their disruption of colonial society and bureaucratic administration. In Spanish America, the bureaucracy juggled the discordant interests of groups and institutions. But as the pace of economic change accelerated in response to commercial reforms (*comercio libre*), the colonial bureaucracy faced difficulties on several fronts. It had to somehow accommodate a new merchant class, and it had to placate established groups threatened by new economic activities. At the same time, its ability to act was undercut by the divisive administrative reforms introduced from Madrid. In the situation of uncertainty created by Napoleon's invasion of Spain, bureaucratic authority collapsed. The independence movement began as a struggle for control of the bureaucratic system. It culminated in its destruction. The process of emancipation in Spanish America was considerably more painful, complex, and socially disruptive than was true of the revolution in English America.[10] Goya's gruesome painting of Saturn devouring his children vividly portrays the character of independence. That revolution in Spanish America was simultaneously civil war is directly related to the nature of bureaucratic organization and the character of the Bourbon reforms.

In Spanish America, the revolts that began in 1810 must be seen in relation to the preceding decades of reform. The Bourbon reforms altered the relationship of the bureaucracy to society. Following the example of other enlightened despots, the bureaucracy—headed by the new Bourbon bureaucrat—became more overtly an extractive apparatus. Taxes were no longer farmed out to local corporations such as the *cabildo*; instead, they were collected more efficiently by treasury officials appointed directly from Madrid. A concerted effort was made to replace Creole officials with Peninsular Spaniards. The political role of the church was reduced. The new Bourbon order was more overtly secular; salvation was less important. The intendancy reform was the high-water mark of the new Bourbon institutions. It was opposed by a combination of interests that varied in each *audiencia*. The structure of political and economic power shifted, both as a consequence of structural changes in the bureaucracy and as a result of more autonomous changes in other areas of society. Free trade and the creation of new political units—intendancies and viceroyalties—

---

[10] Charles C. Griffith, "Economic and Social Aspects of the Era of Spanish American Independence," *Hispanic American Historical Review* 29 (1949): 174–176.

resulted in the emergence of new centers of political and economic power. The Bourbon reforms set in motion a transformation of colonial society.

As this transformation gained momentum, the fortunes of different groups—Creoles and Peninsular Spaniards, the old monopolistic merchants and the new merchants of free trade, the army and the church, the *corregidores* and the intendants, planters and textile producers—rose and fell in different combinations throughout the New World. The conflict engendered by reform gravitated to bureaucratic institutions. Individuals, loosely organized groups, corporations, and institutions clashed as they attempted to influence the bureaucracy. This in itself was not a novel situation. But the role played by the bureaucracy itself in such confrontations was dramatically shifting. It served less as a mediator between conflicting groups or as the guardian of a normative order, and became instead the partisan instrument of the Crown. Its function was to overcome the opposition of local groups—by force if necessary—to the financial and administrative program of the Bourbon state. Whether resisted by the Jesuits, Creole bureaucrats, Peninsular merchants, or local *cabildos*, the Crown's policies were to be enforced. Over widespread and often violent opposition, reform continued.[11] In the process, the new bureaucracy alienated in different ways and with varying degrees of intensity practically every important group in colonial society. Moreover, this conflict occurred at a time of rapid social change. New economic interests and centers of power—such as the merchants of Guadalajara and Buenos Aires—challenged more established groups and the political dominance of the old viceregal capitals, Mexico City and Lima.

The long period of Bourbon reform (1765–1805) alienated the bureaucracy from society. It was no longer meshed with local structures of power that protected colonial interests. It no longer sustained a traditional, normative order. The bureaucracy stood exposed as the naked, authoritarian agent of the Bourbon state—an unmasking that was especially serious in the ideological atmosphere created by the independence of English America. The Spanish American revolts coincided with a far-reaching transformation in the colonies. The deep divisions caused by the Bourbon program carried over into the independence movements.

Independence began in the complicated maneuvering that took place in response to events in Spain. Faced with the question of whether or not to recognize the Junta of Seville as the legitimate representative of Spanish

---

[11] Sergio Villalobos R., "Opposition to Imperial Taxation," in *The Origins of the Latin American Revolutions 1808–1826*, ed. R. A. Humphreys and John Lynch (New York, 1965), pp. 124–137.

authority, the bureaucracy could not provide a united response. Colonial interests quickly formed behind the viceroy, *audiencia*, or *cabildo*. The struggle that began in 1810, when the *cabildos* of Caracas and Buenos Aires rejected the authority of superior bureaucratic units, was bitter, prolonged, and destructive. It was a civil war in the midst of revolution. The Bourbon reforms banished the old gods of the Hapsburg order. They were never to return.

In Spanish America, independence occurred as the concordant framework sustained by the colonial bureaucracy deteriorated. In English America, when revolution occurred, the assembly was already a key institution—a focus of social integration. Representative of important colonial interests, the assembly was the agent, rather than the enemy, of local power. The revolt pitted colonial groups against the Crown rather than against each other. The revolution did not take place in the midst of any comprehensive process of social reorganization comparable to the significant changes that were occurring in Spanish America on the eve of revolt. This was not a period that witnessed a dramatic growth or decline in colonial exports or industry, a shift in basic internal economic networks or external commercial ties. The struggle against the Crown arose in a social environment that was relatively stable. The proponents of independence in Spanish America had, at all times, to contend with a turbulent social and economic environment.

The program of the new British ministry (1760) was not posited on the philosophic principles of Enlightened Despotism. It was not a grandiose plot to destroy the "rights of Englishmen." But it did represent an important shift in policy from commercial to fiscal considerations. Given the size of the national debt and the growing burden placed on the treasury by the expanded postwar empire, the executive was determined to ease this burden by levying taxes in America. But it was precisely the right to control taxation that gave the assembly its political leverage against the Crown. What appeared to Parliament to be moderate tax reforms amounted to a constitutional revolution in America. It was the support the assembly enjoyed in various provinces—its harmonious relationship to society— that made possible a concerted response to the financial reforms of the British executive and Parliament. In a sense, the assembly had become more legitimate than its rival, the royal executive. Since the executive did not maintain a class of civil and ecclesiastical bureaucrats who controlled access to vital resources, significant colonial interests were not committed to the maintenance of royal government with the tenacity that characterized the situation in many parts of Spanish America. It was difficult for the Crown to find a wedge to drive between competing groups. The two most important economic interests—merchants and planters—were not involved in competition for political ascendancy in the same institution. They exerted their political power in separate provincial assemblies. In Spanish America, especially New Spain, Creoles and Peninsular Spaniards were arrayed against each other at almost every bureaucratic level.

In English America, colonial society did not simmer for several decades in the face of unpopular reforms. Reaction to the Stamp Act was almost immediate. The assemblies played a central role in shaping this reaction. The Crown attacked the center. The center resisted. Resistance to the mother country in English America was organized by the most comprehensive political institution, the assembly. The Continental Congress was its creation. The problem of authority was resolved before the revolution commenced. In Spanish America, the institutional base of the revolt was the *cabildo*, the least comprehensive political unit. The problem of authority, the issue of who should govern and to whose benefit, was at the heart of the rebellion. The independence movement in Spanish America faced a situation fundamentally more complex than the difficulties experienced by revolutionary leaders in English America. The assembly could levy taxes, raise armies, and issue currency. It was an established institution that held together the dominant interests of colonial society. The revolution in English America sustained and defended a basic, operating, legitimate institutional framework. The ideology of the revolution came from the assembly. The *cabildo* had none of these advantages. It did not have the legitimacy of the assembly. It represented local interests and was not structured to contain the diverse interests of colonial society. The independence movement in Spanish America was directed against an established institutional order. It faced the enormously difficult task of both dismantling and constructing institutions simultaneously. In English America, the assembly was instrumental in setting up a single, independent state. But in the aftermath of independence, there was no institution that could play such a role in Spanish America. The revolutions produced weak states whose resources were soon engrossed by Anglosaxon entrepreneurs. The buccaneers returned.

Selected Bibliography

SPAIN IN AMERICA

Aiton, Arthur S. "Spanish Colonial Reorganization under the Family Compact." *Hispanic American Historical Review* 12 (1932): 269–280.

Aiton, Arthur S. *Antonio de Mendoza, First Viceroy of New Spain.* Durham, 1927.

Alden, Dauril, Ed. *Colonial Roots of Modern Brazil.* Berkeley, 1973.

Alden, Dauril. *Royal Government in Brazil.* Berkeley, 1968.

Alden, Dauril. "The Undeclared War of 1773–1777: Climax of Luso–Spanish Platine Rivalry." *Hispanic American Historical Review* 41 (February, 1961): 55–74.

Arcila Farías, Eduardo. *Comercio entre Venezuela y Mexico en los siglos xvi y xvii.* Mexico, 1950.

Ardant, Gabriel. "Financial Policy and Economic Infrastructures of Modern States and Nations." In *The Formation of National States in Western Europe*, edited by Charles Tilly. Princeton, in press.

Bakewell, Peter J. *Silver Mining and Society in Colonial Mexico: Zacatecas, 1546–1700.* Cambridge, Eng., 1971.

Bayle, Constantino. *Los cabildos seculares en la América española.* Madrid, 1952.

Bobb, Bernard. *The Viceregency of Antonio Maria Bucareli: 1771–1779.* Austin, 1962.

Borah, Woodrow W. *Early Colonial Trade and Navigation between Mexico and Peru.* Berkeley, 1954. (Ibero–Americana 38)

Borah, Woodrow W. *New Spain's Century of Depression.* Berkeley, 1951. (Ibero–Americana 35)

Borah, Woodrow W. "Representative Institutions in the Spanish Empire in the Sixteenth Century: The New World." *The Americas* 12 (January, 1956): 246–257.

Borah, Woodrow W. *Silk Raising in Colonial Mexico.* Berkeley, 1943. (Ibero-Americana 20).

Borah, Woodrow W., and Cook, Shelburne. *The Aboriginal Population of Central Mexico on the Eve of the Spanish Conquest.* Berkeley, 1963.

Bourne, Edward Gaylard. *Spain in America.* New York, 1904.

Boxer, Charles R. *The Golden Age of Brazil.* Cambridge, Eng., 1962.

Boxer, Charles R. *The Portuguese Seaborne Empire.* New York, 1969.

Brading, D. A., and Cross, Harry E. "Colonial Silver Mining: Mexico and Peru." *Hispanic American Historical Review* 52 (November, 1972): 545–579.

Brown, Vera Lee. "Contraband Trade as a Factor in the Decline of Spain's Empire in America." *Hispanic American Historical Review* 7 (1928): 662–678.

Brown, Vera Lee. "The South Sea Company and Contraband Trade." *American Historical Review* 31 (July, 1926): 662–678.

Castañeda, C. E. "The Corregidor in Spanish Colonial Administration." *Hispanic American Historical Review* 9 (November, 1929): 446–470.

Chevalier, François. *Land and Society in Colonial Mexico.* Berkeley, 1963. First published in French under the title, *La Formation des grands domaines au Mexique.* Paris, 1952.

Christelow, Allan. "Contraband Trade between Jamaica and the Spanish Main, and the Free Port Act of 1766." *Hispanic American Historical Review* 22 (May, 1942): 309–343.

Christelow, Allan. "Economic Background of the Anglo–Spanish War of 1762." *Journal of Modern History* 18 (1946): 22–36.

Christelow, Allan. "French Interest in the Spanish Empire during the Ministry of the Duc de Choiseul, 1759–1771." *Hispanic American Historical Review* 21 (1941): 515–537.

Christelow, Allan. "Great Britain and the Trades from Cadiz and Lisbon to Spanish America and Brazil, 1759–1783." *Hispanic American Historical Review* 27 (1947): 2–29.

Christian, William A., Jr. *Person and God in a Spanish Valley.* New York, 1972.

Curtin, Philip D. *The Atlantic Slave Trade.* Madison, 1969.

Descola, Jean. *Daily Life in Colonial Peru.* London, 1968.

Dusenberry, W. H. "Woolen Manufacturing in 16th Century Spain." *The Americas* 4 (1947–1948): 223–234.

Elliott, J. H. *Imperial Spain 1469–1716.* New York, 1963.

Elliott, J. H. *The Revolt of the Catalans.* Cambridge, Eng., 1963.

Fairnie, D. A. "Commercial Empire of the Atlantic, 1607–1783." *Economic History Review* 15 (1962): 205–216.

Farriss, N. M. *Crown and Clergy in Colonial Mexico, 1759–1821.* London, 1968.

Fisher, H. E. S. "Anglo–Portuguese Trade, 1700–1750." *Economic History Review* 16 (1963): 219–233.

Fisher, John. "The Intendant System and the Cabildos of Peru, 1784–1810." *Hispanic American Historical Review* 49 (August, 1969): 430–453.

Fisher, Lillian Estelle. *The Last Inca Revolt 1780–1783.* Norman, Ok., 1966.

Fisher, Lillian Estelle. "Teodoro de Croix." *Hispanic American Historical Review* 9 (1929): 489–504.

Fisher, Lillian Estelle. *Viceregal Administration in the Spanish American Colonies.* Berkeley, 1926.
Floyd, Troy S. "The Guatemalan Merchants, the Government and the Provincianos, 1750–1800." *Hispanic American Historical Review* 41 (February, 1961): 90–110.
Gates, Eunice Joiner. "Don José Antonio de Areche: His Own Defense." *Hispanic American Historical Review* 8 (February, 1928): 14–42.
Gibson, Charles. *The Aztecs under Spanish Rule.* Stanford, 1964.
Gibson, Charles. *Spain in America.* New York, 1966.
Goebel, D. B. "British Trade to the Spanish Colonies 1796–1823." *American Historical Review* 43 (1938): 288–320.
Gómara, López de. *Cortés: The Life of the Conqueror by His Secretary López de Gómara.* Edited by Leslie Byrd Simpson. Berkeley, 1964.
Góngora, Mario. *El estado en el derecho indiana, época de fundación, 1492–1570.* Santiago de Chile, 1951.
Greenleaf, R. E. "The Obraje in the Late Mexican Colony." *The Americas* 23 (1967): 227–250.
Griffin, Charles C. "Economic and Social Aspects of the Era of Spanish American Independence." *Hispanic American Historical Review* 29 (1949): 170–187.
Guthrie, Chester L. "Colonial Economy, Trade Industry and Labor in the 17th Century." *Revista de Historia de America* 7 (December, 1939): 103–134.
Hamill, Hugh M., Jr. *The Hidalgo Revolt Prelude to Mexican Independence.* Gainesville, 1966.
Hamilton, Earl J. *American Treasure and the Price Revolution in Spain 1501–1650.* Cambridge, Mass., 1934. Reprint ed., New York, 1965.
Hamnett, Brian R. *Politics and Trade in South Mexico, 1750–1821.* Cambridge, Eng., 1971.
Hanke, Lewis. *The Imperial City of Potosí.* The Hague, 1956.
Hanke, Lewis. *The Spanish Struggle for Justice.* Philadelphia, 1949.
Haring, Clarence H. *The Spanish Empire in America.* New York, 1947.
Haring, Clarence H. *Trade and Navigation between Spain and the Indies in the Time of the Hapsburgs.* Cambridge, Mass., 1918.
Hartz, Louis. *The Founding of New Societies.* New York, 1964.
Herr, Richard. *The Eighteenth-Century Revolution in Spain.* Princeton, 1958.
Herr, Richard. *Spain.* Englewood Cliffs, 1971.
Humphreys, R. A. *Tradition and Revolt in Latin America.* London, 1969.
Humphreys, R. A., and Lynch, John, Eds. *The Origins of the Latin American Revolutions 1808–1826.* New York, 1965.
Hussey, R. D. *The Caracas Company, 1728–1784.* Cambridge, Mass., 1934.
Kamen, Henry. *The War of Spanish Succession 1700–1715.* London, 1969.
Keen, Benjamin, Ed. *Readings in Latin American Civilization.* Boston, 1955.
Koenigsberger, Helmut. *The Government of Sicily under Philip II of Spain: A Study in the Practice of Empire.* New York, 1951.
Lee, Raymond L. "American Cochineal in European Commerce 1526–1625." *Journal of Modern History* 23 (1951): 205–224.
Lee, Raymond L. "Cochineal Production and Trade in New Spain to 1600." *The Americas* 4 (1947–48): 449–473.
Levene, Ricardo. *A History of Argentina.* Translated by William Spence Robertson. Chapel Hill, 1937. Reprint ed., New York, 1963.
Lockhart, James. *The Men of Cajamarca.* Austin, 1972.
Lockhart, James. *Spanish Peru, 1532–1560; A Colonial Society.* Madison, 1968.

240

Selected Bibliography

Lohmann Villena, Guillermo. *El corregidor de Indios en el Perú bajo Los Austrias.* Madrid, 1957.
Lohmann Villena, Guillermo. *Las relaciones de los virreyes del Perú.* Seville, 1959.
Lovett, Gabriel. *Napoleon and the Birth of Modern Spain.* New York, 1965.
Lynch, John. "Intendants and Cabildos in the Viceroyalty of the Rio de la Plata." *Hispanic American Historical Review* 35 (1955): 337–362.
Lynch, John. *Spain under the Hapsburgs.* 2 vols. Oxford, 1964–1969.
Lynch, John. *Spanish Colonial Administration, 1782–1810; The Intendancy System in the Viceroyalty of the Rio de la Plata.* New York, 1958.
McAlister, Lyle N. *The Fuero Militar in New Spain 1764–1800.* Gainesville, 1957.
McAlister, Lyle N. "Social Structure and Social Change in New Spain." *Hispanic American Historical Review* 43 (1963):
Mariluz Urquijo, José Mariá. *Ensayos sobre los juicios de residencia indianos.* Seville, 1952.
Marzahl, Peter. "Elite and Government: The Cabildo of Popayan." *Hispanic American Historical Review,* forthcoming.
Maxwell, Kenneth. "Pombal and the Nationalization of the Luso–Brazilian Economy" *Hispanic Historical Review* 48 (1968): 586–607.
Moore, John P. *The Cabildo in Peru under the Bourbons.* Durham, 1966.
Moore, John P. *The Cabildo in Peru under the Hapsburgs.* Durham, 1954.
Neasham, Aubrey V. "Spain's Emigrants to the New World." *Hispanic American Historical Review* 19 (1939): 147–160.
Nelson, George H. "Contraband Trade under the Asiento 1730–1739. *American Historical Review* 51 (October, 1945): 55–67.
Nettels, Curtis. "England and the Spanish American Trade, 1680–1715." *Journal of Modern History* 3 (March, 1931): 1–32.
Pagden, A. R. *Hernan Cortés: Letters from Mexico.* New York, 1971.
Parry, John H. *The Establishment of the European Hegemony.* New York, 1966. Earlier published under the title, *Europe and a Wider World.*
Parry, John H. *The Sale of Public Offices in the Spanish Indies under the Hapsburgs.* Berkeley, 1953. (Ibero–Americana 37)
Parry, John H. *The Spanish Seaborne Empire.* New York, 1966.
Parry, John H. *The Spanish Theory of Empire in the 16th Century.* Cambridge, Eng., 1940.
Phelan, John L. "Authority and Flexibility in the Spanish Imperial System." *Administrative Science Quarterly* 5 (June, 1960): 47–65.
Phelan, John L. *The Kingdom of Quito.* Madison, 1967.
Pike, Frederick. "The Municipality and the System of Checks and Balances in the Spanish Colonial System." *The Americas* 15 (October, 1958): 139–158.
Prado, Caio. *The Colonial Background of Modern Brazil.* Berkeley, 1967.
Prescott, William H. *The History of the Conquest of Mexico.* [1843] Abridged and edited by C. Harvey Gardiner. Chicago, 1966.
Prescott, William H. *The Conquest of Peru.* [1847] Edited by Victor W. von Hagen. New York, 1961.
Priestly, Herbert Ingram. *José de Gálvez, Visitor General of New Spain 1765–1771.* Berkeley, 1916.
Romiro, Emilio. *Historia económica del Perú.* Buenos Aires, 1949.
Rowe, John Howland. "The Incas under Spanish Colonial Institutions." *Hispanic American Historical Review* 37 (1957): 156–191.

Rubio y Moreno, Luis, Ed. *Pasajeros a Indias*. 2 vols. Madrid, 1930.
Schäfer, Ernesto. *El consejo real y supremo de las Indias*. 2 vols. Seville, 1934–1947.
Schurz, William Lytle. *The Manilla Galleon*. New York, 1939.
Simpson, Leslie Byrd. *The Encomienda in New Spain*. Berkeley, 1950.
Simpson, Leslie Byrd. *Many Mexicos*. Rev. ed. Berkeley, 1971.
Sluiter, Engel. "Dutch–Spanish Rivalry in the Caribbean Area, 1594–1609." *Hispanic American Historical Review* 28 (1948): 165–196.
Smith, Robert. "The Institution of the Consulado in New Spain," *Hispanic American Historical Review* 24 (1944): 61–83.
Stein, Stanley, and Stein, Barbara. *The Colonial Heritage of Latin America*. Oxford, 1970.
Swanson, Guy E. "To Live in Concord with Society." In *Cooley and Sociological Analysis*, edited by Albert J. Reiss, Jr. Ann Arbor, 1968.
Swanson, Guy E. *Religion and Regime*. Ann Arbor, 1967.
Vicens Vives, Jaime. *Historia Social y económica de España y América*. 5 vols. Barcelona, 1957–1959.
Vicens Vives, Jaime. *Manual de historia económica de España*. Barcelona, 1964. Translated by Frances López–Morillas as *An Economic History of Spain*. Princeton, 1969.
Woodward, Margaret L. "The Spanish Army and the Loss of America, 1810–1824." *Hispanic American Historical Review* 48 (November, 1968): 608–631.
Zimmerman, Arthur Franklin. *Francisco de Toledo: Fifth Viceroy of Peru, 1569–1581* Caldwell, 1938.

ENGLAND IN AMERICA

Andrews, Charles M. *The Colonial Background of the American Revolution*. Yale, 1924.
Andrews, Charles M. *The Colonial Period of American History*. 4 vols. New Haven, 1934–1938.
Andrews, Charles M., Ed. *Narratives of the Insurrections 1675–1690*. New York, 1915.
Armytage, Frances. *The Free Port System in the British West Indies: A Study in Commercial Policy 1766–1822*. London, 1953.
Ashton, Trevor, Ed. *Crisis in Europe 1560–1660*. New York, 1967.
Bailyn, Bernard. *The Ideological Origins of the American Revolution*. Cambridge, 1967.
Bailyn, Bernard. *The New England Merchants in the Seventeenth Century*. New York, 1964.
Bailyn, Bernard. *The Origins of American Politics*. New York, 1968.
Bailyn, Bernard. "Politics and Social Structure in Virginia." In *Seventeenth-Century America*, edited by James Morton Smith. Chapel Hill, 1959.
Barnes, Viola. *The Dominion of New England*. New Haven, 1923.
Barrow, Thomas C. *Trade and Empire: The British Customs Service in Colonial America 1660–1775*. Cambridge, 1967.
Bassett, John S. "The Regulators of North Carolina, 1765–1771." *American Historical Association Annual Report*, 1894.
Beer, George L. *British Colonial Policy 1754–1765*. [1907] Gloucester, 1958.

Bertelson, David. *The Lazy South*. New York, 1967.

Black, John B. *The Reign of Elizabeth 1558–1603*. 2d ed. Oxford, 1959.

Boorstin, Daniel. *The Americans: The Colonial Experience*. New York, 1958.

Boxer, Charles R. *The Dutch in Brazil*. New York, 1965.

Boxer, Charles R. *The Dutch Seaborne Empire*. New York, 1965.

Bridenbaugh, Carl. *Myth and Realities: Societies of the Old South*. New York, 1952.

Bridenbaugh, Carl. *No Peace Beyond the Line*. Oxford, 1972.

Bridenbaugh, Carl. *Vexed and Troubled Englishmen*. New York, 1968.

Brown, Richard M. *The South Carolina Regulators*. Cambridge, Massachusetts, 1963.

Brown, Robert E., and Brown, Katherine B. *Virginia, 1705–1785: Democracy or Aristocracy?* East Lansing, 1964.

Bushmen, Richard L. *From Puritan to Yankee*. Cambridge, Massachusetts, 1967.

Campbell, Mildred. "Social Origins of Some Early Americans." In *Seventeenth-Century America*, edited by James Morton Smith. New York, 1955.

Clark, Dora Mae. *The Rise of the British Treasury*. New Haven, 1960.

Craven, Wesley Frank. *The Colonies in Transition, 1660–1713*. New York, 1968.

Craven, Wesley Frank. *The Southern Colonies in the Seventeenth Century*. Baton Rouge, 1949.

Craven, Wesley Frank. *White, Red and Black: The Seventeenth-Century Virginian*. Charlottesville, 1971.

Crouse, N. M. *The French Struggle for the West Indies 1665–1713*. New York, 1943.

Davis, Ralph. "English Foreign Trade, 1660–1700." *Economic History Review* **7** (1954): 150–166.

Davis, Ralph. "English Foreign Trade, 1700–1774." *Economic History Review* **15** (1962–1963): 285–299.

Davis, Ralph. *The Rise of the English Shipping Industry in the Seventeenth and Eighteenth Centuries*. London, 1962.

Degler, Carl N. *Out of Our Past*. New York, 1959.

Diamond, Sigmund. "From Organization to Society: Virginia in the Seventeenth Century." *American Journal of Sociology* **63** (March, 1958): 457–475.

Dickerson, Oliver M. *American Colonial Government 1696–1765*. [1912] New York, 1962.

Dickerson, Oliver M. *The Navigation Acts and the American Revolution*. Philadelphia, 1951.

Dorn, Walter L. *Competition for Empire, 1740–1763*. [1940] New York, 1963.

Dunn, Richard S. *Puritans and Yankees*. Princeton, 1962.

Dunn, Richard S. *Sugar and Slaves*. Chapel Hill, 1972.

Elkins, Stanley M. *Slavery*. Chicago, 1959.

Elkins, Stanley M., and McKitrick, Eric. "Institutions and the Law: The Dynamics of Unopposed Capitalism." *American Quarterly* **9** (1957): 3–21.

Erikson, Kai T. *Wayward Puritans: Studies in the Sociology of Deviance*. New York, 1966.

Gipson, Lawrence Henry. *The Coming of the Revolution*. New York, 1954.

Goebel, Dorothy Burne. "The 'New England Trade' and the French West Indies, 1763–1774: A Study in Trade Policies." *William and Mary Quarterly* **20** (1963): 331–372.

Goodman, Paul, Ed. *Essays in American Colonial History*. New York, 1967.

Goslinga, Cornelis. *The Dutch in the Caribbean 1580–1680*. Amsterdam, 1971.

Gray, Lewis Cecil. *History of Agriculture in the Southern United States to 1860*. Washington, 1932.

Greene, Jack P. "Foundations of Local Power in the Virginia House of Burgesses 1720–1766." *William and Mary Quarterly* 16 (October, 1959): 485–506.
Greene, Jack P., Ed. *Great Britain and the American Colonies 1606–1763*. Columbia, 1970.
Greene, Jack P. *The Quest for Power: The Lower House of Assembly in the Southern Royal Colonies, 1689–1776*. Chapel Hill, 1963.
Greene, Jack P., Ed. *The Reinterpretation of the American Revolution 1763–1789*. New York, 1968.
Haffenden, Philip S. "The Crown and the Colonial Charters 1675–1688." *William and Mary Quarterly* 15 (1958): 297–311, 452–466.
Hall, Michael G. "The House of Lords, Edward Randolph and the Navigation Acts of 1696." *William and Mary Quarterly* 14 (1957): 494–515.
Handlen, Oscar, and Handlin, Mary. "Origins of the Southern Labor System." *William and Mary Quarterly* 7 (1950): 199–222.
Harper, Lawrence A. "The Effects of the Navigation Acts in the Thirteen Colonies." In *The Era of the American Revolution*, ed. Richard B. Morris.
Harper, Lawrence A. *The English Navigation Acts*. [1939] New York, 1964.
Hawke, David. *The Colonial Experience*. New York, 1966.
Heimert, Alan, and Miller, Perry, Eds. *The Great Awakening*. New York, 1967.
Hill, Christopher. *The Century of Revolution: 1603–1714*. New York, 1961.
Hoetink, H. *Slavery and Race Relations in the Americas*. New York, 1973.
Jameson, John Franklin. *The American Revolution Considered as a Social Movement*. Princeton, 1926.
Jordan, Winthrop D. *White Over Black*. Chapel Hill, 1968.
Katz, Stanley. *Newcastle's New York: Anglo–American Politics 1732–1753*. Cambridge, Mass., 1968.
Kellogg, Louise P. "The American Colonial Charter." *American Historical Association Annual Report*, 1903.
Kennedy, William. *English Taxation, 1640–1799*. [1913] London, 1964.
Klein, Herbert. *Slavery in the Americas*. Chicago, 1967.
Knollenberg, Bernhard. *Origin of the American Revolution 1759–1766*. New York, 1961.
Labaree, Leonard. *Royal Government in America*. New York, 1930.
Labaree, Leonard. *Royal Instructions to British Colonial Governors, 1670–1776*. 2 vols. New York, 1967.
Laslett, Peter. *The World We Have Lost*. London, 1965.
Laurie, Nancy O. "Indian Cultural Adjustment to European Civilization." In *Seventeenth-Century America*, edited by James Morton Smith. Chapel Hill, 1959.
Lockridge, Kenneth A., and Kreider, Alan. "The Evolution of Massachusetts Town Government." In *Colonial America*, edited by Stanley N. Katz. Boston, 1971.
Lovejoy, David S. *The Glorious Revolution in America*. New York, 1972.
McLoughlin, William. *Isaac Backus and the American Pretistic Tradition*. Boston, 1967.
Middleton, Arthur Pierce. *Tobacco Coast: A Maritime History of Chesapeake Bay in the Colonial Era*. Newport News, 1953.
Miller, John C. *Origins of the American Revolution*. Boston, 1943.
Miller, Perry. *Errand into the Wilderness*. New York, 1956.
Miller, Perry. *Nature's Nation*. Cambridge, Mass., 1967.
Miller, Perry, and Johnson, Thomas, Eds. *The Puritans: A Sourcebook of Their Writings*. 2 vols. New York, 1963.
Moore, Barrington. *The Social Origins of Democracy and Dictatorship*. Boston, 1966.

Morgan, Edmund S. "The American Revolution: Revisions in Need of Revision." *William and Mary Quarterly* 14 (1957):

Morgan, Edmund S. "New England Puritanism: Another Approach." *William and Mary Quarterly* 18 (1961): 236–242.

Morgan, Edmund S. *The Puritan Dilemma: The Story of John Winthrop.* Boston, 1958.

Morgan, Edmund S. *The Puritan Family.* New York, 1966.

Morgan, Edmund S., and Morgan, Helen M. *The Stamp Act Crisis.* Chapel Hill, 1953.

Morris, Richard B. *Government and Labor in Early America.* New York, 1946.

Morton, Richard L. *Colonial Virginia.* 2 vols. Chapel Hill, 1960.

Ness, Gayl D. *The Sociology of Economic Development.* New York, 1970.

Nettels, Curtis P. "British Mercantilism and the Economic Development of the Thirteen Colonies." *Journal of Economic History* 12 (Spring, 1952): 105–114.

Nettels, Curtis P. "The Economic Relations of Boston, Philadelphia and New York, 1680–1715." *Journal of Economic and Business History* 3 (1930–1931): 185–215.

Nettels, Curtis P. "England's Trade with New England and New York, 1685–1720." *Publications of the Colonial Society of Massachusetts* 28 (1930–1933): 322–350.

Newton, A. P. *The Colonizing Activities of the English Puritans.* [1914] Yale, 1966.

Newton, A. P. *The European Nations in the West Indies 1493–1688.* London, 1933.

Notestein, Wallace. *The English People on the Eve of Colonization.* New York, 1954.

Ogg, David. *England in the Reigns of James II and William III.* Oxford, 1955.

Ostrander, Gilman. "The Colonial Molasses Trade." *Agricultural History* 30 (April, 1956): 77–84.

Pares, Richard. *Merchants and Planters.* Cambridge, Eng., 1960.

Pares, Richard. *War and Trade in the West Indies, 1739–1763.* London, 1936.

Pares, Richard. *Yankees and Creoles: The Trade between North America and the West Indies before the American Revolution.* London, 1956.

Parry, J. H., and Sherlock, P. M. *A Short History of the West Indies.* London, 1959.

Peckham, Howard H. *The Colonial Wars: 1689–1762.* Chicago, 1964.

Plumb, John H. *England in the Eighteenth Century: 1714–1815.* Cambridge, Eng., 1950.

Plumb, John H. *The Origins of Political Stability: England 1675–1725.* Boston, 1967.

Pomfret, John E. *Founding the American Colonies, 1583–1660.* New York, 1970.

Price, Jacob M. "The Economic Growth of the Chesapeake and the European Market, 1697–1775." *Journal of Economic History* 24 (1964): 496–511.

Price, Jacob M. "The Rise of Glasgow in the Chesapeake Tobacco Trade, 1707–1775." *William and Mary Quarterly* 11 (1954): 179–199.

Root, Winfred T. "The Lords of Trade and Plantations, 1675–1696." *American Historical Review* 23 (1917): 20–41.

Rose, J. Holland, Newton, A. P., and Benians, E. A., Eds. *The Cambridge History of the British Empire.* 8 vols. Cambridge, Eng., 1929–1936. Vol. 1, *The Old Empire.*

Schlesinger, Arthur M., Sr. *The Colonial Merchants and the American Revolution 1763–1776.* [1917] New York, 1957.

Seiler, William H. "The Anglican Parish in Virginia." In *Seventeenth-Century America,* edited by James Morton Smith. Chapel Hill, 1959.

Smith, Abbot E. *Colonists in Bondage.* Chapel Hill, 1947.

Soltow, J. H. "Scottish Traders in Virginia, 1750–1775." *Economic History Review* 12 (1959): 83–98.

Supple, Barry E. *Commercial Crisis and Change in England 1600–1642.* Cambridge, Eng., 1959.

Tannenbaum, Frank. *Citizen and Slave.* New York, 1947.

Tilly, Charles. "Clio and Minerva." In *Theoretical Sociology,* edited by John C. Mc-
Kinney and Edward A. Tiryakian. New York, 1970.

Tilly, Charles. "Reflections on the History of European Statemaking." In *The Formation of National States in Western Europe,* edited by Charles Tilly. Princeton,
in press.

Tilly, Charles. "Revolutions and Collective Violence." In *Handbook of Political Science,*
edited by Fred I. Greenstein and Nelson W. Polsby. 8 vols. Forthcoming.

Tilly, Charles. *The Vendee.* New York, 1964.

Tolles, F. B. "The American Revolution as a Social Movement: A Re-evaluation."
American Historical Review 60 (October, 1954): 1–12.

Ubbelohde, Carl. *The American Colonies and the British Empire.* London, 1968.

Ubbelohde, Carl. *The Vice Admiralty Courts and the American Revolution.* Chapel
Hill, 1960.

Ver Steeg, Clarence L. "The American Revolution Reconsidered as an Economic Movement." *Huntington Library Quarterly* 20 (1957): 361–372.

Ver Steeg, Clarence L. *The Formative Years.* New York, 1964.

Walzer, Michael. "Puritanism as a Revolutionary Ideology." *History and Theory* 3
(1963): 3–36.

Washburn, Wilcomb. *The Governor and the Rebel.* Chapel Hill, 1957.

Wertenbaker, Thomas J. *The Planters of Colonial Virginia.* Princeton, 1922.

Wertenbaker, Thomas J. *Torchbearer of the Revolution.* Princeton, 1940.

Williams, Basil. *The Whig Supremacy 1714–1760.* Oxford, 1949. Rev., 1962.

Wilson, Charles. *England's Apprenticeship.* London, 1965.

Wilson, Charles. "Mercantilism: Some Vicissitudes of an Idea." *Economic History Review* 10 (1957): 181–188.

Wolf, Eric R. *Peasant Wars of the Twentieth Century.* New York, 1969.

Wood, Gordon S. *The Creation of the Republic.* Chapel Hill, 1969.

Wright, Esmond. *Fabric of Freedom 1763–1800.* New York, 1961.

Wright Louis B. *Religion and Empire: The Alliance between Piety and Commerce in
English Expansion, 1558–1625.* Chapel Hill, 1943.

Index